the Scots *of Chicago*

the SCOTS *of Chicago*

Quiet Immigrants and Their New Society

Wayne Rethford
and
June Skinner Sawyers

KENDALL/HUNT PUBLISHING COMPANY
4050 Westmark Drive Dubuque, Iowa 52002

Library of Congress Catalog Card Number: 96-79713

ISBN 0-7872-2837-0

Printed in the United States of America

10 9 8 7 6 5 4 3 2 1

CONTENTS

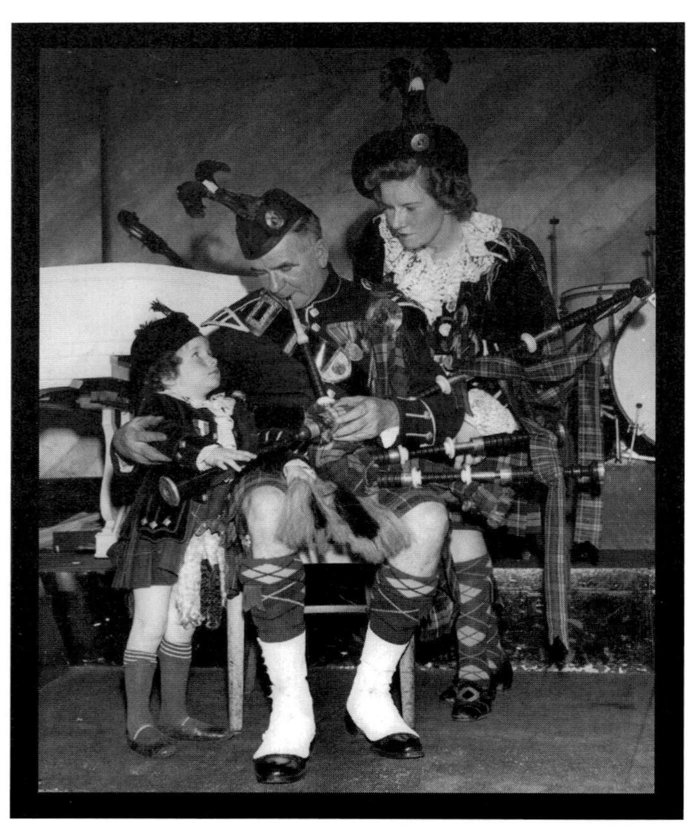

Pipe Major Robert H. Sim, of the Illinois Saint Andrew Society, four-year-old Margaret Anne MacDonald and Margaret Baikie MacDonald, December 1, 1953.

FOREWORD

Scotland's immortal bard, Robert Burns, wrote, "O wad some Power the giftie gie us, To see ourselfs as ithers see us!"

In the book *The Scots of Chicago,* Wayne Rethford and June Sawyers have indeed presented a gift to Scottish Americans, particularly to those Scottish Americans residing in the Midwest and, above all, to the members of the Illinois Saint Andrew Society. On the occasion of the 150th anniversary of the founding of the Society, this book presents an eye-opening appraisal of the many contributions of Scots to America's progress—contributions to politics, to education, to science, to philosophy, to sports, and to many other subjects. Numerous indeed have been the gifts of Scots to their adopted country. Few have taken the time to chronicle these gifts of a proud minority whose fiber has been a strong part of the American scene from pre-Revolutionary days to the present.

When Wayne Rethford came to the Scottish Home as its administrator in 1985, he was a little like Columbus discovering a new land, complete with a new people, people not foreign on the outside but with a depth of difference internally; a difference he discovered, often to his consternation, that was the basis for much of the strength and endurance of Scots everywhere.

The character of the many contributions that Scots have given as gifts to our society, as well as the characteristics of the gift givers, is set forth in this book. This is no treatise on some of the more popular aspects of Scottishness—the kilts, tartans, haggis, and pipers. On the contrary, it is a definitive work celebrating the accomplishments rather than the trappings of the Scottish American. As Iain Finlayson has said, "Scots, like seeds windblown from the corners of the Earth, must recognize some dilution of Scottish traditions as they were in reality in Scotland and a corresponding vigorous development of traditions immortalized and ameliorated by myth. Regardless of however rough the transplantation is, the Scottish seedling will normally flourish safe in unfamiliar, often positively hostile territory, and retain their characteristics against all odds."

In this country—in this city—Scots have achieved much, yet rarely have they been recognized for their ethnicities. This latter fact is because they have become so totally assimilated into mainstream society. In Chicago, even from the beginning, rarely did any true major Scottish pockets exist that would correspond to areas inhabited by other ethnic groups. Instead the Scots have gone their own way, contributing wherever they go to the advancement of the world they live in, to its history and to its cultural traditions. I strongly support the conclusion that is evidenced in this work that Scots are endowed with ample doses of patriotism, industry, and responsibility.

I join with the authors in saluting the Illinois Saint Andrew Society for its 150 years of "aiding the distressed" and, in particular, saluting those of Scottish birth and background for their contributions to the country in which they live. A personal salute to Wayne Rethford, and thanks for this "giftie."

ROBERT J. BLACK

President, Illinois Saint Andrew Society, 1988–90

ACKNOWLEDGMENTS

Appreciation is warmly extended to Ann Adee, Robert J. Allan II, Penny Aylor, Dr. Rowland Berthoff, Robert J. Black, Larry Bruce, Bill Currie, James John D'Anza II, Kathryn Elaine D'Anza, Alexander D. Kerr, Jr., Scott C. Elliott, Donald A. Gillies, Tammi Longsjo, Ruth McGugan, Roberta Nichols, Jay Pridmore, Philip M. Puckorius, Catharine Regan, Elaine Rethford, Mary Ellen Rethford, Suzanne D'Anza, Edward C. Rorison, Jane Samuelson, Elizabeth Sherman of the John D. and Catherine T. MacArthur Foundation, Norman Standish, Ian Swinton, James C. Thomson; and the staffs of the Chicago Historical Society, the Newberry Library, Loyola University Chicago Library, and Northwestern University Library, and the Board of Governors, Illinois Saint Andrew Society.

INTRODUCTION

The purpose of this book is to give credit to those Scottish men and women who have influenced the city of Chicago, the state of Illinois, and, indirectly, the country itself. It is an almost impossible task since so few Scots in America have taken the time to write down their own history.

Much of our emphasis here will be on the Scottish influence in Chicago, especially as it relates to the Illinois Saint Andrew Society, the oldest charitable institution in Illinois.

Historian Charlotte Erickson has referred to the Scots as "invisible immigrants." Like their British cousins, the English and the Welsh, the Scots have not so much assimilated into the American mainstream, rather they have—until very recently—all but disappeared. Unlike their more ethnic-conscious Irish counterparts, it has been rare to hear Americans of Scottish descent refer to themselves as second or third generation Scottish Americans. Usually immigrant Scottish children or the children of immigrants—and most certainly the grandchildren of immigrants—considered themselves simply American, giving no or little thought to their ethnic ancestry.

The problem with writing about Scottish settlements in Chicago is that much of the information that is available is sketchy at best—fragments that lead nowhere, all-to-brief newspaper articles from another century, faded scrapbooks in worn-out shopping bags. Sadly, many important papers relating to Scottish settlement in Chicago—including entire libraries—were destroyed during the Great Fire of 1871. What's more, few Scots in Chicago felt compelled to write down their memoirs; consequently, a rich lore of local ethnic history and culture has been lost forever.

In general, compared to other ethnic groups, the literature on Scottish emigration is scant. Locally, the Scots are one of the least examined ethnic groups in Chicago. There has been no comprehensive study of the Scots in either city or state, for example.

More damaging, perhaps, is the attitude of benign neglect among historians. For the most part, Scottish American history is looked upon as a curiosity, hardly taken seriously from a scholarly perspective.

Not as cohesive as the Irish, not as organized as the Jews, not as numerous as the African Americans, the Scottish Americans of Chicago are admittedly elusive people to track down. The Irish may have their heritage center, the Poles their museum and cultural center, the

Ukrainians their stunningly beautiful churches, the Swedes their historical archives nicely situated on a well-known college campus, but the only long-lasting institution that Chicago Scots have to call their own is the Illinois Saint Andrew Society and the Society's chief concern, the Scottish Home in North Riverside. Most other Scottish organizations in the city—and there were many—have been long forgotten.

For the most part, Scots made a mark on America, at least in Chicago, not as members of an identifiable ethnic group but as individuals. The vast majority of the Scots who settled here came from the industrial Lowlands. Unlike the Gaelic-speaking Highlanders, Lowland Scots typically did not consciously choose to settle in Scottish American communities. With a few exceptions, they went to the place that offered the best opportunity for economic improvement. Only once they were "dug in" did they give any serious thought to forming ethnic organizations. For, on the whole, Scots were not joiners.

The focus of this study, then, is on individual Scots who made an impact on the city, with brief explorations of Scottish communities outside Chicago. These are the Scots who established the ethnic and regional organizations, formed the mutual help societies, sponsored the Highland games, and participated in the Burns's club activities. The story of the Scots in Chicago did not occur in a vacuum, though. Hence, it is important to get a sense of what was going on in the city itself. For this reason the Scottish story is set in the framework of the larger Chicago story.

Yet there is much to celebrate within the Scottish community. Today, for example, there is a revived interest in Scottish activities across the country. Highland games and Scottish concerts appeal to Scot and non-Scot alike. Most encouraging of all perhaps is the growing interest among Chicagoans to learn about authentic Scottish culture, not just the tartan and kitsch variety. In recent years there has been a valuable and welcome exchange of information between Chicago and Scotland itself. Chicago Scots and native Scots are no longer the strangers they once were, separated by an ocean and the passage of time. These ongoing stories are also addressed.

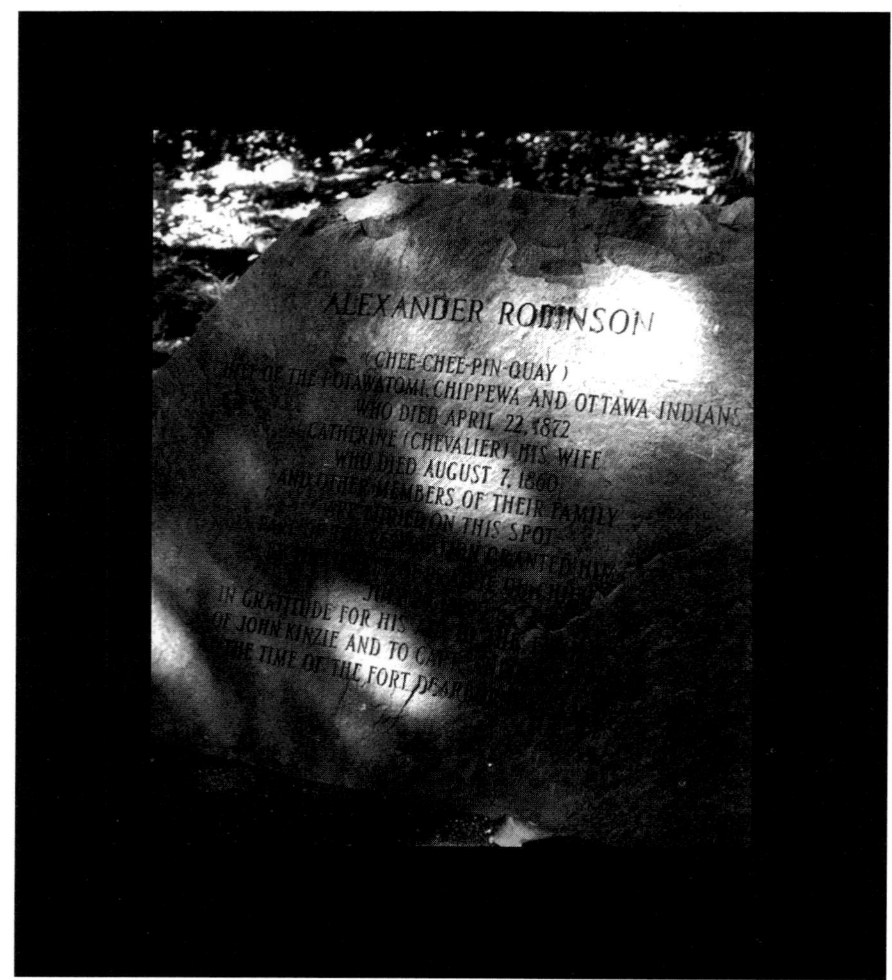

Robinson family burial ground

ONE

Beginnings

Although a long neglected minority in Chicago history, Scots have played an important if largely unheralded role, especially within the city's business, economic, and educational life. Much the same can be said about Scottish influence in the United States. According to some accounts, more than 10 million Americans today can claim some Scottish heritage and more than 142,000 sole Scottish ancestry (Aman 1991, 13). In the Chicago area, some scholars estimate that at least 10 percent of the population has ancestral links to Scotland (Kokmen 1995).

SCOTLAND IN THE NINETEENTH CENTURY

Scotland is a small country that shares its southern boundary with England. For much of its history it also has been a poor country, wracked by the twin evils of unpredictable weather and meager natural resources. Warfare, poverty, and various forms of oppression have taken their toll, yet for all the country's troubles over the centuries, the people have displayed a remarkable resiliency and a determination to make the best of their rather inhospitable surroundings.

Scotland's greatest export has been its people. It is a truism that has been repeated many times yet it is nevertheless still valid. For centuries ambitious Scots saw very few opportunities in their native land except to leave. For many a Scot, America was the Promised Land; the best place for a poor man—or woman—to better himself or herself. Between 1760 and 1775 alone, some 40,000 Scots emigrated to North America (Bailyn 1986, 26). Once started, it was difficult to stem the flood of emigration, and by 1773 none other than the eminent Dr. Samuel Johnson observed that the Scots seemed to be afflicted with an "epidemick disease of wandering" (40); indeed this contagious "disease" was evident throughout Great Britain and Ireland.

Yet by the nineteenth century conditions in Scotland had improved considerably. The union with England, the marvelous achievements during the glory years of the Scottish Enlightenment, the economic expansion in the Lowlands—all these factors and more helped to improve the country's morale and increase the value of the individual Scot's pocketbook. Although hardly a prosperous country, conditions were definitely on the upswing. Yet there were disturbing signs of trouble ahead, both in the Highlands and the Lowlands. Once again, emigration—the inevitable consequence of domestic turmoil—would be on the rise.

HIGHLAND CLEARANCES

The chief causes for emigration from the Highlands in the nineteenth century were overpopulation, poverty, and high rents. Unlike earlier migrations, the majority of Highlanders were poor people who chose to leave their homeland in search of a better life elsewhere.

The bulk of what has come to be known as the Highland Clearances occurred in the nineteenth century, primarily from 1800 to 1850. During this tragic phase in Scottish history, landlords converted their property into more profitable sheep farms. People who had lived on the land for generations and who knew no other home or way of life were unceremoniously forced to leave. Since most did not want to leave, there were ugly scenes of forced evictions occurring throughout the Highlands from Sutherland in the vast northwest to Skye in the Western Isles. Homes were burned, sometimes with people still inside. Entire families were put onto emigrant ships and sent across the ocean. The sheer brutality of these evictions, or "clearances," lived on in the folk memory and made the people bitter for a very long time. Even today, the Clearances remain a palpable part of the psychological makeup of the Scottish Highlander.

Some people moved to small fishing villages along the coast. Unfortunately, they were not accustomed to making a living this way. Rather than stay, many decided to move to Edinburgh or Glasgow to find work. Others, though, chose to leave Scotland entirely. In later years, when sheep farms proved uneconomic, the sheep were removed and replaced with deer forests in which the affluent classes could leisurely slaughter deer and grouse (Mackie 1978, 345). But the lands remained mostly empty, with vast expanses devoid of human habitation, leaving later generations to marvel at the grandeur of this most decidedly humanmade of "wildernesses."

UNEMPLOYMENT IN THE LOWLANDS

The Union of Parliaments of Scotland and England in 1707 generally led to improved economic conditions in Scotland. Consequently, commerce grew and some industries in particular, such as linen and textiles, even thrived. Advancements also took place in the cotton, woolen, and fisheries industries. Later, heavy industries, such as coal, iron, and especially shipbuilding in Glasgow and Clydebank, flourished (Mackie 1978, 324). A flurry of activity took place—mines were opened, roads were improved, and canals were built. Consequently, the population in the burgeoning urban centers mushroomed.

But this tremendous activity had a dark side. In the 1830s automation had transformed a number of the traditional industries, leaving many laborers out of work. Later years saw countless linen workers in places like Paisley and Glasgow replaced by machines. With increased population came a concomitant rise in poverty and crime. Much of the work that ushered in the Industrial Revolution was often boring and dehumanizing. Whether factory work or shipbuilding, the effort was both hard and numb. Worse, the Scottish working class tended to congregate in crowded tenements in the large urban centers, huddled together under appalling living conditions. For many Lowland Scots, life in the nineteenth century meant enduring long periods of chronic unemployment.

MIGRATIONS

> *My love of home, placed in juxtaposition with my restless desire to leave it, would appear to those unacquainted with the character of the Scottish people to savor of inconsistency. The migratory spirit of the Scotch is not altogether an optional matter with the individual. (Johnston 1885, 8)*

According to the 1790 census, there were 189,000 people of Scottish origin living in the United States, although it is highly probable the figure may have also included Ulster Scots (Brander 1982, 89; Donaldson 1966, 108).

The Revolutionary War had virtually stopped all Scottish emigration to the United States as did the outbreak of the War of 1812. Indeed there was no substantial emigration from Scotland to the United States again until about 1845 (Donaldson 1966, 112).

From the Civil War era to the turn of the century, the greatest number of Scots were found on the East Coast in New York, Pennsylvania, and Massachusetts, followed by Illinois, Michigan, and Ohio. But Scots also settled as far west as California. Among cities during this period, New York, Chicago, Philadelphia, and Detroit had the highest number of Scots (Brander 1982, 104). By 1850 there were almost 5,000 Scots in Illinois alone (Donaldson 1966, 120).

During the Scottish economic depressions of the 1860s, thousands of Scottish miners emigrated to the New World. As many as 2,000 of these miners were said to be in Illinois in the post–Civil War era. Many were from Lanarkshire in the Scottish Lowlands and tended to congregate as groups, such as those who ultimately settled in Braidwood, Illinois, an industrial community south of Chicago (Hewitson 1993, 88).

As homegrown industry developed within the United States, Scottish expertise was no longer as highly valued. Thus, according to Gordon Donaldson (1966, 120), by 1870 the iron and steel industries placed less emphasis on hiring Scottish workers. A similar situation occurred in the coal industry about 1880 and in the textile industry around the turn of the century. Shipbuilding, though, was another story. Scots were so prominent in the American shipbuilding industry in 1905 that it was said there was "hardly a man . . . who did not speak with a strong Scottish accent" (Thernstrom 1980, 913).

During the first half of the nineteenth century, the majority of Scots who emigrated chose Canada. Thus, between 1820 and 1851, only 10,525 Scots came to the United States (Aman 1991, 71). From the 1850s to 1880s, however, several thousand Scots immigrated to the States every year. After 1870, the number was more than 10,000 a year. "In all, 478,224 Scots immigrated to the United States between 1852 and 1910," writes one historian. By 1870 immigrants from England, Scotland, and Wales made up nearly 14 percent of the population in the United States (Berthoff 1953, 6). Indeed, during the latter half of the nineteenth century and in the first two decades of the twentieth—that is, between 1870 and 1920—most of the people leaving the United Kingdom chose to settle in the United States. The level of emigration reflected the economic conditions in the Mother Country. During times of depression, emigration increased; during times of relative prosperity, on the other hand, emigration waned (10). A large number of the emigrants during this period were experienced artisans (21). Earlier emigrants had likely been farmers and peasants (107). Most came to America in search of a better life. For many Scots, accustomed as they were to hardship and survival, the greatest ambition of all was to own a piece of the good earth. Mostly though, they just wanted a chance, a chance to start over, a chance to improve their lot in life. Chicago, the boom town of the prairie, offered the chance of a lifetime.

EARLY CHICAGO

If one were to travel back in time and visit Chicago during the early decades of the nineteenth century, it would have not been very pleasing to the eye. A gentleman from London, William N. Keating, said as much during his stopover in 1825. On the contrary, he described the landscape as a "fatiguing monotony" of "thin and scrubby woods . . .

John Law

In 1717 the Scots entrepreneur John Law, a native of Edinburgh, obtained a charter from the French government to colonize Prairie du Rocher (Field of the Rock) in southwestern Illinois on the Mississippi River. He established the Company of the West, bringing in immigrants from France, Italy, Switzerland, and Germany. The Company was given exclusive control of the trade in Canada and the Mississippi River.

Law was a risk taker and offered the immigrants the promise of making grand profits. However, his "Mississippi Bubble" eventually burst in 1720, leaving the settlers stranded. Most chose to stay on, though. In that same year Fort de Chartres was completed. Today, parts of the reconstructed fort are located within a state park.

George Rogers Clark

Another important figure in the early history of Illinois is George Rogers Clark. His great- grandfather, John Clark, came to Virginia in 1630 from southwestern Scotland. He had married a Scottish girl who was described as "a red-haired beauty," and they lived for some time in the parish of Drysdale, in King and Queen County, Virginia.

When Clark was only nineteen he made several trips back and forth to Virginia on behalf of the settlers in Kentucky. He also served in various campaigns against the Indians. During the Revolutionary War, Clark, commanding Kentucky and Virginia rebels, who were, like himself, mostly of Scottish descent, captured British garrisons at Vincennes and Kaskaskia, checkmating the plans of the British leader Lieutenant Governor Henry Hamilton at Detroit. Clark's quick actions virtually guaranteed the entire Northwest, including the then obscure Chicago portage, would remain in American hands. Clark eventually received a pension of $400 from the Virginia government for his services. The city of Chicago commemorated his achievements too by naming a street in his honor. Clark died in February 1818 (Angle 1975).

William, his younger brother, accompanied Meriwether Lewis on the famous Lewis and Clark Expedition of 1805. President Jefferson sent the pair to explore the recently acquired territory of the Louisiana Purchase. They made a remarkable journey from St. Louis to the Pacific coast and back. William Clark was later appointed governor of the Missouri Territory and died in St. Louis on September 1, 1838. The records maintained by Lewis and Clark on their great journey would give the nation its first detailed account of the vast lands of the West.

Arthur St. Clair

Arthur St. Clair was a major general during the Revolutionary War and, later, the first governor of the Northwest Territory, which included what was to become the state of Illinois. He fought in the battles of Trenton and Princeton and served as a delegate to the Continental Congress. Born in Thurso, Caithness, Scotland, St. Clair, a proud and vainglorious man, created a county seat in downstate Illinois, naming it after himself and giving his cousin, William St. Clair, the title of county clerk (Howard 1972, 64–65).

John Regan

Scots found the open prairie a fascinating place. In 1852 a Lowlander by the name of John Regan left Scotland when he was twenty-three and settled for a time in a small village in western Illinois called Virgil:

> *The village stands upon the banks of the Spoon, which is here about the size of the Clyde at Glasgow. A wooden bridge crosses the stream, of no mean construction. There were two shops or stores, a post-office and tavern, a grist and saw-mill, blacksmiths, wagonmakers, tailors, but no shoemakers.* (Regan 1859, 57)

Regan built a log cabin, raised crops, and taught school before returning to Scotland, where he published in 1847 *The Emigrant's Guide to the Western States of America.* His guide is now considered one of the great if neglected accounts of Illinois literature. In it he describes the local surroundings in great detail, its communities and characters, and his own experiences as an immigrant in a strange new land. Regan was so impressed with Illinois, he encouraged others to settle here.

here and there" populated with little more than a few huts and "filthy" log houses (Gilbert and Bryson 1929, 43). Clearly, Chicago did not make a very good first impression.

Yet, despite its rather shabby appearance, Chicago would soon be playing an important role in local politics. When Cook County was created on January 15, 1831, Chicago became the county seat (Pierce 1937, 33). The town of Chicago was incorporated in 1833. Four years later, in 1837, with a population of 4,170, Chicago received its charter as a city. The boundaries were Twenty-second Street on the south, Wood Street on the west, Lake Michigan on the east, and North Avenue on the north (Gilbert and Bryson 1929, 86).

The 1840s saw the beginning of a great westward movement. By 1848 the population of Chicago was more than 20,000 (Pierce 1937, 44). Still, Chicago was enough of a frontier town as late as the 1850s that it was not unusual to see riders on horseback with pistols in their holsters.

Chicago had the advantage of being located on the shore of Lake Michigan at the head of a great waterway that led to central Illinois and the Mississippi Valley. In 1836 the proposal to build the Illinois and Michigan Canal virtually guaranteed the city a bright future. The canal provided links between Chicago and the Mississippi, opening up in the process an extensive market for goods. It also increased the corn, wheat, and lumber trades.

But it was the vast network of railroads that emanated from Chicago that was the single greatest reason for the city's phenomenal growth and that, consequently, made Chicago the commercial center of the Midwest. The euphoria of life in the boom town diminished somewhat during what came to be known as the Panic of 1837. At that time President Andrew Jackson ordered the U.S. land office to accept nothing but gold or silver in payment for public lands. Further, Jackson removed public funds from the Bank of the United States. Up until this time, the country had enjoyed a spate of prosperity, which led many people to indulge in wild speculation and inflated credit.

Consequently, during the next few years a fair number of Chicago's leading citizens went bankrupt (Pierce 1937, 68) and property values declined. For this reason, many believed the future of the city and the short-term health of the struggling real estate market depended on the building of the I & M canal (70). Unfortunately, in 1841, work on the canal came to a standstill as funds all but evaporated (71).

Despite the town's financial woes, the population of Chicago continued to grow (76), so much so that by 1845 the city was beginning to establish the foundations of a stable society. The Saloon Building, which was erected in 1836 at the corner of Lake and Clark Streets, was the center of Chicago life in the late 1830s and 1840s. The city's first literary and debating society held its meetings there. The building also housed the federal and county courts, the U.S. Land Office, and the Second Presbyterian Church. Robert Fergus, an early pioneer Scot, printed the first of his Historical Series there (Jensen 1953, 154).

In 1848, the first telegraph line was completed in Chicago (Pierce 1937, 105), allowing communication with the outside world. It would soon bring word that gold had been discovered in California. Internally, too, the city was developing. The first waterworks had been completed, and the streets were being covered with wooden planks. In the same year the first railway station in Chicago, the Galena and Chicago Union, opened at the corner of Canal and Kinzie Streets (Gilbert and Bryson 1929, 95).

As early as the 1840s criminal activity had grown along with the city, so much so that by 1849 "more gambling establishments were flourishing in Chicago than in Philadelphia and more in proportion to population than in New York" (Pierce 1940, 432). There were also countless brothels, saloons, and dram shops. Consequently, temperance societies sprung up to address the increasingly serious alcohol consumption. Organizations such as the Chicago Juvenile Temperance Society, the Total Abstinence Benevolent Association, and the Scottish Temperance Society "urged state prohibition of the making of sale of liquor a crime" (436). The Chicago Temperance Society existed as early as 1832.

But not all of life in early Chicago was grim. Chicagoans found time to pursue cultural activities and exercises in self-improvement. The works of such popular authors as Charles Dickens, William Makepeace Thackeray, and Sir Walter Scott as well as such Scottish Americans as Washington Irving and James Fenimore Cooper found their place on the bookshelves of many a Chicagoan (Pierce 1937, 294).

Meanwhile, a number of girls' schools addressed the crudeness of life on the prairie by teaching such subjects as reading, grammar, geography, writing, enamel painting, and pianoforte. As early as 1834, for example, Edinburgh-born Catherine Bayne opened her boarding school on Randolph between Clark and Dearborn Streets (281) Language lessons were also given, such as the French instruction offered to young ladies by another Edinburgh woman, Isabella Kay, in 1836 (282). Chicago could even claim the talents of a fine young artist from Scotland, one James Forbes.

Despite earnest attempts to improve the standard of living in the community, Chicago still had some very serious problems. Health issues, of course, were an ongoing concern. There were various cholera outbreaks in the 1840s and 1850s and even as late as 1866, when 990 people died (Gilbert and Bryson 1929, 113).

Undoubtedly, one of the most vexing problems was mud. After all, Chicago was mostly built on a drained marsh. The streets were unpaved. The mud was not only a constant dilemma but also a persistent source of civic embarrassment. Poor drainage created additional headaches. Dogs, pigs, and cattle were allowed to roam free.

Yet Chicago was making some progress. In 1857 a method was devised that raised an entire city one block at a time. George Pullman, the railroad pioneer, elevated the Tremont House, the largest hotel in the city at the time, some eight feet, using the efforts of 1,200 men and the power of 5,000 jackscrews (Cromie 1958, 5). Thus began an extraordinary transformation of the physical layout of the city. All over town street levels and buildings were raised. The "raising" of Chicago soon became a subject of endless fascination. Visitors from around the world came to see this miracle for themselves. David Macrae, who published a two-volume set called *The Americans at Home: Pen-and-Ink Sketches of American Men, Manners and Institutions in 1870* for an Edinburgh-based publishing house, described the raising of the Briggs House at the northeast corner of Randolph and Wells Streets in 1857:

> *The Briggs House, a gigantic hotel, five storeys high, solid masonry, weighing 22,000 tons, was raised four and a half feet, and new foundations built below. The people were in it all the time, coming and going, eating and sleeping—the whole business of the hotel proceeding without interruption. (Mayer and Wade 1969, 96)*

Meanwhile, there were repeated efforts to resolve the city's harbor problems, and many requests were made to Washington, D.C., for financial help. As early as March 1833 the federal government gave the town $25,000 to build a harbor (Pierce 1937, 91–92). A decade later the city was able to secure a total of $55,000 in federal assistance. The work was under the direction of Captain George B. McClellan and was to include the extension and elevation of the North Pier. The pier was finally extended some 3,900 feet and a lighthouse of pine timber constructed at the eastern end. Unfortunately, the effort proved to be only a temporary solution, and the problem continued for several more years. A lighthouse had been built in 1832 (Mayer and Wade 1969, 20).

The first railroad to actually reach Chicago from the East arrived on February 20, 1852. Two years later a line was extended to the Mississippi River and by 1855, ten trunk lines and eleven branch lines entered the city. Ninety-six trains were entering Chicago every day. There were nearly 3,000 miles of railroads in operation in Illinois at the time. Chicago was now the center of the largest rail network in the world. In 1856 four of the principal railroads had carried 639,666 passengers westward from Chicago and 532,013 in the opposite direction. Thus, the city had also become the supply point of the westward movement.

Public houses and taverns played an important role in pioneer Chicago since there were few places where visitors could stay or be entertained. Some of the early taverns included the Green Tree Tavern, Wolf Point Tavern, the Exchange Coffee House, the Eagle Hotel, and probably the most famous, the Sauganash Hotel. Here in this humble two-story frame building Mark Beaubien, the hotel's amiable host and resident fiddler, held court (Pierce 1937, 213).

Saint James Church, a Protestant Episcopal Church, served the spiritual needs of the community's elite in the 1830s. It opened on Easter Sunday in 1837 and boasted a $4,000 mahogany pulpit. Much of the wealth of the church was courtesy of the generous donations of John H. Kinzie, son of the famous Scottish American pioneer. It was frequently known as the "Kinzie Church" (229).

In a span of a few brief years Chicago had developed from frontier town to urban community. Despite its many problems, early Chicago was essentially an optimistic city. Chicagoans believed in progress. Conditions, they were certain, could only get better.

EARLY SCOTTISH IMMIGRATION TO CHICAGO

The Scottish community in Chicago did not settle as a group. Indeed, they hardly formed a cohesive unit in the traditional sense at all. The Scots seldom congregated in communities of their own kind. There were no Scottish neighborhoods in Chicago that were comparable, say, to later Irish, Italian, or Polish neighborhoods. Lowlanders, in particular, usually dispersed within the larger community with little or no bother.

Hence, the Scots assimilated fairly easily into the American mainstream. Unlike other immigrants, they already knew the language and many, at least among the Lowlanders, were skilled laborers or members of the professional or merchant class. Young Scotsmen, especially those from Glasgow, established their own dry-goods stores, which eventually expanded into department stores (Berthoff 1953, 120). Carson Pirie Scott and Company, for example, was cofounded by John T. Pirie, a native of Scotland, while another Scot, Andrew MacLeish, later became president of Carson's. Still later, the Glasgow-born Scot James Simpson would become president of Carson's competitor, Marshall Field and Company.

Indeed, Scots almost passed unnoticed into the American landscape. According to Rowland Berthoff (1953, 132), Americans "seldom thought of their English, Welsh, or Scottish neighbors as foreigners." At the same time, many of the new arrivals did not really consider America a foreign land, either, but rather something along the lines of a "greater" Britain or, in the case of one Scotsman, simply an extension of the homeland, sort of "another Scotland on a large scale and who, after speaking of the Scotsmen, from [Alexander] Hamilton to Andrew Carnegie, who had helped to make America what it is, declared . . . that America would have a poor show if it had not been for the Scottish" (139).

Another difference is that many of the key players in the Scottish community who emigrated directly from Scotland to America and settled in Chicago were from the Lowlands of Scotland. Robert Fergus, Chicago's first printer, for example, hailed from Glasgow as did Andrew MacLeish and other prominent Scots. Consequently, unlike their Gaelic-speaking Highland brethren, language was usually not a problem.

Hence, the story of the Scottish community in Chicago is one of individuals from Scotland who came to this city on the lake to better themselves. They were emigrants who happened to be Scots and who, on occasion, formed organizations with like-minded Scots. But, as a whole, Scots were not joiners.

FOUNDING OF THE ILLINOIS SAINT ANDREW SOCIETY

Philanthropic societies were among the earliest of immigrant societies within the Scottish American community. The first philanthropic society in the United States was reportedly the Scots Charitable Society of Boston, founded in 1657. In the eighteenth and nineteenth centuries comparable societies, taking the name of Scotland's patron saint, Saint Andrew, were established. Gasdon Donaldson believes that the first Saint Andrew Society (sometimes spelled Saint Andrew's), got its start in New York in 1756, while others say Charleston, South Carolina, which founded its branch as far back as 1729, holds the honor (Thernstrom 1980, 915). Chicago did not have its own Saint Andrew Society until the mid-nineteenth century, however. "None but Scotchmen, or the sons or grandsons of a native of Scotland, shall be admitted as members of the Society," Society records report.

General George McClellan the famous Civil War soldier, was living at the Lake House, working on the city's intractable harbor problem, when he called for Scottish men to help celebrate the birthday of Saint Andrew. And so it was that probably fewer than twenty persons gathered for the anniversary dinner at the Lake House on that November 30, 1845. The first official meeting, however, was held on January 26 of the following year. This meeting, also held at the Lake House, was chaired by James Murray of Buffalo, New York. It was said that seventeen men attended the meeting, and fourteen were elected to the office. The official name adopted that evening was the Illinois St. Andrew Society of the City of Chicago. The officers elected that night included the following:

George Steel, president

George Barnett, first vice president

John Crawford, second vice president

Alexander Brand, treasurer

Patrick Ballingall, secretary

John Ross, assistant secretary

"Relieve the Distressed" was adopted as the motto of the Society. A later statement was issued, elaborating the Society's purposes and motives: "Organized thus to mitigate the evils and vicissitudes incident to life, the Society will seek to advance, by all legitimate means, the social improvement of its members—encouraging and stimulating, under its auspices, the formation of clubs which shall have for their object the development of physical energy and the elevation of moral character."

George Anderson of Chicago, John McGlashan of Bridgeport, James Michie of Summit, and R. Raddler of Naperville were elected as managers. The *Daily Journal* carried the story of the meeting on January 26, 1846:

> *As the Society embraces at present, the whole State, and is solely for benevolent purposes, it is earnestly requested that Scotsmen residing in the City and neighboring counties will attend the next meeting.*

General George McClellan (right)

The Journal also suggests that a constitution was adopted, and the date of the next meeting established. They were to meet on Thursday morning, February 12, at 7 p.m. in the office of the secretary, Mr. Ballingall, at 92 Lake Street.

It was already dark and cold that evening when George Anderson made his way to the Lake House. From his small home, where he also conducted his business, at 117 Clark Street, he walked briskly north to the river and then east on South Water Street to the ferry at Michigan Avenue.

What a great evening it must have been. These young men desperately needed the solace of a gathering such as this, being so far from their beloved Scotland, homesick for families and friends and living in such an untamed environment.

After the first meeting, Anderson was appointed chairman of a committee to draft a constitution and bylaws. If a constitution was in fact adopted at the first meeting, it cannot be verified since the earliest copy was destroyed in the Great Fire of 1871. The first constitution that can be identified comes from the annual report of the Society in 1889. However, it may be safely assumed that much of the preamble dates back to an earlier time. It seems likely, for example, that the constitution and bylaws were adopted in 1850 and a charter obtained in 1853. In fact, the Society was incorporated as a special act of the Illinois legislature on February 10, 1853, making it the oldest philanthropic organization in the state. A later revision was made of the constitution and bylaws in 1858 by a committee consisting of Anderson, John H. Kedzie, Peter McFarlane, and John Stewart.

The following statement comes from the preamble and clearly identifies the purpose of the Society:

> *A sacred obligation to aid the unfortunate among our countrymen, or their families, who may, in pursuit of labor of business, have come here, and having deliberated on the most effective means to promote and compass these most desirable object, we hereby form ourselves into a society bearing the name of the Illinois St. Andrew Society of Chicago.*

Organized thus to mitigate the evils and vicissitudes incident to life, the Society also sought to advance, by all legitimate means, the social improvement of its members—encouraging and stimulating, under its auspices, the formation of clubs that shall have for their object "the development of physical energy and the elevation of moral character."

The annual report of 1890 also contained the following statement:

> *The benevolent feelings implanted by the Creator in the hearts of men are given for practical development, and if it is true that no braver hearts beat than those that throb under a Scottish plaid, much more so is it true that nowhere does the development of the benevolent feelings find a readier expression than amongst Scotsmen. The expression of these benevolent prompting is not confined to individuals. It assumes an organized form and thus becomes more efficient, and concentrates individual efforts into a well-digested and laudable system of benevolence.*

Since 1846 members and friends of the Society have held an annual festival on or near Saint Andrew's Day. From the small number of members little or no revenue accumulated from these anniversary dinners until 1851. The Society lost everything to fire—in 1849 and again in 1871.

EARLY PRESIDENTS OF THE SOCIETY

GEORGE STEEL

George Steel, the first president of the Society, was born in Forfarshire, Scotland, in 1797. One of twelve sons, Steel arrived in Chicago in 1837. As a contractor on the Illinois and Michigan Canal, he built the works at Utica, Illinois, known as the Clark Cement Works.

When work on the canal stopped, Steel began several business ventures in Chicago. He owned a pork-packing plant on South Water Street, for example. He was also in the produce business with an office and warehouse located at the foot of LaSalle Street. In 1856 a new three-story building was erected on this site, and it became the first permanent home for the board of trade. Steel was very active in the board of trade and attended its first organizational meeting. He served as president of the board in 1852 and again in 1853.

Steel's company built the first steam-operated grain elevator in Chicago, which was capable of operating from the canal as well as the railroads. It was destroyed by fire in 1854.

In 1830 Steel married Anna Stein Morrison of Montreal, Canada. They had nine children. Steele served two terms as president of the Saint Andrew Society. He was a very popular man during his lifetime and perhaps fairly representative of the "typical" businessmen of the era. He died in March 1865.

ALEXANDER BRAND

Alexander Brand was elected as the first treasurer and would later serve three terms as president, in 1848, 1850, and 1851. He arrived in Chicago from Scotland in the summer of 1839 and took up residence at the Lake House. He opened an exchange house, establishing a partnership and calling the firm Murray and Brand. The company was involved in most forms of banking, including the buying and selling of real estate. In 1844 Brand's partner, James Murray, had apparently moved to Buffalo, New York, and the name was changed to Alexander Brand and Company. The directory of Chicago in 1845 reads:

> *Alexander Brand—private banker and exchange broker, 127 Lake Corner Clark St., residence—Lake House*

Thus, four of the men who attended the first anniversary dinner in 1845 lived at the Lake House. They were Brand, Captain George B. McClellan, John S. Ross, and his brother, Daniel E. Ross, who according to the directory, was the "bar keeper" at the House. Brand later returned to his home in Aberdeen, Scotland.

JAMES MICHIE

James Michie served one term as president of the Society in 1847. It appears that in 1848 he may have moved to Lyons, Illinois. This would not have been considered unusual since many people believed that Lyons had a great future and would be a large city due to its location on the Des Plaines River. The township of Lyons was organized in 1850, and Michie was elected the town clerk. He was reelected in 1851. Michie was also a justice of the peace.

The first road in Lyons township was privately owned by Michie, Eden Eatron, and Samuel Vail. In 1854 Michie was elected supervisor and also was "the overseer of the poor." He died in 1876 at age sixty-eight.

In 1876 the Board of Governors passed the following resolution "of respect to the memory of the late James Michie and Alexander Brand":

> *It having pleased the Almighty Ruler of the universe, in whose hands are the issue of life and death, to remove from this, the scene of their earthly labors, our late friends and brothers James Michie and Alexander Brand, both ex-presidents, valued and esteemed members of this Society since its organization.*
>
> *And whereas, this Society has learned, with feelings of profound regret, of the demise of our fellow-members at nearly the allotted time of man, three-score-and-ten.*
>
> *We would bow with humble submission to the Divine Will, who doeth all things as seemeth good in His sight, whose arm none can stay, nor say to Him, "What doeth Thou?"*

THE LAKE HOUSE

Chicago's first important hotel was the Lake House, a three-story brick building between Rush and Kinzie. The Lake House opened to the public in 1836. It introduced to the frontier town such niceties as "napkins, toothpicks, printed menus and a French chef" (Dedmon 1983, 8). Among the early Chicagoans who donated the nearly $100,000 cost were Gurdon S. Hubbard and John Kinzie.

"When the Lake House was erected there was nothing between it and the shore of Lake Michigan, distant only a few hundred feet, excepting the great cotton wood trees that had sheltered the pioneer Kinzie House," writes historian Josiah Currey. "From three sides the Lake House looked out on the blue expanse, north, east and south. It was finished early in the fall of 1836. The opening was a festive event; it took place during the flush times preceding the crash of 1837, money was plenty, and its prospects for success were excellent" (Currey 1912, 247). The Lake House was frequented by officers, judges, canal contractors, lake captains, politicians, speculators, and travelers; among the celebrities who were entertained there were Daniel Webster, General Winfield Scott, and Governor Lewis Cass. Ultimately used as a rundown tenement, it was destroyed in the fire of 1871.

The Lake House Hotel is located at the base of the Rush Street Bridge (above).

Resolved, that we tender the heartfelt sympathy of the Illinois Saint Andrew Society to the families of our deceased brothers, in this The hour of their sad affliction and bereavement; and that, as a mark of respect to their memories (which the Society will always affectionately remember), the above resolutions be spread on the records of the Society, and that a copy be transmitted to the families of our deceased brothers.

GEORGE ANDERSON

George Anderson was born in Glasgow, Scotland, and came to Chicago in 1841. He attended the first anniversary dinner in 1845 and served as president of the Society in 1852.

Anderson enjoyed much success as a businessman. As an early-day Republican and ardent antislavery champion, he achieved local distinction. He served as deputy under Sheriff L. L. Wilson in 1858, and for years afterward he was employed in the Department of Public Works. He resigned from his post as superintendent of the Twenty-second and State Streets postal station and returned to private life when Grover Cleveland became president. Anderson, a Unitarian, was one of the charter members of the Illinois Saint Andrew Society. Anderson, along with other members of the his family, is buried in the family plot in Oak Woods Cemetery.

JOHN HUME KEDZIE

John Hume Kedzie was born in Stamford, Connecticut, on September 8, 1815. Adam Kedzie, his grandfather, emigrated from Hawick, Scotland, with his wife and eight children. They arrived in 1795 and settled in Delaware County, New York. The maternal grandfather Robert Hume crossed the Atlantic on the same vessel as the Kedzie family. He graduated from Oberlin College in 1841 and was admitted to the bar in 1847.

Kedzie came to Chicago in 1847 and began the practice of law. He gradually switched to real estate and became one of the leading citizens in town. His property dealings were mostly on the west and north sides of the city, and Kedzie Avenue is named in his honor. He saw the city laid to waste by the Great Fire of 1871. In 1868 he moved to Evanston and was instrumental in laying out the Kedzie and Keeney additions, which formed the nucleus of South Evanston. He was also involved in founding and developing Ravenswood. He opposed slavery in the South, espousing the cause of the abolitionist party and met with five or six others in the first meetings held to organize the Republican Party in Illinois. He died April 9, 1903. Kedzie is buried in a family plot at Rosehill. He was president of the Illinois Saint Andrew Society in 1854.

JOHN ALSTON

John Alston was born in Glasgow, Scotland, in 1821. He died in Chicago on January 13, 1899. In the Great Fire of 1871, Alston lost his glass and paint factory at 172 Randolph Street. He served as an alderman from 1859–60. His funeral took place at St. Andrew's Church, Washington Boulevard and Robey Street. Among the honorary pallbearers were John Kedzie, John McArthur, Daniel Cameron, William Stewart, John J. Badenoch, and John Sherriffs.

Alston was a charter member of the Society and served as president in 1855, 1856, 1891, and 1892. At the time of Alston's death John Sherriffs was the last surviving charter member.

ROBERT HERVEY

Robert Hervey was born in Glasgow on August 10, 1820. Hervey's father died when Robert was eleven. At that point his mother decided to emigrate to America. At seventeen, Hervey moved to Canada with the intention of entering the mercantile business with his uncles. However, he began the study of law and was admitted to the bar in 1841. He returned to Chicago in 1852 and entered into practice with Buckner S. Morris and Joseph P. Clarkson at Lake and Clark Streets. Eventually the firm became known as Hervey, Anthony, and Galt—one of the best known in the city. In 1873 he was admitted to practice before the U.S. Supreme Court. He was one of the founders of the Chicago Bar Association.

Hervey became a member of the Society in 1852, serving six terms as president. In the winter of 1865, "during which there was much suffering to be relieved among the poor and unfortunate, the funds of the Society became exhausted, and, at the request of his friends, Mr. Hervey prepared and delivered a lecture on Robert Burns at the old Metropolitan Hall. The receipts of this lecture netted the Society about $450" (*Album of Genealogy and Biography* 1899, 237–38).

The lecture was well received and was repeated several times. A lecture about Sir Walter Scott was also quite popular and brought the Society additional revenue. In 1856 Hervey helped organize the Caledonian Club and was chosen its first president, a position he held for several years.

For more than twenty-five years, Hervey and his family lived near the lake at Twenty-fifth Street, having moved to that location prior to the Great Fire of 1871. His office on Dearborn Street was destroyed in the fire and a valuable law library was also lost.

PIONEER SCOTS

Many Scots contributed greatly to the growth and development of the thriving frontier town of Chicago.

JOHN KINZIE

Often called the "Father of Chicago," John Kinzie is credited with being Chicago's first permanent white settler and first English-speaking resident. Kinzie arrived in Chicago in 1804, living in a cabin opposite Fort Dearborn. There he earned a reputation as a fair and trustworthy man who traded and established friendly relations with the Native American population (Pierce 1937, 18). It was said that Kinzie had a "good Scotch head upon his shoulders" (Gilbert 1929, 29). He was described by some as easygoing and amiable, strong and courageous. His house was the center of the small town's social life. Indeed, from 1804 to 1812, Kinzie was considered the most powerful man in Chicago.

Kinzie was born in Quebec in 1763, the son of John MacKenzie, or MacKinzie, a surgeon of Scottish descent in the British army. Kinzie was always looking for adventure. When he was just a lad of ten, he became determined to make his way back to Quebec. He did just that, with some help from kind strangers, and began searching the streets of his hometown for work. Kinzie was indentured as a silversmith for three years before joining his family at their new home in Detroit. Then he was off again, this time as a trader.

Life at Fort Dearborn was usually uneventful although it was occasionally punctuated with feuds—sometimes deadly. The ongoing altercation between Kinzie and John Lalime, an Indian interpreter, was one

SCOTS IN THE FUR TRADE

Scots played prominent roles in the fur trade, both in Chicago and elsewhere. Most of the employees of the Canadian-based Hudson's Bay Company, for example, were Scottish. Scots involved in the fur trade in Chicago included William Burnett, Ramsey Crooks, William H. Wallace, John Kinzie's son James Kinzie, and Kinzie's half brothers Thomas and Robert Forsyth. In addition to Hudson's Bay, other fur-trading firms included the North West Company, the XY Company, the Southwest Company, and the American Fur Company. John Kinzie's eldest son, John Harris Kinzie, worked for the American Fur Company alongside fellow Scot Robert Stuart.

"Kinzie Mansion – Near this site stood Kinzie Mansion, 1784–1832, home of Pointe Du Saible, Le Mai, and John Kinzie, Chicago's 'First Civilian' Here was born, in 1805, the city's first white child, Ellen Marion Kinzie." Inscription on the Kinzie monument.

of the worse examples. Apparently, a struggle erupted between the two men. Kinzie was wounded, and Lalime was fatally stabbed. Kinzie pleaded self-defense and, although some bad blood existed for a time between Kinzie and the officers of the fort—Lalime was well regarded by many officers there—Kinzie was ultimately exonerated (Gilbert 1929, 29–32).

The War of 1812 had just begun, placing Fort Dearborn's strategic Chicago location and its small population in danger. With word of a possible Indian attack imminent, the commander of Fort Dearborn, Captain Nathan Heald, was told to evacuate immediately and to proceed to Fort Wayne, Indiana. Kinzie thought evacuating was risky and instead maintained that it was far safer to remain situated at the fort.

Despite his protests, Kinzie agreed to accompany Captain William Wells and his party to safety. Rather than risk his family's health, however, he placed his wife and children on a boat. On August 15, 1812, Wells, Kinzie, and the rest of the party were attacked by a party of Indians, mostly Potawatomi, less than two miles from the fort. Kinzie survived, but twenty-six soldiers, including Wells, twelve children, and two women, were slain. The Fort Dearborn Massacre, as it came to be called, was one of the most tragic and violent episodes in Chicago history.

By the time of the massacre, most of the white settlers had already left Chicago. Kinzie returned in 1816, when the second Fort Dearborn was built, living in a small cottage in the area near what is now the Chicago Tribune Building. He became a trading agent for the new fort (McGowen 1989, 12), but he never really regained his former stature. Kinzie died in 1828 at age sixty-five.

Yet the Kinzie name is important in so many other ways. During the winter of 1810–11, for example, thirteen-year-old Robert A. Forsythe gave lessons to six-year-old John H. Kinzie, John Kinzie's son, in what was reportedly the first recorded tuition in Chicago. The teaching materials consisted of one spelling book, which had been brought from Detroit to Chicago in a chest of tea (Pierce 1937, 268). The younger Kinzie later married Juliette Magill and, in turn, this Juliette Magill Kinzie wrote the popular novel *Wau Bun: The "Early Days" of the Northwest,* a fictionalized account of the Fort Dearborn Massacre. John H. became one of Chicago's leading citizens. He was the first president of the village of Chicago. He also speculated aggressively in the booming real estate market, was active in securing a charter for a Chicago railroad, and was president of the Chicago branch of the second Illinois State Bank (Mayer and Wade 1969, 11). Another son, James Kinzie, built the Wolf Point Tavern in 1823, reportedly Chicago's first tavern, and later, in 1833, the popular Green Tree Tavern at Lake and Canal Streets. Kinzie Street is, of course, named in honor of John Kinzie.

ALEXANDER ROBINSON

Another influential figure of Scots descent was Alexander Robinson, a trader and Indian chief. Also known as Che-che-pin-qua (Blinking Eye), Robinson was born at Mackinaw, the son of a Scottish trader and a half Green Bay Chippewa Indian. He was also a close friend of John Kinzie. At the infamous Fort Dearborn Massacre of 1812 Robinson reportedly helped in the rescue attempt of Captain and Mrs. Heald and took them by boat to the safety of St. Joseph and eventually to Mackinac. Robinson returned to Chicago a few years later in 1814, settling in what is now the corner of Kinzie and Dearborn Streets. With Antoine Quilmette, who was half Potawatomi and half French, he farmed on land that once was used by the soldiers of Fort Dearborn (McGowen 1989, 12).

By 1816 or so Robinson had moved to the north side of the Chicago River near what is now Dearborn and Kinzie Streets and began working in the fur trade. Until 1825 he had a cabin and trading post at Hardscrabble (modern-day Bridgeport). Because he helped

the U.S. government as an interpreter and negotiator with the Indians, he was given in 1828 a frame house between Superior and Chicago Avenues, reportedly Chicago's first frame house. He also ran an Indian store and tavern near Wolf Point.

In 1826 Robinson married Catherine Chevallier. Her father was a Potawatomi chief. After the chief's death and during the 1825 Treaty at Prairie du Chien, Robinson was appointed chief of the Potawatomi, Ottawas, and Chippewas. He later represented them at the famous Chicago Treaty of 1833. As a result of that historic treaty, the tribes left in exchange for "better" land west of the Mississippi River. Robinson, however, chose to stay.

For his governmental services, Robinson and his family received generous portions of land on the banks of the Des Plaines River—about 1,200 acres from south of what is now Irving Park Road to the north to Foster Avenue. Today, these areas bear the names of Che-Che-Pin-Qua Woods, Robinson Woods, and Catherine Chevalier Woods. Robinson died on April 22, 1872. He is buried, along with family members, on a plot of ground on the northwest corner of East River Road and Lawrence Avenue, the heart of his former reservation (38).

"THE OLD DOCTOR" AND THE GROVE

Dr. John Kennicott, or "The Old Doctor," as he was called, came to an area called the Grove in 1836, at that time little more than an untamed prairie northwest of Chicago. Here he built a log house for his family and catered to the medical needs of the area's settlers. The presently standing John Kennicott House dates back to 1856. During the 1840s and 1850s, a visit out to the Kennicott farmhouse became the preferred way of spending a leisurely Sunday afternoon by the city's elite (Drury 1948, 130).

Dr. Kennicott was the father of the Illinois naturalist and Arctic explorer, Robert Kennicott. Robert was the first director of the Chicago Academy of Sciences.

The Chicago Academy of Natural Sciences was incorporated in April 1859 under the name of the Chicago Academy of Sciences. Robert Kennicott collected and documented thousands of Illinois flowers, birds, and insects. It was this collection that became the foundation for the future academy. In that same year Kennicott participated in the most important expedition of his life. It lasted three years and included travels to British North America (Canada) and portions of what is now Alaska. Kennicott received a great deal of assistance from the officers of the Hudson's Bay Company in Canada, most of whom were Scottish and, in particular, Orcadian. Of his reception there, he wrote:

> *The larger part of the gentlemen in the Hudson's Bay Company service are Scotch. They are generally of good families and well educated; and that they are hospitable and companionable, I can testify of all whom I met. (James 1940, 28)*

Kennicott spent the winter of 1862–63 at the Smithsonian Institution in Washington, D.C., cataloging much of the material that he collected during his trip in the North. The following year he accepted the curatorship of the Chicago Academy of Sciences. He later became its director and a trustee (James 1940, 34). In May 1866 Kennicott died during one of his expeditions in the small Russian outpost of Nulato at the age of thirty. He was buried at the Grove (38n. 16).

Another son of "The Old Doctor," John A. Kennicott, himself a successful Chicago

Alexander Robinson (above)

"Kennicott House was built in 1856 by John A. Kennicott, a prominent Illinois physician, horticulturalist, and educational and agricultural leader. Kennicott moved to The Grove from New Orleans with his family in 1836 shortly after the birth of his son, Robert, in 1835 He devoted much of his time to the study and promotion of horticulture and agriculture, developing The Grove into the first major nursery in northern Illinois. Robert Kennicott developed an interest in nature at an early age , studying with his father. He helped found the Chicago Academy of Sciences, and his explorations of Alaska gave the United States its first scientific knowledge of that region and influenced the decision for its purchase." Inscription at The Grove National Historic Site, Glenview, Illinois.

dentist, built an elegant mansion at what is now Forty-eighth Street and Dorchester Avenue on the South Side. He called his home "Kenwood," reportedly after his mother's family estate in Scotland. The name became attached to the surrounding community when General George B. McClellan, who was vice president of the Illinois Central, officiated at the opening of the Forty-seventh Street station and christened it "Kenwood" (Holt and Pacyga 1979, 67). From the 1880s to the 1920s, Kenwood remained a fashionable neighborhood of Chicago. Among its more illustrious residents were architect Louis Sullivan, John G. Shedd, Mayor Edward H. Kelly, and philanthropist Julius Rosenwald (68).

In 1923 the noted nature writer Donald Culross Peattie married the great-granddaughter of "The Old Doctor," Louise Redfield. The couple spent many eventful summers at Kennicott Grove. Louise Redfield's brother, Robert Redfield, an anthropologist at the University of Chicago, also lived and worked at the Grove as did Peattie's brother, Roderick Peattie, a geographer and writer. Two natural history books were set at the Grove, Donald C. Peattie's *A Prairie Grove* and Louise Redfield Peattie's *American Acres* (Drury 1948). Donald's father, Robert Burns Peattie, was a reporter for several Chicago newspapers, including the *Chicago Daily Herald* and the *Chicago Daily News.* Donald's mother, Elia Peattie, was literary editor of the *Chicago Tribune* and author of *The Precipice,* now considered a classic piece of Chicago fiction.

Today the Grove, an eighty-two-acre nature retreat and environmental center, is called the "Walden Pond of the Prairie." In 1976 the Grove, which consists of three houses (the Kennicott House, the Redfield Center, and the Interpretive Center) surrounded by woodlands, gardens, and 500-year-old oak trees, was declared a national historic landmark. In late 1995 the MacArthur Foundation gave an additional forty-one acres that it owned to the Glenview Park District, owner of the Grove. The noted Scottish American philanthropist and businessman John D. MacArthur had bought the land years earlier with thoughts of converting the space for corporate headquarters (Spencer 1995, 7). The Redfield Center was built in 1929 and replaced an earlier structure that had burned down.

ROBERT FERGUS

Robert Fergus was considered the father of the printing industry in Chicago. He came to the small frontier town in July 1839. Fergus was also a charter member of the Illinois Saint Andrew Society.

Fergus was born in Glasgow on August 4, 1815, the youngest son of John Fergus and Margaret Patterson Aitken. At fifteen he was apprenticed to a Glasgow printing house. Around this time he began collecting the works of Scottish authors, which became a lifelong passion.

Fergus first went to Milwaukee before finally settling in Chicago. He worked as a printer in several print shops and then entered into a partnership with William Ellis. His first office was in the old Saloon Building. It was here that he worked on Chicago's first city directory. Fergus, however, is best known perhaps for his Fergus Historical Series. He published some thirty issues, including a reprint of Kinzie's *Narrative* as well as biographical sketches of early Chicagoans, remembrances, and papers of the Chicago Historical Society, of which Fergus himself was a member (Regnery 1993, 13).

During these early years, Fergus lost his shop twice to fires. But it was the Great Fire of 1871 that truly devastated him and the work that he had accumulated over a thirty-year period (11–15).

Fergus was killed on June 23, 1897, while crossing the train tracks during a violent rainstorm in Evanston (14).

LAUGHLIN FALCONER

Another pioneer Scot was a man from Inverness named Laughlin Falconer. In 1848 Falconer bought an eighty-acre site and erected a white frame house at the corner of Cicero and Wellington Avenues. Like many an emigrant, Falconer did not bring much in the way of material goods with him to the new land. But one of his prized possessions was an old flintlock musket, which an ancestor of his who fought in George III's army carried. Laughlin's brother, David, had arrived in Chicago some years earlier, in 1832, when it was little more than a settlement of a few log and frame houses surrounding Fort Dearborn. The Falconer brothers, however, preferred a quieter spot. They decided on a remote area on the prairies some six miles northwest of the fort. Later, the land that the Falconers had settled on was called Grayland, in honor of a pioneer named John Gray. Later, still, it was changed to Kelvyn Grove. In the Falconers' days, the brothers worked as farmers, selling their produce in the old South Water Street Market and driving their creaky wagons down Milwaukee Avenue.

Like many Scots in the city's history, Falconer would have been completely forgotten if not for the school named after him that stands at 3020 N. Lamon Avenue. Other Chicago public schools named in honor of Scots or Scottish Americans include:

Alexander Graham Bell School
3730 N. Oakley Avenue

Robert Burns School
2524 S. Central Park Avenue

Daniel R. Cameron School
1234 N. Monticello Avenue

Andrew Carnegie School
1414 E. 61st Place

Rachel Carson School
5516 S. Maplewood Avenue

George Rogers Clark School
1045 S. Monitor

Stephen A. Douglas School
3200 S. Calumet Avenue

Thomas A. Edison School
6220 N. Olcott Avenue

Alexander Fleming School
4918 W. Sixty-fourth Street

Robert Fulton School
5300 S. Hermitage Avenue

Ulysses S. Grant School
145 S. Campbell Avenue

Alexander Hamilton School
1650 W. Cornelia Avenue

Patrick Henry School
4250 N. St. Louis Avenue

John H. Kinzie School
5625 S. Mobile Avenue

James Monroe School
3651 W. Schubert Avenue

Samuel Morse School
620 N. Sawyer Avenue

John T. Pirie School
650 E. Eighty-fifth Street

Adlai E. Stevenson School
8010 S. Kostner Avenue

Graeme Stuart School
4525 N. Kenmore Avenue

Ella Flagg Young School
1434 N. Parkside Avenue

ANDREW MACLEISH

Andrew MacLeish was born in Glasgow, Scotland, on June 28, 1838. His father, Archibald MacLeish, was an important dry goods merchant. Andrew learned the mechanics of conducting business while in London. When his childhood sweetheart, Lilias Young, decided to emigrate to America and settled in Chicago, MacLeish followed her, arriving in 1856. Two years later he married her.

MacLeish found work with the firm of J. D. Sherman on Lake Street. He was so well liked and respected that he was given the responsibility of opening a store in the small town of Kewanee, Illinois. Kewanee was too quiet for MacLeish, however, and he returned to Chicago to work with J. B. Shay Company, also on Lake Street. He became a partner there until a bigger company, Carson Pirie Scott and Company, offered MacLeish a better position. Under MacLeish's leadership, Carson Pirie Scott and Company flourished as a retail store until it was destroyed in the Great Fire of 1871.

MacLeish was able to salvage some of the store's belongings. There is the perhaps apocryphal story that he personally went to every available person on the street with a wagon or truck and offered them $50 to carry away as much of Carson's property as was possible (Gilbert and Bryson 1929, 740).

Two Carson's stores opened after the fire, one at Madison and Peoria and another on West Twenty-second Street. The flagship store moved several times before settling in at the present location at Madison, State, and Wabash.

After the death of his first wife, MacLeish married M. Louise Little and then, after her death, Martha Hillard. He had three daughters, Lily, Mrs. C.K.G. Billings, and Isabel, and three sons, Norman, Archibald, and Kenneth. Kenneth was killed in action in France during World War I. A modern-day Renassiance man, Archibald was one of the twentieth century's greatest American poets.

MacLeish was a trustee of the University of Chicago, a charter member of the Union League Club, and a founder of the Northern Baptist convention.

SYLVESTER LIND

Born in Aberdeenshire, Scotland, in 1807, Lind was a carpenter by trade. He came to Chicago in 1837 and started a small lumber business. Like many Chicagoans he suffered the up and downs of the young town, winning and losing fortunes several times during his careers in lumber, real estate, and insurance. He once served as water commis-

sioner for Chicago but is probably best know today as being the four-term mayor of Lake Forest. He served as a charter member of the Lake Forest Association. He was also was instrumental in the founding of Lake Forest University. Originally called Lind University, Lind had offered a gift of $100,000 for the establishment of an institution of higher learning. Unfortunately, he was unable to meet his financial obligations and the offer was rescinded (Ebner 1988, 27).

GEORGE SMITH

In 1836 a Scottish businessman named George Smith established the Chicago Marine and Fire Insurance Company, which met with great success. Smith was born in the parish of Old Deer, Aberdeenshire, in the northeast of Scotland. He had made a fortune in Chicago in real estate only two years before establishing his insurance company. Impressed with the little village's possibilities and its land speculation, he returned to Scotland to organize the Scottish Land Investment Company. A few years later he came back to Chicago and with Patrick Strachan and William D. Scott, two Scottish bankers, acted as agents for the company (Pierce 1937, 160). Smith was also a director of the Galena and Chicago Union Railroad and a charter member of the Chicago Board of Trade. He returned to Scotland and died there in 1899.

Other early Chicago Scots included David McKee, reportedly the first blacksmith in what is now Chicago; coroner Orsemus Morrison, who once owned the now demolished Morrison Hotel at the corner of Clark and Madison; real estate speculator and lumber dealer Peter Crawford, for whom Crawford Avenue, the original name of Pulaski Road, was so honored; and baker Hugh Templeton, one of the founders and an elder of the Jefferson Park Presbyterian Church.

VISITORS FROM SCOTLAND

Pioneer Chicago was a favorite destination for many overseas visitors, including quite a few from Scotland.

An early visitor was a Scottish farmer named Patrick Shirreff. As early as 1835 Shirreff could see that the little village held great promise: "Chicago consists of about 150 wood houses, placed irregularly on both sides of the river, over which there is a bridge," he wrote. "This is already a place of considerable trade. . . and when connected with the navigable point of the river Illinois, by a canal or railway, cannot fail of rising to importance. Almost every person I met regarded Chicago as the germ of an immense city (Shirreff 1835, 226).

Several years later an Edinburgh lawyer, James Logan (1838, 104), spent a short time in Chicago, which he described as "rather pleasantly situated, being elevated from the lake; the streets are wide, and the houses are wooden, excepting two large stores, which are of brick. Four years ago it did not contain more than a hundred inhabitants, and now it boasts nearly 5,000. This rapid increase it owes to its favourable position at the head of Lake Michigan, which renders it the port for all sorts of goods to and from New York. Indeed, so favourably is it looked upon by the Americans in general, that many persons from various parts of the States have purchased town lots, and built large frame stores" (Logan 1838, 104).

In 1869 William and W. F. Robertson (1871, 54) visited when Chicago had grown to 350,000

Sylvester Lind House, Lake Forest, Illinois (above)

inhabitants. "This city is admittedly the most go-a-head in the whole Union." Although generally impressed with the town's robust vitality, the Robertsons were "greatly disappointed" by the low caliber of accommodations, "which was about the worst we met with in the States, Omaha always excepted, and quite unworthy of the city." They were only too glad to leave behind the "mosquitoes and dirt of the famed Sherman House" (59).

Some Scots were struck by what they considered the wickedness of the city and its notorious reputation for immorality. "What she does she does with all her might. Her good people are very good, her bad people are very bad." But what really struck the first-time visitor was Chicagoans mad rush for wealth. "Chicago is a young New York. The deep-mouthed roar of the Empire City becomes a Babel of shrill voices in the West, but the universal cry is the same 'Dollars and cents, dollars and cents' " (Macrae 1870, 1:197).

Scots, for the most part, received a cordial welcome. "Everywhere, from the New England farm-house to the Georgian plantation, the fact that I was a stranger from Scotland seemed sufficient to secure me a kindly welcome" (xxii).

More than forty years after Chicago was incorporated, another visitor made his way here. Undoubtedly he was the most famous Scot to visit Chicago in the nineteenth century.

On August 7, 1879, Robert Louis Stevenson set sail for the New World, leaving Glasgow and bound for New York on the *Devonia*. Like many before him, he experienced the confined quarters on one of the immigrant trains that crisscrossed the country, stopping briefly in Chicago. The city did not make a particularly good first impression:

Chicago seemed a great and gloomy city. I remember having subscribed, let us say sixpence, toward its restoration at the period of the fire; and now when I beheld street after street of ponderous houses and crowds of comfortable burghers, I thought it would be a graceful act for the corporation to refund that sixpence or, at the least, to entertain me to a cheerful dinner. But there was no word of restitution. I was that city's benefactor, yet I was received in a third-class waiting room, and the best dinner I could get was a dish of ham and eggs at my own expense.

I can safely say, I have never been so dog-tired as that night in Chicago. I sat, or rather lay, on some steps in the station, and was gratefully conscious of every point of contact between my body and the boards. My one ideal of pleasure was to stretch myself flat on my back with arms extended, like a dying hermit in a picture, and to move no more. I bought a newspaper, but could not summon up the energy to read it; I debated with myself if it were worth while to make a cigarette, and unanimously decided that it was not.

When it was time to start, I descended the platform like a man in a dream. It was a long train, lighted from end to end; and car after car, as I came up with it, was not only full but overflowing. . . . I was hot, feverish, painfully athirst; and there was a great darkness over me, an internal darkness, not to be dispelled by gas. When at last I found an empty bench, I sank into it like of bundle of rugs; the world seemed to swim away into the distance; and my consciousness dwindled within me to a mere pin's head, like a taper on a foggy night. (Stevenson 1985, 120)

Cyrus McCormick

TWO

Drovers, Soldiers, and Civil War

In 1850 the population of Chicago was almost 30,000. By that time the city had made significant strides toward becoming the premier town of the West. More than half of the inhabitants were foreign born, with the Irish and Germans posting the highest tallies. But there were also English, Swedes, Norwegians, Danes, and French (Mayer and Wade 1969, 30). Trailing far behind were the Scots at 610. A decade later the figure had jumped to 1,641 and on the eve of the Great Fire of 1871 to 4,197 (Pierce 1940, 16).

The city grew in all directions. By 1856 it had a system of public transportation that carried some 7 million passengers annually. These horse-drawn street railroad cars were uncomfortable and by present-day standards extremely slow. However, they were much faster than walking and allowed people to live farther from the city.

As the heart of the city grew, it also changed. After the Civil War the commercial heart moved from Clark and Lake Streets to State Street. In 1867 Potter Palmer, a merchant from back East, bought property along State Street. He soon persuaded others to follow him and even convinced the city council to widen the street (Mayer and Wade 1969, 54). In the 1860s anyone desiring fashionable living followed Marshall Field and Philip Armour to an area along Prairie Avenue and Twenty-second Street. The Second Presbyterian Church would become the place of worship for the Prairie Avenue residents and the religious home for many prominent Scottish American families.

The immense growth that the city witnessed was made possible by the railroads. Chicago had become the terminal between East and West, the Atlantic and the Pacific. Not only did railroads bring livestock, wheat, and oats, they also brought the immigrant to the New World. How the railroads entered the city was also very important since they needed to reach the industries that were positioned along the Chicago River. The Illinois Central purchased part of old Fort Dearborn and also land along the river. From Senator Stephen A. Douglas they purchased water rights south of the city. Douglas, of Scottish descent, played an important role in Chicago's history and the shape of its downtown area. He had speculated in land along the lake shore and the Lake Calumet region, and he was also instrumental in obtaining federal land grants for the Illinois Central. His monument on Thirty-fifth Street overlooks the railroad he helped create.

The coming of the railroad, however, did not eliminate the growth of traffic on the lake. Iron came from the northern Great Lakes and lumber from Michigan and Wisconsin. By 1869 shipping to Chicago harbor reached 3 million tons. Hundreds of vessels would often arrive in one day. Individuals moving to the west needed lumber for houses and barns, and Chicago became the lumber capital of the world. Stretching along the South Branch of the Chicago River were miles and miles of lumber mills and related industries.

Chicago also became the grain center of the world. In 1859 the city had exported 16,000,000 bushels of grain. A year later the figure had almost doubled to 31,000,000. By 1862 the grain export reached 65,400,000 bushels. Cyrus McCormick, a Presbyterian of Ulster Scot ancestry, and his reaper must be given credit for this dramatic increase. As the war progressed more and more reapers were produced to harvest the grain. Even though every third man was in the army at that time, grain production on the prairies rose.

THE STOCKYARDS

If corn and wheat were a sign of the growing importance of the city, so was the livestock industry. One-third of all the slaughtering in the West was done in Chicago. Originally the slaughtering plants were located along the river, but in the 1860s the meatpacking industry moved some four miles southwest of the city. The first cattle shipments were made from Chicago.

By 1880 refrigerator cars had revolutionized the meatpacking industry, making shipment possible to the East Coast and even as far away as Europe. The slaughtering and packing industries in the United States, worth less than $30 million in 1860, expanded to being worth more than $300 million in 1870 and more than $564 million in 1890 (Brander 1982, 103–4). It didn't take long before Chicago could claim the title of the meatpacking capital of the country. The Big Five companies—Armour, Swift, Nelson Morris, Continental Packing Company, and Libby, McNeill, & Libby Company—were

located here (Hirsch and Goler 1990, 60).

The stockyards—the pride of Chicago—opened on Christmas Day, 1865. The Union Stock Yard was located at Halsted Street and Thirty-ninth Street and covered nearly 350 acres (Pierce 1940, 94). It could house 21,000 cattle, 75,000 hogs, and 20,000 sheep. With its hotels and restaurants, it was practically a city within a city. There were seven miles of streets, paved with wooden blocks. Thirty-one miles of sewers kept the area sanitary. Troughs, three miles in length, brought clear water from a well drilled a thousand feet below the surface. Time would see many Scots laboring in the stockyards of Chicago.

Indeed, the stockyards were built by Scottish Americans, Scottish immigrants, and the Scotch Irish—including the Armours, the Wilsons, and former president of the Stock Yards William Wood Prince, among others—while many of the cattle owners and drovers were themselves Scottish immigrants. More than a few of the original cattle breeders and livestock personnel were also of Scots descent.

Philip Danforth Armour, one of Chicago's wealthiest citizens, built the largest meatpacking company in the country in the city. He was born May 16, 1832, in Stockbridge, New York. The Armours for generations had lived in an area of Scotland known as Argyllshire, the chief city being Campbeltown. The Armours arrived in the colonies from Scotland during the mid-eighteenth century. Armour was educated at Cazenovia Academy in New York and then worked on the family farm. He later set out across the country to pan for gold in the fields of California. He then moved to Wisconsin with a sizable fortune and started a wholesale grocery business. In association with his brother Herman, he became involved in grain commissions and meatpacking plants.

Union Stock Yard, 1866 (left)

Philip Armour

Out of these ventures came the firm of Armour and Company with its headquarters in Chicago. It was destined to become the nation's largest meatpacker with worldwide operations. Armour revolutionized many modern livestock management techniques. He built low-cost rental apartments for his workers and founded the Armour Institute of Technology, which is now known as the Illinois Institute of Technology. Armour was also a member of the Illinois Saint Andrew Society and, it was said, one of its most generous supporters. He died on January 6, 1901.

The advent of the Civil War helped the stockyards' business tremendously. Cattle and hogs from the yards went to feed the hungry soldiers of the Union army (Wade 1987, 32–33). Within a fairly short amount of time the stockyards had become world famous. No visitor wanted to leave without visiting them. Going to Chicago without seeing the stockyards, said one *Chicago Tribune* reporter, was like visiting Rome without seeing the Coliseum (84). John Kerr Campell, a visitor from Scotland, agreed. His most vivid memory was the sound of "thousands of cattle bellowing . . . hogs squealing and so many men roaring" (183).

SCOTS ABOLITIONISTS

While the abolitionist movement was very much an international movement, Scotland played a small but significant role. The first printed protest against slavery was reportedly published by a Scottish Quaker by the name of Reverend George Keith as far back as 1693, while the first antislavery governor of Pennsylvania, James Pollock, was a Scot (MacDougall 1992, 37).

Chicago Daily Drovers Journal, 1955

THE STOCK YARD INN

The Stock Yard Inn, a three-story Tudor-style hotel on South Halsted Street said to be modeled after Shakespeare's home in Stratford-on-Avon, England, was built in 1912. Politicians roamed its corridors during five national political conventions held at the nearby (and now demolished) International Amphitheatre. Some of the more famous guests included Calvin Coolidge, Herbert Hoover, Franklin Delano Roosevelt, Harry Truman, Dwight Eisenhower, and John F. Kennedy. But it was also filled with more humble persons—farmers, cattle owners, truck drivers, drovers, ranchers, and cowhands. After fire destroyed the original building, a new inn reopened in 1934. The fire also destroyed the Livestock National Bank, the *Drovers Journal,* and the Livestock Records Building, which housed the equally famous Saddle and Sirloin Club.

It was said that the highest honor you could give packers was to hang their portraits in the gallery of the Saddle and Sirloin Club. The club, whose name was taken from a series of articles about the work of British breeders in Scotland and England, was founded in 1903. Both the portrait gallery and the club were the brainchild of Robert Burns Ogilvie, secretary of the American Clydesdale Association. The original artist hired to paint the portraits was Arvid Nyholm. Ogilvie died in 1923.

Numerous Scots were represented. Among the more prominent included Robert Aitchison Alexander, a Scot who emigrated to Kentucky, where he bred thoroughbred horses and shorthorn cattle; Philip Danforth Armour, founder of Armour and Company; Captain Barclay, a large Scottish landholder and one of the most successful breeders of shorthorn cattle; Walter Biggar, a Scottish breeder, judge, and exporter of cattle; Scots-born Dr. W. J. Butler, long-time director of the International Live Stock Exposition; Alexander Galbraith, early secretary of the American Clydesdale Breeders Association; Murdo Mackenzie, one of the largest cattle ranchers in the world; and Robert Burns Ogilvie himself. Other Scots or Scottish Americans were John Clay, Sr., James I. Davidson, Robert A. Fairbairn, Sir George MacPherson Grant, General Ulysses S. Grant, W. J. Grant, Dr. James Law, Andrew Little, James D. MacGregor, Archibald MacNeilage, William McCombie, John Miller, William Miller, Jr., Andrew Montgomery, Dr. John Gunion Rutherford, W. J. Tod, Hugh Watson, James Wilson, and Thomas E. Wilson (Runnion 1992).

A fire destroyed the Saddle and Sirloin Club ballroom, once an elite club, and all of the 350 oil paintings of the livestock breeders and meatpackers that hung on the halls and in the private dining room of Frederick Prince, an important figure in the stockyards. The baronial hall boasted a paneled and vaulted ceiling (Currie 1976).

In the aftermath of the damage, Robert W. Grafton was commissioned to repaint Nyholm's portraits. Grafton was a Chicago-born portrait painter who studied at the Art Institute of Chicago as well as in Paris, Holland, and England. He completed 164 portraits before he died. His work was then continued by Othmar Hoffler (Runnion 1992).

The Stock Yard Inn was demolished in early 1977. The stockyards themselves closed on August 1, 1971. All that remains of the stockyard era is the Old Stone Gate at 850 W. Exchange Avenue, which was built in 1879 and was most likely designed by the famous architectural firm of Burnham and Root. The portrait collection is now the property of the Kentucky Fair and Exposition Center.

The most influential of Scotland's abolitionist leaders, George Thompson, argued that "as a citizen of the world he claimed brotherhood with all mankind" (Rice 1981, 4). Some Britishers believed that because American society had been created by British government and British law that Britain should claim ultimate responsibility for the unfortunate institution of slavery. Captain Charles Stuart, a Scottish soldier, hence could proclaim:

> *The United States of America are our sister land. Like us, they boast of freedom—like us, they are pouring the Bible and light all over the world—and like us, they disgrace their professions and tarnish their fair name, by keeping slaves. . . .They lay this sin to our charge, and unquestionably the guilt of its origin is ours. They are our progeny—they were long and subject to our laws. (5)*

In nineteenth-century America people still thought highly of British attitudes so that it was not unusual for a Scottish publication, such as the *Edinburgh Review* to have better sales than the indigenous *North American Review* (10). When William Lloyd Garrison, America's foremost abolitionist leader and publisher of the *Liberator* newspaper, toured Britain, looking for support for his abolitionist views, he turned to Thompson for help. With Thompson's influence, emancipation societies were formed in Glasgow and Edinburgh (16). "By 1830, disapproval of slavery could be assumed in all respectable and literate Scots homes," says Rice (23). It is significant that the outspoken Fanny Wright, a Scot from Dundee who was considered the first American woman lecturer, visited America in 1818–20 and was a forerunner in the antislavery movement (MacDougall 1992, 71).

Pinkerton family residence on Ashland Boulevard (above)

Disapproval of the principle of slavery dates back to at least the mid-eighteenth century in Scotland, if not earlier, especially among Scottish intellectuals. The first edition of the then Edinburgh-based *Encyclopaedia Britannica,* for example, denounced the slave trade as "scarce defensible on the foot either of religion or humanity" (Rice 1981, 20).

Scottish influence was felt across the Atlantic, too. Antislavery societies sprang up in Chicago in the 1840s. They included the Chicago Anti-Slavery Society; the Chicago Female Anti-Slavery Society, which held meetings at the First Presbyterian Church; and the Illinois Anti-Slavery Society (Pierce 1940, 244). Although the Fugitive Slave Laws of 1850 had demanded the return of slaves who had fled from their owners, Chicagoans generally did their best to ignore the odious law. Hence, the city council passed a resolution that any lawmakers from the free states who passed such laws were "fit only to be ranked with the traitors Benedict Arnold and Judas Iscariot." The council believed that saving fugitives from "oppression" was not contrary to the law of the land (Freshman 1982, 24). Although Chicagoans largely expressed antislavery sentiments and had noble desires to protect the civil rights of African Americans, they hardly viewed their African American counterparts as equals, however. (12).

ALLAN PINKERTON

Allan Pinkerton's West Adams Street house was a famous stop on the Underground Railroad. Many African Americans stayed there before making their journey to freedom. The Glasgow-born Pinkerton and his wife immigrated to America in 1842. He spent his first year in Chicago working at a local brewery before opening a cooper's shop in the little Scottish community of Dundee, some forty miles west of the city. Pinkerton, an avowed supporter of laborer's rights in his native Scotland, inadvertently started his career as a detective when he accidentally came across the hideout of a gang of counterfeiters and helped to bring them to justice.

Pinkerton founded his famous detective agency in 1850. Its original purpose, according to some accounts, was to help runaway slaves escape to freedom on the underground railroad—Pinkerton was a staunch abolitionist—but it didn't take long before Pinkerton began pursuing the criminal element on a full-time basis. By 1860 Pinkerton had not only become a well-known crimestopper but he also had become one of the most prominent abolitionists in Chicago.

When Pinkerton moved west to Dundee he found in the little community many like-minded individuals. Most of the Scots in the area were devout abolitionists. Pinkerton's belief in the rightness of the movement was so strong that he reportedly ran for office in the Abolitionist Party in the county (Dupre 1985, 66).

In 1873 Pinkerton, at the height of his career, moved into a lavish mansion in Onarga, a small community southeast of Chicago. Nine years earlier Pinkerton had acquired a 254-acre farm on the outskirts of town. Here he built his dream house. The villa received the nickname of "The Larches"

Pinkerton burial site, Graceland Cemetery (above)

because of the profusion of larch trees—imported from Scotland—that he planted. It was said that Pinkerton had built his version of the gentlemen's estates that he had admired so much in Scotland. The weekend estate—Pinkerton would take the Illinois Central down from Chicago—reportedly contained a fish pond, a swimming pool, a race track, an immense barn that housed from forty to fifty ponies, a wine cellar called the "Snuggery," and several greenhouses. The walls of the Snuggery were supposedly decorated with murals of Scottish heroes (Drury 1948, 191–93).

STEPHEN DOUGLAS

As far back as 1860 Chicago was a Democratic city, and Stephen Douglas, a Scottish American and Illinois' favorite son, was the most famous Democrat of them all. Douglas was Chicago's first politician to make a name for himself nationally. Short in stature but long known for his integrity and his skills as a great orator, Douglas earned the well-deserved nickname of the "Little Giant."

Douglas was born on April 23, 1813, in Brandon, Vermont, the son of a New York physician. In 1834 he obtained a license from the Supreme Court to practice law and opened an office in Jacksonville, Illinois. Douglas held a number of important offices as a young man on the rise. He was a member of the Illinois House of Representatives from 1836 to 1837, then Illinois secretary of state from 1840 to 1841, judge of the Illinois Supreme Court from 1841 to 1847, and finally a U.S. senator from Illinois.

In 1850 Douglas led the campaign in Congress to make land grants to Illinois for the Illinois Central Railroad, which would link Chicago to the West. Many others wanted a southern route for what was then the longest railroad in America. The fact that the Illinois Central ran along lakefront property owned by Douglas only serves to reinforce the "Little Giant's" historical continuity with the Chicago political tradition.

Douglas had a strong connection with the first University of Chicago. An earlier University of Chicago (not the current one) was originally called Douglas University. In 1854 Stephen Douglas donated a parcel of land along Cottage Grove Avenue and Thirty-third Street for the school. The cornerstone of the main building was laid in July 1857, and the doors opened in 1860. Two years earlier he had purchased seventy acres along the lake between Thirty-third and Thirty-fifth Streets. His purpose was to be an urban developer of sorts. He wanted the

Stephen Douglas (above)

land to be (1) donated to an educational institution and (2) to have a portion of the land be set aside for residential parks. His wish came true with the establishment of Groveland Park and Woodland Park. The following year he moved into his Oakenwald estate at what is now 34 East Thirty-fifth Street (Duis and Holt 1979, 49). Economic turmoil and the outbreak of the Civil War, however, waylaid the plan. The university never really got off the ground—it finally closed in 1886—but eventually the present University of Chicago would prove to be wildly successful (MacMillan 1919, 21; Duis and Holt 1979, 49).

Douglas was a man of strong principles. He firmly believed in the concept of manifest destiny, for example. He also held firm opinions regarding the sensitive subject of slavery. Whereas Abraham Lincoln, Douglas's erstwhile opponent, advocated federal legislation that would prohibit slavery in any of the territories, Douglas believed that only the will of the people should determine whether or not a territory remained free of slavery. He referred to this notion as *popular sovereignty.*

In 1854 Douglas presented the Kansas-Nebraska bill to Congress. This legislation, passed and signed in June of that year, established Kansas and Nebraska as U.S. territories; more important, it stated that the people of these territories would decide for themselves whether or not to allow slavery on their soil. In other words, it was a direct contradiction of the Missouri Compromise of 1820, which banished any slavery north of the Mason-Dixon line. A great many Chicagoans objected to Douglas's bill. Democratic newspapers rejected it too (Pierce 1940, 207).

Douglas faced considerable opposition during his campaign for reelection to the U.S. Senate. His challenger? None other than Abraham Lincoln, the tall, gaunt, craggy-faced lawyer from downstate Illinois. Lincoln, a member of the newly created Republican Party, favored keeping slavery out of the territories.

After the passage of the Kansas-Nebraska bill, Douglas went on a speaking tour, which included a stop in Chicago. Writes one observer, "To the militant antislavery people here, his arrival was like the Japanese ambassador coming for a visit a couple of days after Pearl Harbor. The church bells of many congregations rang for half an hour in a syncopated, clanging protest. The flags of most of the ships in the Chicago River harbor were lowered to half mast, as if to signify the death of righteousness" (Freshman 1982, 24).

Douglas spoke at Market Hall, near Randolph and State. A crowd of 10,000 gathered, which proceeded to heckle and hiss the politician for hours and hours. Unable to express his views, an angry Douglas gave up in frustration, bellowing, "Abolitionists of Chicago! It is now Sunday morning. I'll go to church, and you may go to hell!" (25). Although none of the famous Douglas-Lincoln debates were held in Chicago, both candidates did speak on successive nights from the balcony of the Tremont Hotel at Lake and Dearborn Streets.

Ultimately, Douglas won the election by a close margin and was returned to the Senate, but his days were numbered. Two years later, Lincoln beat Douglas in the presidential election of 1860. Lincoln was nominated as the Republican Party's choice for the presidency in May 1860 at the Wigwam, a wooden building at the southeast corner of Lake and Market (Wacker) Streets on the site where once stood Mark Beaubien's famous Sauganash Hotel (Gilbert 1929, 116). It was the city's first national political convention.

On November 6, 1860, Chicagoans went early to the polls and gave Lincoln the necessary edge: 10,000 votes to Douglas's 8,000 votes. "By ten o'clock that evening, the telegraph had brought an excited city enough reports to assure the followers of Lincoln that the Midwest had gone Republican"

(Pierce 1940, 248).

Douglas died in Chicago on June 3, 1861.

OUTBREAK

As the Saint Andrew Society was being formed in Chicago, Abraham Lincoln was on his way to Washington to begin his first term as a member of the House of Representatives. After serving two terms, Lincoln returned to Springfield and by 1850 was one of the most eminent lawyers in Illinois. He traveled extensively throughout the state, visiting Chicago often. Many members of the Society supported Lincoln, including George Anderson, whose obituary stated he was "an 'early-day' Republican and a supporter."

At the outbreak of the Civil War patriotic fervor ran high in Chicago. The city's population in 1861 was a little more than 100,000. But some 15,000 men—mostly volunteers—went off to war. "Men tended to go into the army with men they were associated with. There were ethnic units of Irish, Hungarians, Germans, and Jews. There were occupational units of railroad men, firemen, board of trade workers, and bridge tenders" (Freshman 1982, 25) Altogether there were 140 volunteer units representing Illinois.

But the volunteer units were not nearly enough. Union armies had already been defeated at places like Bull Run and Lexington. Consequently the local units were combined to form the Fifty-first Illinois Infantry, which included the Chicago Light Guard, the Wentworth Light Infantry, the Ellsworth Zouaves, the Anderson Rifles, the Garden City Guard, the Bryan Light Guard, the Chicago Citizen Corps, the Fremont Fencibles, the Union Railroad Guard, and the Sturges Light Guards (29). After a long line of Union commanders had lost in disgrace, President Lincoln ordered the command of the entire Union forces to a soldier from Galena, Illinois, named Ulysses S. Grant.

In 1919, Thomas MacMillan made a detailed study of the state adjutant general's complete roster of Civil War volunteers from Illinois. "Of the officers who attained the rank of Lieutenant-Colonel, and above," he wrote, "more than sixty are of Scottish birth and ancestry. The officers from Major to Second Lieutenant of Scots descent number into the hundreds."

During the duration of the war Chicago took the lead in providing necessary goods, commodities, and men. The city became the leading center for guns, bullets, and uniforms, as well as the primary market for pork, beef, and bread. The Rand McNally printing and publishing house was formed; iron and brass foundries were established; meatpacking, men's clothing, and agricultural machinery became dominant industries. Cyrus McCormick's reaper factory was so valuable that Secretary of War Stanton once exclaimed that it "[was] worth an army in the field."

Yet Chicagoans were divided about the war. Many residents harbored Southern sympathies, had relatives in the South, or hailed from the South themselves. Clearly, the conflict was more than a matter of North against South, Union against Confederate. It produced complex emotions that took years to resolve.

JOHN MCARTHUR AND THE HIGHLAND GUARDS

The Civil War devastated the nation and seriously affected the members of the Illinois Saint Andrew Society. Many Chicago Scots served with the Twelfth Illinois Infantry commanded by Colonel John McArthur. McArthur later became a general as well as president of the Society in 1871.

The Highland Guards were one of the earliest military groups to form during the Civil War. Composed almost exclusively of Scots under the command of John McArthur, they soon became known as one of the best disciplined and most picturesque

John McArthur of the Highland Guards (right)

outfits in the West. The members of the regiment wore the kilt. According to Thomas MacMillan (1919, 44), they were mustered in as Company E of the Nineteenth Illinois Volunteer Infantry on May 3, 1861. A few years earlier, in 1859, when the city celebrated the centennial of Robert Burns's birth – "probably the largest and most striking procession which Chicago had witnessed up to that time" (44) — the Highland Guards took part.

McArthur was born in 1826 at Erskine, Renfrewshire, Scotland. His parents hoped he would enter the Presbyterian ministry one day. Instead he emigrated to America one year after marrying Christina Cuthbertson in 1848 to join his brother-in-law Carlisle Mason in Chicago. Standing more than six feet tall, the strong, broad-shouldered McArthur soon found work as a mechanic and was involved in the construction of engines, boilers, and general machinery. With Mason, he started the firm of Mason and McArthur, builders of heavy machinery. In 1859 their plant, located at Canal and Carroll Streets, was destroyed by fire, and the firm was dissolved.

One year before the war broke out McArthur rose from the rank of third lieutenant and was chosen as captain of the Guards. When Fort Sumter was hit, McArthur volunteered his services and became a captain in the Twelfth Illinois Infantry. He was quickly promoted to lieutenant colonel and then colonel. For his performance at Fort Donelson, Tennessee, he earned the title of brigadier general. General Ulysses S. Grant was impressed with McArthur, calling him "zealous and efficient." He was wounded at the Battle of Shiloh. Despite his injuries, he returned to the front (45), leading the Sixth Division, Army of the Tennessee, at Corinth. He also fought at Vicksburg and Nashville. At Nashville he achieved his most impressive victory, charging and crushing the left wing of the enemy and effectively turning the battle into a Confederate rout. For this he received the honor of brevetted major general.

After the war, McArthur served as commissioner of public works from 1866 to 1872. From 1873 to 1877 he was postmaster in Chicago. Unfortunately during his term more than $70,000 disappeared in "a bank crash." A court decision forced him to use most of the monies he had saved over the years to pay the balance. He retired in 1885 although he continued to be active in the church and the Illinois Saint Andrew Society. McArthur died on May 15, 1906, and was buried in Rosehill Cemetery (MacMillan 1919, 45; Malone 1933). He served three terms as president of the Society, in 1869, 1870, and 1871.

DANIEL ROSS CAMERON

The Sixty-fifth of Illinois, nicknamed the Scotch or Second Scotch Regiment, was organized by Daniel Ross Cameron, and the unit was composed exclusively of men from Chicago and Cook County. The Glengarry Guards, a private military and marching unit of Scots, comprised Company H of the Sixty-fifth. Cameron served as president of the Society in 1862.

CAMP DOUGLAS

From September 1861 to April 1865, Camp Douglas, a prison camp for captured Confederate soldiers, occupied a portion of the late Senator Douglas's Oakenwald estate, between Thirty-first and Thirty-third Streets and Cottage Grove and what is now King Drive. Originally a military training and recruitment center, between 25,000 and 30,000 members of various Illinois regiments were trained for battle there (Holt and Pacyga 1979, 50). It was converted to a prison camp for Confederate prisoners in February 1862 following the capture of 8,000 to 9,000 Confederate troops by General Ulysses S. Grant at Fort Donelson, Tennessee.

Camp Douglas consisted of more than 150 buildings, most of them flimsy wooden barracks, and a large yard that was surrounded by a twelve-foot wooden stockade fence.

Visiting the camp on Sundays became a regular routine for quite a number of Chicagoans. Many were concerned about the welfare and good health of the prisoners. Collections were taken by church groups and medical supplies were sent there. Even so, conditions were still dreadful. One of the camp's more famous and articulate prisoners was Sir Henry Morton Stanley, a young Englishman who fought for the Confederacy:

> *Our prison pen was like a cattle-yard. . . . Left to ourselves, with absolutely nothing to do but to brood over our positions, bewail our lots, catch the taint of disease from each other, and passively abide in our prison-pen, we were soon in a fair state of rotting while alive. (Chicago Landmark Commission 1976, 5–6)*

Stanley later became a famous journalist. It was he who found the Scots missionary David Livingston in Africa.

More than 30,000 prisoners were held at Camp Douglas at one time or another, and nearly 6,000 Southern soldiers died in the camp's squalor. They lie now in muted silence in Oak Woods Cemetery, on East Sixty-seventh street (Freshman 1982, 30).

AFTERMATH

The Civil War officially ended in April 1865 with the surrender of General Robert E. Lee to General Grant at Appomattox Courthouse in Virginia. Chicago suffered dearly during the bloody conflict, posting 4,000 casualties from the city alone, including George Anderson's son Alexander, who died in circumstances unclear on June 28, 1862, at the age of twenty-four. In total, Cook County sent more than 22,000 to war, 15,000 of whom came from Chicago (Karamanski 1993, 235).

By August 1865, most of the 12,000 prisoners of war who still remained in Camp Douglas had sworn allegiance to the U.S. government and were released. In November the barracks were torn down and other buildings were sold at auction. A single row of barracks was moved from the camp to East Thirty-seventh Street before being destroyed in 1940.

Chicagoans welcomed the end of the war with a collective sigh of relief and immense joy. But the good feelings were short-lived for the unthinkable happened. At 4 a.m. on April 15, Chicagoans woke up to the heart-

THE DOUGLAS TOMB

The only physical reminder of Camp Douglas today in the area is the Douglas tomb, which is commemorated by a monument that is located in a small park near where the camp once stood. Nearby is St. Joseph's Carondelet Child Center, a portion of which dates back to the Civil War era and was used as a home for sick and disabled Civil War veterans.

In the late 1860s sculptor Leonard Volk was commissioned to design the Stephen A. Douglas Monument at 636 East Thirty-fifth Street. The war and economic difficulties, including the loss of the designs in the Great Fire of 1871, delayed its completion until May 1881. Douglas's body was interred in a white Vermont marble sarcophagus under the base of the statue. A nine-foot nine-inch bronze figure of Douglas tops the forty-six-foot column some ninety-six feet above the ground. The monument, which is located on land that was part of Douglas's Oakenwald estate, was declared a national historic landmark on September 28, 1977 (Bach and Gray 1983, 217–18).

SCOTTISH AMERICAN SOLDIERS MONUMENT

John McEwan was a young man when he emigrated to America and settled in Chicago. At the outbreak of the Civil War, he enlisted as a private in the Sixty-fifth Illinois Volunteer Infantry. At war's end he had risen to the rank of sergeant major. The Sixty-fifth was commanded by Brigadier General Daniel Cameron, who was president of the Illinois Saint Andrew Society in 1862. His regiment was known as the Second Scotch and was also called the Highlanders.

At the end of the war McEwan's health was broken and so he returned to Scotland where he married and had three children. Times were very difficult for the family, and McEwan never was able to properly support his wife and children. When he died it was necessary for his loved ones to bury him in a pauper's grave.

In 1890 McEwan's widow appealed to Wallace Bruce for help in getting her pension from the U.S. government. At the time, Bruce was serving as the U.S. Consul in Edinburgh. He was shocked to discover that a veteran of the war was buried in a potter's field. He was so distraught that he made the decision to resolve the situation himself. He felt that there should be a better place for the burial of Scottish American soldiers in Edinburgh.

Returning to the United States, Bruce began a campaign to raise money for a monument to Abraham Lincoln and a burial place for some of the veterans of the war. Contributors to the memorial consisted of such famous individuals as Waldorf Astor, Andrew Carnegie, Cornelius Vanderbilt, William Rockefeller, and J. Pierpont Morgan. The Illinois Saint Andrew Society made a contribution through Robert Clark, Jr.

The sculptor chosen for the proposed monument was George E. Bissell, himself a war veteran. The date for the dedication was August 21, 1893. The ceremony began with the Argyll and Sutherland Highlanders marching from Edinburgh Castle to Waterloo Place at the east end of Princes Street. The band, pipers, and the guard of honor numbered 250 strong as they led the procession to the Old Calton Burying Ground.

A large crowd gathered and waited in the rain. A strong southwest wind had been blowing all day and a great gust arrived at the same time as the Highlanders. So strong was the wind that umbrellas were of little use. The monument was draped with the Union Jack, the Stars and Stripes, and the Scottish Standard. Around the platform was an edging of heather. There were many visitors from America, including veterans from both sides of the war. The highest officials in Edinburgh were also in attendance, including the Lord Provost of the city. The dedicatory prayer was given by the Bannockburn-born Reverend Professor Christie from Pennsylvania. In spite of the weather there were several speeches.

The daughter of Wallace Bruce unveiled the statue. She was wearing a long, flowing white dress, her hair encircled in a band of gold, representing Columbia. At the appropriate moment, she pulled a cord that removed the flags and exposed the statue to full view. A loud and prolonged cheer came from the crowd. The Highlanders began playing "Hail Columbia" and "Rule Britannia."

The figure of Abraham Lincoln stood on a large pedestal with a freed African-American slave at his feet. Recorded on the base were the names and regiments of five Scottish soldiers who fought in the Civil War:

Sergeant Major John McEwan
Vo. H 65th Reg. Illinois Vol. Infantry

William L. Duff
Lt. Col. 2nd Illinois Reg. of Artillery

Robert Steedman
Lt. 5th Reg. Maine Infantry Volunteer

James Wilkie
Co. C 1st Michigan Cavalry

Robert Ferguson
37th Rect. New York Infantry Volunteer

Carved in Aberdeen granite in the base of the statue were the words of Abraham Lincoln, "To preserve the jewel of liberty in the framework of freedom." To the left of the statue stands the circular tower designed by Robert Adam, which is the burial place of David Hume, the great historian and philosopher. Also buried nearby is the grandfather and father of author Robert Louis Stevenson. Significantly, many of the ordinary citizens of Edinburgh are also resting here.

The main address of the day was given by the Honorable Wallace Bruce. Bruce was born in Columbia County, New York, of Scottish parents. He was educated at Yale University and after his graduation traveled throughout Europe, including many stops in Scotland. He became a lecturer and poet and was even regarded as one of the most brilliant figures in America. He lectured about Robert Burns, Sir Walter Scott, and Washington Irving. He visited Chicago several times. For several years he was the U.S. Consul to Scotland and was greatly loved and respected by the Scottish people. Even after he returned to America, he held the office of poet laureate of Canongate Kilwinning Lodge in Edinburgh, regarded as a position of great honor and high esteem. Bruce concluded his eloquent address by proclaiming:

We celebrate today . . . by unveiling a monument to the last great martyr in the cause of Saxon freedom—an honest man, who saved us in our hour of peril. May it stand to all time as a memorial to your heroes who fought for their adopted home beyond the sea—as a resting place for those who have returned, and have no shelter in the last hour, and as another bond of widening love and friendship between Great Britain and the United States of America.

In accepting the memorial on behalf of the citizens of Edinburgh, the Lord Provost, Sir William Arrol, said:

We also accept gratefully the custody of this monument as an act of courtesy and friendship to the United States of America. . . . We owe them a great debt of gratitude for helping us on in the path of freedom. . . . Edinburgh is, as has been said, rich in historic memories. It is rich in memories of great men and of their works, and we are proud to see so many of our kinsmen from across the sea coming here to claim their patrimony in our history. . . . I have the greatest pleasure, therefore, on behalf of the Town Council of Edinburgh, in accepting the custody of this monument; and I can promise you, Sir, that we shall guard it carefully and see that it suffers no loss.

The pipes and drums of the Argyll and Sutherland Highlanders then played "Auld Lang Syne." Hence, the body of John McEwan lies buried beneath the life-sized, bronze statue of the Great Emancipator in Edinburgh, Scotland.

Lincoln funeral procession, Chicago. At least five members of the Illinois Saint Andrew Society, along with other Scots, were among the 100 who acompanied the Lincoln funeral train from Chicago to Springfield.

breaking news that President Abraham Lincoln had been assassinated "at the hands of a daft theatrical," John Wilkes Booth (Johnston 1885, 195). Flags, which only a few brief days before proudly hung from public buildings, now rested at half mast. The court rooms were adjourned, the saloons remained closed. The city was in a state of shock (Pierce 1940, 283).

The assassination plunged the Union into a deep, national mourning. Thousands of Illinoisans lined the tracks as the train bearing the body of the fallen leader passed through the state. On May 1, the casket, in a black hearse pulled by ten black horses, was escorted by some 40,000 Chicagoans through muddy streets to the Court House, where the president lay in state overnight and where a crowd estimated at 125,000 honored him for the last time (Pierce 1940, 284; Karamanski 1993, 247).

Now the long journey was almost over. That evening the funeral train left the Chicago and Alton Railroad Depot enroute to its final destination of Springfield, Illinois. Thousands of torches lit the way. Two hours earlier, a committee of 100 prominent citizens was selected to represent Chicago at the funeral of the president in Springfield. They had traveled in a separate train to the state capital to participate in the funeral proceedings. The committee represented the city's elite—Mayor John B. Rice, ex-mayors Benjamin W. Raymond, Alson S. Sherman, James H. Woodworth, Isaac L. Milliken, John C. Haines, Charles M. Gray, Alexander Lloyd, and Julian Rumsey. Other prominent members included John V. Farwell, Matthew Laflin, Gurdon S. Hubbard, Mark Skinner, George P. Healy, James H. McVicker, Dr. Daniel Brainard, Joseph Medill, John Jones, Timothy B. Blackstone, W. W. Boyington, John H. Kinzie—and several past presidents of the Illinois Saint Andrew Society, including George Anderson, Robert Hervey, and John Alston (Currey 1912, 155).

Yet the bloody conflict also had a positive effect on Chicago. The city's population tripled during the war years, much of it from an influx of immigrant labor. The Union Stock Yards had opened in late 1865. Two years earlier Bridgeport had been annexed to the city, and the city limits extended from Thirty-first Street to Thirty-ninth Street (Freshman 1982, 30). After five years of interminable bloodshed, though, Chicagoans were looking forward to a more peaceful future.

View from the Court House after the fire.

THREE

The Unforgettable Fire

As the city grew in prosperity and influence, so did the Illinois Saint Andrew Society. Men of significant wealth became members and shared their good fortune with others. The Society increased its giving and enlarged its plans to ensure the fulfillment of its mission statement. By 1870 the population of Chicago was about 300,000, populated by mostly northern European types, principally English, Scots, Irish, German, French, and Scandinavian, either by descent and, quite often, by birth (Gilbert 1929, 154).

In the first twenty-five years of the Society's existence, eighteen men served as president. Robert Hervey, a distinguished attorney, served five terms. Business leaders, attorneys, generals, land developers, and common men would all find a place of leadership during those early years. One in particular will always be remembered by the Chicago street named in his honor—John H. Kedzie, president in 1854.

The Society celebrated its twenty-fifth anniversary dinner on November 30, 1870. George Anderson was the lone representative from the Society's first dinner in 1845. It must have been an emotional moment as he rose to speak:

> *Gentlemen, we may all feel proud of the standing and confidence that the Society has now attained all over this broad and mighty land. It being a child of my early affections and love, I have watched and nursed it in its almost helpless infancy, until it has, as exemplified here tonight, attained the stature of a stalwart man.*

The Society had great plans for the future. Members had already begun raising money to build a charitable Old Peoples Home, a Scottish hospital, and an office building to house all the Scottish organizations that flourished at the time. It was believed the second twenty-five years would be tremendous. Yet few could anticipate the bittersweet irony of Robert Burns's prophetic words: "The best laid plans of mice and men. . . ."

A City Made of Wood

The summer of 1871 had been particularly hot and dry. There was so little rain in fact that the prairies west of Chicago were always on fire. Residents lived in constant fear, since there had already been several serious conflagrations in the city itself. Heat and drought had left the ground parched. Between July and October there had been a total of five inches of rain (Cromie 1959, 9). Worse, Chicago was a city made of wood—a virtual tinderbox—from the South Side slums to the West Side working-class district, from the fashionable North Side to the tawdry West Side. Few would escape the consequences of a disastrous fire.

The potential for serious fire damage, while somewhat neglected, was not entirely ignored, however. After all, the city's fire department had turned professional in 1858, and local authorities had purchased more than a dozen steam-driven fire engines (12–13). The engines commonly were given nicknames, such as the *Waubansia* and *Winnebago*, or *Long John* and *Little Giant* (13). The city also had a new alarm system. Despite these assets, the fire department consisted of only 185 active firefighters (15).

Michigan Avenue, running north and south along the lakefront, had in recent years become one of the most stylish residential streets in town. Toward the northern end of Michigan Avenue, in Dearborn Park, was the small stadium of the Chicago White Stockings. Railroad tracks ran up along the breakwater to the Illinois Central depot standing near the site of Fort Dearborn. On land reclaimed from the lake were several freight yards and two large grain elevators.

Behind Michigan Avenue, stretching from the river almost a mile south to Harrison Street, was the principal business section of the city. Wabash Avenue had become a commercial area from Madison Street to the river and contained several large wholesale stores and warehouses. Many of the city's finest retail stores—including Field and Leiter's "marble palace," Carson Pirie Scott and Company, and Booksellers' Row—were located on State Street, along with the Palmer House (68–69).

Modern office buildings stood on Dearborn Street, including the Times and Tribune buildings. Near the center of the business district was the Court House. The

THE RAM'S HEAD

The ram's head, or sheep's head, as George Anderson called it, was made into a movable humidor complete with a holder for cigars and snuff. On the top was a large cairngorm stone surrounded with Scottish thistle. Back of that was the cigar case and on the center of the lid, the arms of Scotland with the inscription, "Nemo me impune lacessit" (No one dares meddle with me). To the right, the arms of the United States bears the inscription, "E pluribus unum," and to the left the arms of the city of Chicago with the date of incorporation. On the tips of the horns are two large thistles with stones of amethyst; on the top of the forehead is the plate with the inscription: "Presented by George Anderson to The Illinois Saint Andrew Society as a mark of his love and esteem. Chicago, 30th November, 1871."

Court House contained the mayor's office, the board of police and the chief marshal, the fire-alarm telegraph, county records, and the county jail in the basement (82). It was considered virtually fireproof. The six-story Grand Pacific Hotel took up the entire block by Quincy, Jackson, Clark, and La Salle; completed but not yet open for business. In front of it stood the Sherman House, one of the largest and most modern hotels in the city (69). Several of these buildings were also supposed to be fireproof.

On the West Side were mills, warehouses, small factories, and lumberyards. One of the largest plants was the South Side Gas Works. On the Near South Side Conley's Patch was lined with dilapidated frame buildings that housed brothels, dance halls, pawn shops, boardinghouses, and saloons (70). Many of the city's Irish immigrants had settled in this part of town. It was here where Patrick and Catherine O'Leary lived.

GEORGE ANDERSON'S GIFT

In the spring of 1871, George Anderson left Chicago to make a return trip to Scotland. He had not been back home to Glasgow for some thirty years, and this was to be his only visit. Before leaving, he gathered with his friends from the Illinois Saint Andrew Society, who wished him bon voyage and presented him with many valuable gifts as an expression of their esteem. Anderson had been a tireless worker in behalf of the Society, and it was an honor justly deserved.

It is unclear how long Anderson was gone, but if one looks at his itinerary it must have taken most of the summer. As he traveled throughout England and Scotland, he was constantly seeking that special item to purchase for his friends back in Chicago.

It was while visiting a castle in Perth that he found his gift. "After being shown all over it [the castle] and about to leave," he remarked, "we were asked to look at the ancient armor and other curiosities. There was a fine tip's head that attracted my attention. I said to my friend the Baillie, not thinking of it being heard, that if I could get a sheep's head [such] as that, I would have it mounted and present it to the Illinois Saint Andrew Society. Scarcely had I uttered my wish when the ram's head was presented to me."

Anderson was living on the South Side, where he previously had served as the postmaster at Twenty-second and South State Streets. The ram's head, now finished, lay resplendent in a magnificent oak box. The twenty-sixth anniversary dinner was scheduled for November 30, 1871. George Anderson could hardly wait to present his gift to the Society.

FIRE

The dress rehearsal for Chicago's greatest disaster occurred on the Saturday night of October 7, when fire broke out between Canal and Clinton Streets. But it was quickly contained, and people went about their business.

The next day, Sunday, was unseasonably warm for early October. Chicagoans took advantage of the good weather, for they knew that another long winter lay ahead of them. That evening around 8:30 p.m. a small fire started in the barn behind Patrick O'Leary's house at 137 DeKoven Street. The O'Leary's lived in a tiny cottage in an area dominated by working-class Irish and Bohemian families south of the industrial district. Patrick O'Leary, a laborer, had bought the property for $500 back in 1864 (25). Catherine O'Leary, his wife, kept five cows, a calf, and a horse (26). The origin of the fire may still be unknown, but there is little dispute that it started in Mrs. O'Leary's barn (31).

The flames spread. Once again, Chicagoans were not terribly worried, expecting the fire to die out like it had done the night before. But this time around it would be different, tragically and devastatingly different.

The fire department was short-handed from the previous night's outbreak. Those who were still on duty were, of course, exhausted. More disturbing, "no alarm was registered from any box in the vicinity of the fire until it was too late to do any good" (35).

Around midnight, flames jumped across the Chicago River, fanned by the twenty-mile-per-hour winds, laying in ruins the slums of Conley's Patch and continuing its terrible journey north. At 2:30 Monday morning the flames engulfed the Court House. Less than two hours later the flames had reached the Water Tower.

"The North Side is burning!" someone cried.

The Scottish American editor Harriet Monroe, founder of *Poetry Magazine*, was then just a young girl, yet she recalled the sights and sounds of that night vividly years later:

> *I remember a confused jumble of shouting people and pushing teams; and the air strangely full of an ashen dust, blinding and odorous in the gale that was still blowing. . . . I remember how we children gathered together in groups, excited and almost jubilant as we discussed "the greatest fire in the history of the world." (Monroe 1938, 20–21)*

Unfortunately, her father's downtown law office was one of the casualties.

The fire raged on and on until there was nothing but charred ruins as far as the eye could see. Ultimately, the flames would reach as far east as the lakefront and as far north as Fullerton Avenue. Finally, around 11 p.m. on Tuesday night a merciful rain began to fall (242).

The fire destroyed the holdings of many important Chicago institutions, including those of the Chicago Library Association, the Chicago Historical Society, the Chicago Academy of Science, the Young Men's Christian Association, and many others (Pierce 1957, 419). In addition, gone were the largest retail stores, newspaper offices, the depots of the Michigan Southern and Illinois Central Railroads, and most of the shipping on the Chicago River.

Members of the Chicago Club, a social club consisting of the city's wealthiest businessmen, stubbornly defied the flames—and the destruction of their businesses—with a champagne breakfast. Before they could finish, however, the fire reached their exclusive headquarters. They quickly jammed their pockets with cigars and whatever liquor they could carry and picked up the red satin sofas from the lobby and transported them to the lakefront, where they sat down and finished their meal (Dedmon 1983, 106).

Most people, though, took the fire much more seriously. Andrew MacLeish, the Scottish-born partner at Carson Pirie Scott and Company, had been aroused from his bed at 2 a.m. by his brother-in-law, James Chalmers. MacLeish drove from his home on the West Side to pick up George Schott, who lived near Union Park, still farther west.

The two men then tried to cross every bridge from Madison to Kinzie, when they learned the fire had reached the North Side. They had to drive all the way down to Twelfth Street to reach the store. By then it was too late. "Efforts to hire express wagons or trucks proved futile, and little could be saved" (Cromie 1959, 162).

A predawn telegram from Mayor Roswell Mason to Mayor Harrison Ludington of Milwaukee sent a disturbing message:

> *Chicago is in flames.*
> *Send your whole department to help us.*

The First Congregational Church at Washington and Ann (Racine Avenue) Streets was converted into a temporary city hall and relief headquarters (244). Public buildings were set aside as refuge areas, and volunteers were encouraged to serve as part of the city's emergency police force. The responsibility of preserving order was given to General Philip H. Sheridan. Some 500 soldiers were placed on alert. Eyewitness accounts tell of two men who attempted to set houses afire on the West Side and how they were immediately "hung to lampposts," which effectively succeeding in discouraging other "thieves and murderers."

Throughout the ordeal, other communities gave generously to the stricken city. Schools and churches were used as emergency centers. Fire engines came from Milwaukee, Detroit, Aurora, Quincy, and Indianapolis (Pierce 1957, 7). Words of sympathy and offers of monies came from as far away as Canada, Britain, Germany, and France (8). Mass meetings were held in Cincinnati, and hundreds of thousands of dollars were earmarked for Chicago. The Cincinnati Chamber of Commerce alone contributed some $5,000 to the cause.

England donated about 7,000 volumes to be used toward the foundation of a Chicago public library (Weimann 1981, 353). Thomas Hughes, author of *Tom Brown's School Days,* was especially involved in this literary crusade. Other prominent donors included Charles Kingsley, John Stuart Mill, Dante Gabriel Rossetti, Benjamin Disraeli, and even Queen Victoria (Cromie 1959, 262).

Trains, with all manner of provisions and supplies, began arriving in Chicago. Various foodstuffs arrived for days after the fire, including bread, chickens, crackers, flour, sugar, cabbage, beef, pork, coffee, bacon, doughnuts, cheese, sauerkraut, cake, and fruit. In St. Louis, an impressive $70,000 was reportedly collected in one hour. The New York Stock Exchange contributed $50,000. From the president of the United States to governors as well as local, county, and civic organizations, offers of assistance and funds continued to flood in. President Grant reportedly sent $1,000 from his own pocketbook. Altogether, the final total of monies donated to the city amounted to $4,820,148.16, of which $973,897.80 came from twenty-nine foreign countries.

THE SOCIETY COPES

Meanwhile, members of the Society did their best to help one another. According to the Society's annual report, some 8,000 Scottish residents were living in Chicago at the time or, according to Bessie Louise Pierce (1957, 31n. 36), about 2.9 percent of the population. It's been estimated that nearly 90 percent of the Society membership suffered a complete loss of homes and property.

Among the 250 or so people who died in the tragedy were two Society members—Robert Clark, Sr. and William George. Clark, seventy-one, had just returned from a visit to Scotland. He was the father of Robert Clark, Jr., president of the Society in 1885, and chief of the Chicago Caledonian Club. "The old gentleman . . . perished in the burnt district while striving to escape from the fire," according to Society records. William George died of injuries several days later.

David Johnston, a carpenter who joined the Society in 1864, lost all his tools in the fire. He received $135 from various Scottish societies abroad, $100 from the Society itself, and $35 from the Caledonian Club (Johnston 1885, 202). Unable to get on his feet again, he became a book peddler in St. Louis before returning to Chicago. On his way back he visited the little Scottish community of Elmira, which he had visited when he first came to Illinois. "I found the whole community in a very thriving condition," he cheerfully reported (204).

Appeals for help went out to Scots throughout America and Canada; indeed, around the world. Donations poured in from everywhere—Saint Andrew societies, companies, individuals, churches, towns, and cities. The city of Glasgow sent £5,000. The Saint Andrew Society of Boston canceled their own anniversary dinner and sent

EYEWITNESS ACCOUNT BY SOCIETY MEMBER

The following eyewitness account of the Great Fire of 1871 by a Society member was contained in the Society's annual report of 1871 (for the complete description, see the appendix):

The telegraph has already told to the world the story of the terrible fire in Chicago. "Send us food for the suffering, our city is in ashes" is the appeal of the Mayor and his brief description of the scene. . . . At present, we have no trustworthy estimate of the total value of the property destroyed or of the lives lost. One report states that the total loss can scarcely fall below one hundred fifty million dollars, and it is believed that over one hundred thousand persons have been rendered homeless and destitute by the calamity. Over an area four miles long and one mile wide, the fire swept, reducing all the finest public buildings in the city, the churches, hotels, theaters, banks, railroad depots, newspaper and telegraph offices, to ashes.

Measures for the relief of the sufferers have been already taken in all the large cities .... In this work of charity, we believe that Scotsmen of America can do, is to take care that their countrymen, in Chicago, shall not suffer long from the late terrible disaster.

The Scottish Sufferers

On the 8th of October, a conflagration, unparalleled in the history of the world, doomed the "Garden City of the West" to destruction, poverty, wretchedness and death. The telegraph has already sent the news of the sad calamity to the utmost part of the earth. Both pen and pencil have endeavored to portray the more striking incidents of the scene, but all have failed to give more than an epitome of what transpired during the progress of that fiery avalanche which, with one fell swoop, in the space of twenty-four hours, rendered homeless about 150,000 men, women, and children; destroyed some two hundred millions of property, devastated nearly 20,000 homes and places of business, and destroyed several hundred lives. We will not attempt to detail the progress of the fire from its first commencement up to the present hour. The record would fill a volume of horrors. But for the benefit of absent friends in Auld Scotland, and all parts of this broad land, I will endeavor to mention what more particularly will be of interest to our countrymen in relation to the losses sustained by a few of the 8,000 Scottish residents of Chicago.

Mr. Robert Hervey, and **Mr. Wm. M. Johnston** lost valuable law libraries on Dearborn St.; **Thomas Dougall,** soap factory and houses on Elm street; **David Wylie** house and furniture, on Elm street; **Hugh Ritchie,** soap factory and house on Grand Haven street; **James Thomson,** nine houses and furniture, on Wells and Dearborn streets; **John Alston** & Co., 172 Randolph street, glass and paints, valued at $200,000; **A. Barnett,** brassfounder, Franklin street, loss of entire stock; **William Hendrie,** watchmaker, Franklin street, loss of entire stock; **Alex. Murray,** plumber, Franklin street, loss, $3,000; **Hugh Cooper,** tailor, Madison street, entire stock and furniture, $3,000; **A. B. McLean,** clothing, Randolph street, entire loss of stock; **Thomas Hastie,** boots and shoes, Randolph street, $60,000 in U. S. bonds and $30,000 on buildings and stock; **Robert Fergus** & Sons, office on Clark street, printing house on Illinois street and residences on North Dearborn and Huron streets, $75,000; **John M'Glashan,** office furniture, on Washington St.; **George Irons,** liquor dealer, stock on LaSalle street and furniture on Madison street; **Thomson & Templeton,** bakers, stores and homes, $40,000 on Randolph street; **Frank Farrish,** importer, office and stock of goods on LaSalle street; **Robert Ritchie,** seven houses on Franklin and Maple streets, furniture and stock, $25,000; **George Frazier,** baker, Division street, furniture and stock; **A. M. Thomson,** Western Coffee and Spice Mills, South Water street, $40,000; **Wm. Stewart,** South Water street, wholesale grocer, $150,000; **James C. Stewart,** Thistle Saloon, Clark street, stock of liquors; **James Peat,** household furniture, Cass street; **Thomas Lees,** plumber, house and store and furniture, on North Clark street; **J. Rattray,** printer, house and furniture, on North Clark street; **James Furnett,** printer, Lake street; Robert Clark, house and foundry on Erie and Kingsbury streets; **John Raffen,** foundry on Kingsbury street; **D. Johnson,** photographer; **Wm. M. Dale,** druggists, South Clark street, loss about $10,000; **James Hamilton,** tailor, stock and furniture; **James Sims,** saloon, Dearborn street; **James Paterson,** plumber, entire stock; **Alex. Raffen,** plumber, Dearborn street, stock; **Charles Glen,** saloon; **Fred. J. Smith,** agricultural implement maker, South Canal street, stock; **Peter and Arthor Devine,** boiler makers, Polk street, building and stock; **Wm. T. Noble,** picture frame maker and gallery of art, State street, loss $30,000; **D. J. McKellar,** office furniture; **Alex. Elder,** painter, Franklin street, house and furniture; **John King,** bookbinder, tools and furniture, Kinzie street; **Peter McFarlane** (at present in Montreal), furniture and a valuable collection of nick nacks; **Arthur C. Ducat,** insurance agent, office furniture; **John Rankin,** china merchant, Randolph street, whole stock; **James Bell,** Dearborn street, furniture; **W. H. Waters,** Illinois Central Land Development, valuable property; **Henry Ross,** glass cutter, furniture; **James Ross,** North Wells street, furniture; **Thomas Haddon,** furniture; **John Kennedy,** Ohio street, four houses, workshop and furniture; **James Ferguson,** watchmaker, Randolph street, whole stock; **John Gabriel,** Tremont House, personal property; **Wm. George,** Tam O'Shanter Saloon, stock and furniture; **James Sym,** confectioner, State street, valuable stock; Smith, Massasoit House, personal property; **D. Kendall,** Larrabee street, furniture; Caledonian Club Rooms, library, pictures, and property valued at $4,000; St. Andrew's Society, pictures, etc.

The writer, on behalf of his fellow-sufferers, would earnestly call on every Scotsman in the United States and Canada, to aid the sufferers in the hour of their trial and distress. The winter will soon be here, and it will find many an empty pocket and many a cauld hearthstone.

Special Relief Fund

St. Joseph, Mo.; $50

Albany, New York; $600

New York City; $1200

Schenectady, N.Y.; $270.50

Ogdensburg, N.Y.; $10

Whitley, Canada; $54.40

Cumnock, Scotland; $337.98

Baltimore (proceeds of Draft); $498.75

Selkirk, Manitoba; $229

Cleveland; $100

Memphis; $100

Savannah, Ga.; $50

Scottish Charitable Society of Boston; $220

Total; $3720.73

By amount paid out, as per Orders of Board of Managers, to date; $2882.85

Amount on hand; $837.78

All of which is respectfully submitted,

John McArthur,
Treasurer Special Relief Fund

FAMOUS SCOTS AND ULSTER SCOTS IN CHICAGO CEMETERIES

Graceland

Philip D. Armour, meatpacker

George Grant Elmslie, Scots-born architect and associate of Louis H. Sullivan

John Kinzie, early Chicago pioneer

A.C. McClurg, publisher and bookseller

Cyrus McCormick, inventor of the reaper

Joseph Medill, editor of the *Chicago Tribune* and mayor of Chicago

Allan Pinkerton, Chicago's first detective

James Simpson, president of Marshall Field and Company

Rosehill

George Buchanan Armstrong, founder of the U.S. Railway Mail Service

Illinois Saint Andrew Society plot

John H. Kedzie, realtor

John Kirk, soap manufacturer

Family plot of James McVicker, founder of McVicker's Theater

(Sclair 1994; Lanctot 1988)

Monument in Rosehill Cemetery marking the 100th anniversary of the Illinois Saint Andrew Society.

the proceeds to Chicago. The Caledonian Club of San Francisco held a second series of games in 1871 to raise funds for the victims of the fire, of which a total of $1,200, was collected (Donaldson 1986 34).

THE SOCIETY'S ANNIVERSARY DINNER GOES ON

Despite the terrible consequences of the Great Fire, the anniversary dinner went on as planned in the Briggs House on West Madison Street. The dining hall was filled with long tables. The walls, however, were left unadorned since flags, pictures, and banners that usually decorated previous celebrations had been destroyed in the fire. Men who once were wealthy found themselves penniless. Still, 120 guests managed to show their support, including George Anderson.

With the words "Tam O'Shanter, Tam O'Shanter, ah! Tam! Tam!" echoing down the hall, Anderson enthusiastically answered the cry. He rose in the center of the room to a great outburst of applause and addressed the membership directly. He told the crowd the story about how he came across the ram's head and then officially presented it to the Society with the admonition that it "remain in your possession during your term of office, and to be handed over to your successors on each succeeding Saint Andrew's Day, as long as the Society shall exist, to be always placed on the dinner table on each recurring anniversary, with this additional request, that the President having the custody of it, will always place it on his table on each and every New Year's Day, the first of January, whether he keeps open house or not; and it be well filled with snuff . . . or cigars or both."

RESILIENCY

It is somewhat difficult to further trace the history of the Society during this period. The Society held its quarterly meetings in the Court House and, thus, their records were destroyed during the Great Fire. From a speech given by George Anderson on November 30, 1870, we can infer several things, however. First, the growth in membership remained rather small, although the exact number is not known. For a number of reasons peculiar perhaps to the Scottish mentality, many refused to join. The financial resources to care for needy Scottish immigrants also remained limited. Only after the Civil War would the funds increase substantially.

However, one event did occur that helped the Society meet the obligations of its mission statement. From its inception in 1846 the Society wished that no deserving Scot or person of Scottish descent would ever be buried in a potter's field. To fulfill this part of the mission, a large plot of land was purchased in 1858 in Rosehill Cemetery. Acquired a year before the cemetery was incorporated, it is located near the main entrance and across the road from the Civil War monument. The plot was dedicated for the burial of "poor and friendless Scots" and became a source of great self-respect for the Society. Several prominent members of the Society have served with pride on the Cemetery Committee. Additional lots were purchased in 1872 and again in 1895. Today more than 200 persons of Scottish descent lie buried in the peaceful surroundings of Rosehill. It was a purchase that brought to the membership a tremendous amount of pride and satisfaction.

The Society received the following letter in September 1870:

No. 464 Dumbarton Road
Glasgow
30 September 1870

Mr. George Anderson
Chairman, Board of Managers
Illinois St. Andrews' Society

Dear Sir:

We received your kind and sympthizing note, informing and condoling with us at the awful, sudden and untimely death of our son, on the 7th day of September, by drowning. While the news, so sudden and unexpected to us, has almost broken our hearts, yet we are consoled in our great grief, by the kindness your Society has shown to our poor boy, in having him decently buried in the Society's grounds.

May the blessing of Almighty God be with you in your Charitable and Benevolent Institution, for this kindness to us, to our son a stranger in a strange land. Please, Sir, convey to your Society our undying thanks, and those of our family; and we hope that your Society will prosper in all its Benevolent Intentions.

If there are any letters or papers of Alexander's in your hands, please be so kind as to forward them to us, with the amount spent by the Society on our Son's funeral and it will be promptly forwarded. And now may God bless you and the Society with which you are connected, in your work of love and mercy, and make you a blessing to the poor and needy, is the sincere prayer of:

Alexander & Margaret Fraser

The twenty-five years after the Great Fire were spent rebuilding the lives of the members. Money was loaned without interest to provide housing, purchase inventories, and rebuild factories. Gradually, the money would be returned through repayment, gifts, or legacies and this would form the basis of the Endowment Fund established by James B. Forgan (1924, 233), in 1919.

In 1871 James Kirk and Company, reportedly the largest soap and perfume manufacturing factory in the country at that time, stood on North Water Street. After the fire, the firm wrote off a loss of $250,000—but there was never any thought of giving up. The factory was rebuilt, and the grandsons of James Kirk, a native of Glasgow, Scotland, carried on under the original name (Gilbert 1929, 180).

Even though by 1871 the Society had already raised $10,000 to build a charitable home, the plans were never finished. The question of a Scottish hospital and downtown office building were never raised again either. The proposed statue to Sir Walter Scott never became more than a dream. The Scottish Old Peoples Home would not become a reality until 1910 and will be discussed in a later chapter.

The charitable work of the Society, however, would continue. Their mission to "relieve the distressed" was never forgotten in spite of their own personal hardships and difficulties. John Crerar, a member, left a great deal of money at his death. Indeed, the Crerar Fund helped many needy Scottish families. A few years after the fire, the Society had 300 applications for relief. Seven persons were buried at Rosehill and seventy-five people were sent to relatives in various parts of the country or back to Scotland. In addition, a gift was sent to the Saint Andrew Society in Memphis, Tennessee, to aid "the sufferers of yellow fever."

Thirteen men served as president of the Society during these second twenty-five years. Two of the men were officers in the Union Army: General John McArthur and Colonel R. Biddle Roberts. Godfrey Macdonald was president of the Lake Shore and Nickel Railroads. Daniel Ross Cameron was an owner of Cameron, Amberg and Company, a large printing company with offices in Chicago, New York, and London. Andrew C. Cameron was an owner of newspapers in Chicago and editor of the *Workingman's Advocate.* Judge Egbert Jamieson served with distinction in the federal court system. John Joseph Badenoch, a successful businessman, had once been the police chief of Chicago. Robert Hervey, a distinguished attorney, served his fifth term as president of the Society over a period of

Rebuilding. Reconstruction after the fire.

twenty years, a feat unparalleled in its history.

The last surviving member of those who met on November 30, 1845, George Anderson, died shortly before the anniversary dinner on October 30, 1887. The voice that had recited "Tam O'Shanter" for more than forty years was now silent. His funeral service was conducted by members of the Society, and his body was buried with dignity and honor in Oak Woods Cemetery.

With the death of John Sheriffs in 1895, all of the founding members of the Society were gone. New leaders emerged, bearing such names as Bogle, MacMillan, Williamson, Crerar, McGill, Cormack, and Forgan.

Although the names may have changed, the Society's mission to help kith and kin remained the same. In fact, the charitable work of the Society grew stronger after the Great Fire because the need was greater than ever.

STARTING OVER

In the aftermath of the fire, Chicagoans wasted no time in getting back on their feet again. Rebuilding began almost immediately. Barracks and tents were erected for the homeless. Laborers flocked to the city, looking for work. And there was plenty of work to do. Skilled workers from the British Isles were especially welcomed.

By October 1872—one year after the terrible tragedy—Chicago was well on its way back toward normalcy. Indeed, only nineteen days after the fire had devastated the city, S. C. Griggs and Company felt confident enough of its future to publish Elias Colbert's and Everett Chamberlin's *Chicago and the Great Conflagration.* (Pierce 1957, 170).

The transformation of the city was so remarkable that a visitor from Scotland in June 1874 could proclaim that "no traces of the fire were visible; the warehouses and hotels had been built on a grander scale than ever; the rate of progress in the population had not been sensibly retarded; nay, it appeared as if the fires through which she had passed, like the fires of affliction in which the Christian is purified, had only enabled rejuvenescent Chicago to start, from a fresh and more secure basis, on a more glorious career than ever" (Ferguson 1878, 250). Two years later, another Scot, journalist Sir John Leng, wrote: "One's first impression on seeing the Chicago of to-day is that it is scarcely possible the magnificent business streets we see extending over a vast area can all have been built in so short a time" (Ebner 1988, 47).

Yet no one could deny the damage that the fire had done to the city. Nearly 90,000 to 100,000 persons were made homeless while seventy-three miles of streets and almost 18,000 buildings were destroyed. The North Side suffered the most property damage with approximately 13,000 buildings leveled (Cromie 1959, 245; Pierce 1957, 6n. 6). Emmett Dedmon (1983, 107) says that the fire ruined 2,124 acres in the central city. Some accounts reported that some 300 men, women, and children died in the fire, and thousands more suffered injuries (Gilbert 1929, 160). Others say that no one knew for sure exactly how many perished. "Only 120 bodies were recovered after the fire but official guesses of the number of dead ranged from two to three hundred," according to Robert Cromie (1959, 247).

Perhaps realtor William Kerfoot best represents the typical Chicagoan's reaction to the tragedy. His sign said it all:

> *All gone except wife, children, and energy*

Kerfoot's makeshift shack was the first building to be erected after the fire (Dedmon 1983, 109–10).

Joseph Medill's editorial in the *Chicago Tribune* three days after the fire had run its course left no room for self-pity:

> *"We have lost money, but we have saved life, health, vigor and industry. . . .*
>
> *"Let the Watchword henceforth be: Chicago Shall Rise Again."*

It was time to get back to work.

Burns Memorial and Monument Association. Prominent members of the association include Magnus Flaws (12), Mrs. R. Ballantine (17), and William Gardner (21).

FOUR

The Bard and the Fair

THE BURNS'S STATUE

The desire to erect a monument to Scotland's literary heroes began long before steps were ever taken to make it a reality. The idea actually occurred before the Great Fire of 1871. At that time, however, the discussion was for a monument to Sir Walter Scott. After the fire, though, thoughts turned to building a memorial for Robert Burns, Scotland's national poet.

The statue was supposed to cost no more than $12,000, and the money was to be raised among the "common folk" in Chicago's Scottish American community. On October 25, 1888, the first practical steps were taken for the erection of a monument when the Caledonian Society issued the call for a meeting. Some sixty-three gentlemen, representing the various Scottish societies of Chicago, met at the Grand Pacific Hotel and organized the Burns Memorial and Monument Association.

William Gardner, president of the Illinois Saint Andrew Society in 1896 and 1897, called the meeting to order and explained the objectives of the gathering. Thirteen organizations were present at the first meeting. In addition to the Illinois Saint Andrew Society, they included the Caledonian Society; Clan MacDuff; Clan Campbell; Clan Ogilvy; Clan Gordon; Clan MacDonald; Orkney and Shetland Society; Highland Association of Illinois, Scottish branch; British-American Association; Scotch Church Literary Society; and the West End Scottish Society.

Robert Clark, president of the Illinois Saint Andrew Society in 1885 and 1886, was elected president of the association. The secretary was Charles Gordon MacDonald and his assistant was James Duncan. The elected treasurer was Gardner. The remaining persons present formed the executive committee. The presidents of all the Scottish societies in the city were made vice presidents as follows:

Judge Egbert Jamieson, Illinois Saint Andrew Society
William Murdoch, Caledonian Society
John Ramsay, Clan Campbell
James L. Campbell, Clan Campbell
A. G. Hodge, Clan Gordon
John Findlay, Clan Ogilvy
Alexander McLachlan, Clan MacDonald

Charles M. McFarlane, Scotch Church Literary Society
A. G. Murray, Highland Association of Illinois
Magnus Flaws, Orkney and Shetland Society
D. R. Goudie, Scottish branch, British-American Association
Robert Aitchison, South Chicago Caledonian Club
John Moffat, West End Scottish Society
J. S. MacDonald, Highland Association of Chicago

Thus, on November 22, 1888, the Burns Memorial and Monument Association was incorporated under the laws of Illinois with the following listed: Robert Clark, Thomas C. MacMillan, William Gardner, John Ramsay, A. C. Cameron, William Forest, James Duncan, A. G. Hodge, and Charles Gordon MacDonald.

James Murray donated funds to the association on the eve of his departure for South Africa in the form of a silver dollar. The coin was marked with a Saint Andrew's cross and was to be placed, with other mementos, in the foundation when the proposed monument was scheduled to be erected.

The first effort to raise money by the association was the issuance of subscription books. Then, on January 24, 1889, a mass meeting was held in the Central Music Hall. The principal address that evening was given by Governor Moonlight of Wyoming. His subject, of course, was Robert Burns. Later that year, on August 10, a picnic and games were held at Elliott's Park in Matteson, Illinois. The picnic turned a profit of $278.44. Various Scottish societies, including the Scotch Church Literary Society, South

Chicago Caledonian Club, Waverly Club, and Clan McKenzie of Braidwood, Illinois, made liberal contributions during the early months of 1889. In December a concert by the Balmoral Choir of Glasgow was held in the Central Music Hall. These and other events helped to raise the funds for the project.

Many members of the Society were involved in the Burns Memorial and Monument Association, including Robert Clark, Daniel Ross Cameron, Walter Scott Bogle, John C. Hunter, Thomas C. Macmillan, and William Gardner. With the exception of Bogle, all had served at least one term as president of the Society.

Yet times were extremely difficult. Periods of financial panic and depression followed the world's fair of 1893. For twelve years there was little interest in the monument; meetings would be called from time to time, but few people attended. The association also suffered from internal dissension, often resulting in mass resignations of the entire board.

For example, on June 23, 1891, at a general meeting of the association, the executive committee, including all the officers, resigned. It appears there was a dispute on how the monies were being handled. Allegations of misappropriation of funds surfaced. The rumor was determined to be unfounded since a thorough audit revealed that the financial matters were scrupulously maintained. Even so, changes were made in the manner of reporting the net proceeds of each event to the treasurer. Obviously it was not an easy effort for so many Scottish groups to work together in harmony.

On September 28, 1891, another general meeting was held, and new officers were elected: Robert Clark as president; Thomas Watson as first vice president; Peter McEwan as second vice president; James Duncan as secretary; A. G. Hodge as assistant secretary; and William Gardner as treasurer. Three directors were elected: A. C. Cameron, William Forest, and R. Aitchison.

The following month, on October 12, 1891, a series of important recommendations were adopted concerning the most practical method of raising money and related matters. It was, at this meeting, that a large number of prominent Scottish Americans were made honorary vice presidents of the association.

On February 7, 1893, Robert Clark resigned as president due to ill health, and Daniel Ross Cameron was elected in his stead. During the world's fair there was little interest in the project. Meetings were called for time to time, but it seemed impossible to revive enthusiasm. Toward the end of 1901, however, the association began to show renewed sparks of life.

Back in March 1892 a resolution had been presented by James Duncan to invite plans

THE SOCIETY BANNER

The banner of the Illinois Saint Andrew Society was presented to the Society at the Tremont House in November 1881 by a committee composed entirely of women. The design consisted of a Scottish thistle on a red silk background with light margins and pendants of white silk, a yellow silk fringe, cord, and tassels. The thistle is surrounded by the words "Illinois St. Andrew's Society, instituted at Chicago, January 26, 1846; incorporated February 10, 1853." The banner is fifty-five inches wide by fifty-eight inches long.

William Gardner (above)
Union Picnic Committee (left). Magnus Flaws (22) and J. D. Williamson (37) are among the members.

and specifications for a monument that was not to exceed $12,000 in expenses. Gardner, John Asher, Hugh Shirlaw, Forest, and Cameron were chosen to head the design committee. A subcommittee, consisting of A. M. Thomson, John Alston, and John Keith and two sculptors were later appointed to assist. Thus, a competition to design the Chicago Burns monument was underway. The first-place award prize of $200,000 was awarded to W. Grant Stevenson, a well-known Edinburgh sculptor. Unfortunately, a combination of circumstances delayed the project until nearly twelve years later.

The association now began the task of finding a suitable location. A committee consisting of John C. Hunter, James Duncan, William Gardner, Thomas C. Macmillan, and Walter Scott Bogle was assigned the task. Ultimately, it was determined that the statue was to stand in Garfield Park on the west side of Chicago at the Washington Boulevard entrance. Garfield Park had been laid out by Frederick Law Olmsted in 1869. Later the members of the Burns committee agreed with the park system's landscape architect Jens Jensen that the proper place "was not where only the automobiles and equipages of the rich whisked past, but 'amid the trees and flowers which he loved' in the part of the park most frequented by the people."

On December 8, 1902, the association enacted a constitution and by-laws. The bank balance at that time had grown to $927.08. It was during this period that the Ladies' Auxiliary of the Caledonian Society became a strong force. Auxiliaries were usually founded by the wives of members of the various Scottish American societies. On the initiative of Chief James D. Currie the Caledonian Society issued an invitation to Scottish ladies—by birth, descent, or marriage—to meet at the Sherman House on June 25, 1902, at 7:30 p.m. to form a Ladies' Auxiliary.

A large number of women responded. Mrs. Robert Ballantine chaired the meeting. Its primary purpose was to secure the necessary funds to build the proposed Burns monument. The ladies then organized the Ladies' Auxiliary of the Caledonian Society with Mrs. Ballantine as president; Mrs. George Fraser as vice president; Margaret B. McCollum as secretary; and Mrs. James Graham as treasurer.

Several months later members of the auxiliary met with the directors of the Burns Memorial group. In 1903 Ballantine made a trip to Scotland and visited with Stevenson. Consequently, installments were agreed upon, and the first payment was made for the completion of the work. By early the following year, the ladies were authorized to assume the title of Ladies' Auxiliary of the Burns Memorial and Monument Association. Mrs. George Fraser represented Scottish societies from the North Side, Isa McArthur from the South Side, and Mrs. R. MacWatt from the West Side, and from that time forward the two groups worked in complete harmony. On May 8, 1905, the association was notified that the statue and panels for the pedestal had been successfully cast.

The women's efforts were many. They made and sold an autographed quilt, which featured some 900 famous names. A second quilt was equally successful. They also presented three popular bazaars. Through these and other activities, they were able to raise more than $2,000 for the memorial. Yet it was Ballantine in particular, a woman of tremendous energy and ability, who made all the difference. Without her leadership as president of the Ladies' Auxiliary it is unlikely that the project would have ever reached fruition.

On November 17, 1905, Clan MacDuff and

W. Grant Stevenson (above) Mrs. R. Ballantine, president, Ladies Auxiliary (next page, top right)

Clan Campbell held a grand ball at the Second Regiment Armory, which had been furnished free of charge by Colonel James E. Stuart. At the installation of new officers on December 11, 1905, President Dr. W. A. Barclay pledged that the monument should be erected in 1906. And so began the final and most eventful year of the association's history.

Earlier, on April 9, 1905, a contract for the erection of the pedestal had been awarded to Welsh and Mitchell, a well-known Scottish American stone firm. The final installment was paid to Stevenson, and the statue and panels were sent to Glasgow. In early 1906 the Anchor Line of steamships offered to transport the Burns monument from Glasgow to New York at a reduced price. The statue and its panels arrived in Chicago in May 1906 and were placed in the Sibley Warehouse on North Clark Street. Members of the Municipal Art Commission later approved them. A committee representing the commission, the West Park Board, and the Burns Memorial and Monument Association then visited Garfield Park and approved the site in front of the Refectory Building in the park's north section.

THE DEDICATION CEREMONY

The dedication ceremony began on Saturday, August 25, 1906, with a giant parade starting from the Van Buren Opera House located at West Madison Street and California Avenue. At 1:15 p.m. the proces-

Ladies' Auxiliaries Burns Memorial and Monument Association
Mrs. Ballantine (17) is seated in the second row.

MONUMENT DESCRIPTION

The statue of Robert Burns is ten and a half feet in height and stands on a pedestal of Vermont granite, twelve and a half feet high. The name "Burns" appears in relief on the base of the pedestal, and underneath it, chiseled in the granite, the legend, "A man's a man for a' that." On the front is an episode from "The Cottar's Saturday Night," with the quotation: "From scenes like these old Scotia's grandeur springs." In the rear is an image from "Tam o' Shanter"—the witch clutching at the grey mare's tail—with the motto:

"But pleasures are like poppies shred
You seize the flow'r, its bloom is shed."

On one side is "Burns at the Plough" turning up the mouse's nest, with the sage maxim:

"The best laid schemes o' mice an' men
Gang aft a-gley."

On the other side is a representation of "The Twa Dogs" with the adage:

"In fair virtue's heav'nly road
The cottage leaves the palace far behind."

Over time the plaques on each side have disappeared.

Burns's statue in Garfield Park.

sion headed by a Captain Tyrell and a platoon of police on horseback began the march to Garfield Park. They were followed by the Highland Pipe and Drum Band and the various Scottish societies. The ceremonies in Garfield Park began at 2:30 p.m. with a call to order by Dr. W. A. Barclay. A choir of more than 100, conducted by Clement B. Shaw, sang such favorites as "Ye Banks and Braes," "There Was a Lad Was Born in Kyle," and "My Love Is Like a Red, Red Rose." Several speeches were made, including one by Illinois Governor Charles S. Deneen. Kate Campbell Saunders, elocutionist, read several poems by Robert Burns. The Reverend James MacLagan, pastor of the Scotch Presbyterian Church, gave the invocation. The orator of the day was to have been Wallace Bruce of Hillsdale, New York, but, according to some accounts, he was not able to attend, and his place was taken by the Reverend W. J. McCaughan, pastor of the Third Presbyterian Church. The monument was unveiled by four-year-old Barbara Evelyn Williamson.

The events of this dedication day closed with the singing of Robert Burns's immortal song "Auld Lang Syne" by both the choir and the audience.

Should auld acquaintance be forgot
An' never brocht tae min';
Should auld acquaintance be forgot
For auld lang syne.

For auld lang syne, my dear,
For auld lang syne,
We'll tak a cup o' kindness yet,
For auld lang syne.

We twa hae paidled [paddled] in the burn
Frae morning sun till dine [dinner],
But seas between us braid [broad] hae roar'd
Since auld lang syne.

Then, here's a hand, my trusty frien'
An' gie's a hand o' thine;
An' we'll take a richt guid-willie [full of good-will] waught
For auld lang syne.
For auld lang syne, my dear,

For auld lang syne,
We'll tak a cup o' kindness yet,
For auld lang syne.

Even Andrew Carnegie sent a congratulatory message from Skibo Castle in Dornoch, Sutherland, in Scotland's far north.

> *It is a great disappointment that I cannot be with you during the ceremony of unveiling the statue to the Immortal Bard, that child of pure genius, the great Democrat who, proclaiming the "Royalty of Man, struck down Rank with one hand and the old hard Theology with the other, dispelling the false conceptions of a Heavenly Father who sent 'ane to heaven and ten to hell a' for his glory." I feel that he also gave us the great rule of life, "Thine own reproach alone do fear."*
>
> *In greater degree than any man who ever lived he became the embodiment of the national spirit of his country.*
>
> *There cannot be too many statues erected to the memory of Burns*
>
> Andrew Carnegie

The Burns monument is an expression of the deep-rooted regard of the rank and file of the Scottish people for their beloved bard. Nearly all the money was collected in small amounts by members from the Scottish and Scottish American working class. Only five persons gave as much as $100 each. An unspecified donation came from a James Dalrymple, a Glasgow traction expert. William Forrest, one of the original incorporators, made and donated a violin. The largest contribution received was $250 from Robert Clark. In addition to cash, the people gladly offered their time and expertise. George Bain donated the hauling of the statue and granite blocks for the pedestal. Dolese and Shepard gave crushed stone for the foundation. James McClintock of the Knickerbocker Company provided the cement. James Steven and Son Company set the monument. George Thomson and Son built the foundation.

The monument to Robert Burns is also important because it marked the first time that there was an united effort among the Scottish people of Chicago. It was the only

Dedication ceremony, Robert Burns Monument.

Wallace Bruce

time that all of the societies and all of the clans would cooperate toward the completion of a project. It was fitting, therefore, that the dedication on August 25, 1906, close with a grand demonstration—including a splendid concert, huge dinner, and gala ball—at the Second Regiment Armory. The program consisted of speeches by prominent Scots and other citizens; solos by Elizabeth M. Steward, James H. Rodger, and William McKenzie; readings from Burns's works by Kate Campbell Saunders and Andrew McLarty. The singing and dancing continued until the wee hours of the morning. For the Scottish people of Chicago, this was indeed their finest hour.

Robert Burns still has a special meaning to members of Chicago's Scottish community, as anyone who has visited the Scottish Home well knows. On April 18, 1993, a portrait of the poet was unveiled during a champagne reception and dedication at the Home. Created in 1910 by Dana Ripley Pond, a prominent New England artist, the painting hung for many years in Caledonia Hall in Lowell, Massachusetts. When the hall closed some fifty or so years ago, the painting was brought to the Chicago area by Samuel Scott. Eventually the portrait hung in the Evanston home of Scott's granddaughter, Roberta H. Johnson. Upon her death and through the intervention of Society member James A. Williams, the Society was fortunate enough to receive the painting as a gift. Hence, Burns's presence continues to be strongly felt at the home.

WORLD'S COLUMBIAN EXPOSITION

While members of the Burns Memorial and Monument Association were busy making plans to build their monument to Scotland's beloved bard, a handful of well-connected citizens of Chicago were laying the groundwork for a much larger and all-encompassing celebration. The biggest event in Chicago's young history occurred in 1893 when the World's Columbian Exposition opened to the public. City leaders believed Chicago was long overdue to let the world know of its many accomplishments.

MONEY, POWER, AND GOOD CHRISTIAN VALUES

Chicago in the 1890s was a boom town. And like any up-and-coming youngster on the verge of maturity, it wanted to blow its own horn. Everything had to be the biggest and the best, whether it be the tallest build-

Highland Pipe Band

ing or the biggest department store.

The city grew and with it came growth in new houses and apartments. People flocked to Chicago to work in the big factories that were opening and labor in the railroad and Stock Yards. This mass influx of people led to increasingly complex social problems, especially among the working class. The key to Chicago's growth was mass production, which often meant using more machines and hiring workers with fewer skills. Thus, the urbanization of the city led to increasingly inhumane working conditions and less opportunity for self-expression.

By the 1880s Chicago had earned a reputation as the socialist capital of the country. Most of the socialist and anarchist organizations were operated by immigrants, primarily Germans or Americans of German descent. It was not until the 1890s that a new American-bred socialism emerged with the leadership of Eugene Debs, Clarence Darrow, and Henry Demarest Lloyd. Significantly, the most important publisher of socialist material during this period was Charles H. Kerr, a Scot.

In the Chicago of the late nineteenth century, a sanitation system was not very highly maintained. An inadequate sewer system often led to disease, illness, and, quite often, death. Residents lived in constant fear of outbreaks of typhoid, cholera, and similar epidemics. During the 1890s, however, sanitary conditions improved somewhat with the completion of the Sanitary and Ship Canal.

Members of the city's elite felt increasingly frustrated and indeed embarrassed by the absence of world-class cultural institutions. In order for Chicago to truly qualify as a great metropolis, they believed, it had to have grand boulevards, beautiful parks, and good museums and cultural institutions. Conventional wisdom of the time maintained that the mark of a cultured person was not only the accumulation of wealth but also the nurturing of the proper amount of cultural sensitivity. Not surprisingly many

A TALE OF TWO CITIES

"Glasgow is the most exciting city of its kind east of Chicago." —Andrew Porter, *New Yorker*

The following is a list of similarities between the two former Second Citys.

Glasgow	Chicago
"Second City"	"Second City"
The Clyde	Chicago River
Burrell Collection	Art Institute
Central Station	Union Station
Glasgow Green	Bughouse Square
Robert Owen and New Lanark	George Pullman and Pullman
Glasgow Herald	*Chicago Tribune*
Charles Rennie Mackintosh	Frank Lloyd Wright
Billy Connolly	John Belushi
The Barras	Maxwell Street
Sauchiehall Street	State Street
The shipyards	The Stock Yards
1888 International Exhibition	1893 World's Columbian Exposition
The underground ("Clockwork Orange")	The elevated ("the el")
Glasgow School of Art	School of the Art Institute
Sir Thomas Lipton	William Stewart
Mitchell Library	Newberry Library
"I Belong to Glasgow"	"My Kind of Town"
No Mean City	City on the Make
"Red Clydeside"	"most radical city in U.S."
Music hall	Vaudeville
George Square	Daley Center
University of Glasgow	University of Chicago
City Chambers	City Hall
Chartists	Wobblies
Neil Munro and the *Glasgow Evening Post*	Finley Peter Dunne and the *Chicago Evening Post*"
"Let Glasgow Flourish"	"City in a Garden" (Urbs in Horto)

ROBERT JARVIE (1865-1941)

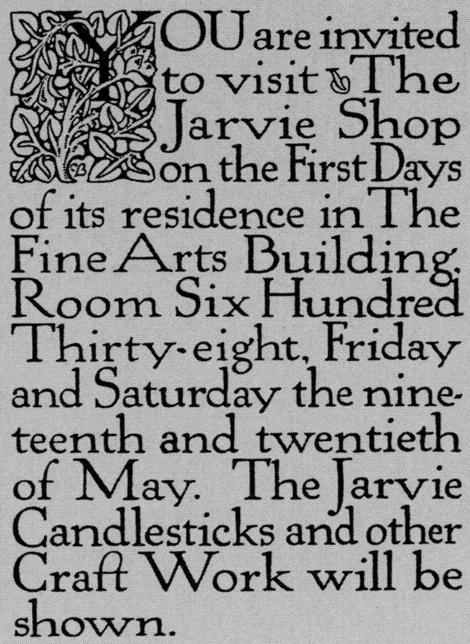

Robert Jarvie, an American of Scottish descent, is considered one of America's finest modern silversmiths. But for many years his work and his life languished in obscurity. In the late 1890s Chicago embraced what came to be known as the arts and crafts movement, an artistic movement that originated in England that sought to create beauty in the design and manufacture of ordinary products. The Chicago Arts and Crafts Society was created in 1897 with a membership of 126 artists, architects, designers, metalworkers, and writers (Edelstein 1992, 151–52).

The Jarvie Shop was located in the Fine Arts Building from 1904–9; at 1340 E. Forty-seventy Street from 1909–12; and at 842 Exchange Avenue in the Stock Yards district from 1912 to about 1920.

Jarvie's work was reminiscent of the Glasgow style made famous by Charles Rennie Mackintosh. At the time the arts and crafts movement gained ground in Chicago Jarvie was working as a clerk in the city's Department of Transportation. Born in Schenectady, New York, the son of Scottish parents, Jarvie came to Chicago in the 1890s.

Jarvie, a largely self-taught artist, specialized in metalwork. In 1900 he entered two of his works—slender metal candlesticks—in a Chicago Arts and Crafts Society show. The show elicited some interest and Jarvie picked up a number of patrons. Soon he began advertising his talents as a "candlestick maker," again to enthusiastic response. He met with so much success in fact that he resigned from his city job to devote more time to his new career. At this point, he opened the Jarvie Shop in the Fine Arts Building.

Jarvie expanded his line to include lanterns, copper bowls, bookends, vases, trays, and other home accessories. He then began to experiment with gold and silver. Art Institute President Charles Hutchinson commissioned Jarvie to design a silver punch bowl for the Cliff Dwellers Club, a prominent Chicago literary social club. Jarvie himself was a charter member of the club. In keeping with the Native American origins of the club's name, Jarvie modeled the bowl after vessels used by the cliff-dwelling Indians of the American Southwest. He also created a similarly designed silver punch bowl as a gift to Hamlin Garland, the founder of the club. The bowl is still in the club's collection.

In 1912 Arthur G. Leonard, president of the Union Stock Yard, asked Jarvie to design trophies for the cattle raisers and cattle breeders who regularly took part in the various livestock fairs. Leonard hoped that the trophies could also be adapted for personal use in the home. Business was so brisk that Jarvie decided to move his base of operations to the upper floor of the Old English Cottage Building in the stockyards. There Jarvie designed livestock exposition, golf club, and country club trophies.

But Jarvie didn't stop there. He began adding tea sets as well as furniture and wool rugs to his line. The outbreak of World War I, however, soon put an abrupt stop to his good fortune. The Jarvie Shop went out of business, and Jarvie and his wife moved to Evanston. Jarvie then found work as a salesman in the silver department at C. D. Peacock Company. In the 1930s the couple retired to the Scottish Home, where they spent their last days together. They both died there, in poverty, in 1941.

Jarvie remains an important, if neglected, figure in Chicago art history. Fortunately, a few samples of his work still remain. Several of his pieces can be found in the collections of the Art Institute of Chicago, the Chicago Historical Society, and the Metropolitan Museum of Art (Patton 1991; Darling 1977).

Jarvie Shop advertisement, 1905 (above). Jarvie's silver punch bowl was inspired by a Navajo basket presented to the Cliff Dwellers in 1910 by Charles L. Hutchinson on the second anniversary of the housewarming of the Cliff Dwellers' Orchestra Hall space, January 6, 1909. (above, right).

wealthy Chicagoans were self-made. If it took large sums of money to buy culture, so be it. One of the wealthiest was John Crerar, a member of the Illinois Saint Andrew Society and a generous supporter. Crerar, like other like-minded persons of his generation, believed that the arts were morally uplifting.

Crerar was a true Christian gentleman. Men of Crerar's background who made a lot of money typically stressed their social achievements rather than their material successes. A merchant and philanthropist, Crerar was born in New York City in 1827, the son of John Crerar and Agnes Smeallie. Both were strict Scottish Presbyterians, and young John received a rigid upbringing. When the elder Crerar died, John's mother married another Scot named John Boyd.

Crerar moved to Chicago in 1862 as representative of the railway supply firm of Morris K. Jessup and Company. A short time later Crerar and the Chicago manager of the firm, J. McGregor Adams, formed their own partnership.

Crerar was also one of the incorporators of the Pullman Palace Car Company as well as a director of the firm. In addition, he was a trustee and an elder of the Second Presbyterian Church. He gave generously to charities, was director of the Presbyterian Hospital of the Chicago Relief and Aid Society, and served as vice president of the Chicago Orphum asylum. He donated generously to the Chicago Historical Society and the YMCA. Although not a great scholar in the traditional sense of the word, he did love books, especially bibles, Presbyterian literature, biographies, and histories of Scotland.

Crerar projected somewhat of a serious demeanor, yet he apparently was quite genial and always ready to entertain with a story or joke (John Crerar Foundation 1989, 14). A life-long bachelor, he lived for many years in the luxurious Grand Pacific Hotel. He died there in 1889. At the time of his death he was worth an estimated $4 million. Of that amount, he bequeathed more than $1 million to religious and charitable institutions, while $2.5 million was given for the establishment of the great science and medical library that still bears his name.

Crerar also requested that the library should serve, without charge, the citizens of Chicago and accommodate the needs of the scientific community. The first librarian of the Crerar Library was a fellow Scot named Clement Walker Andrews. By the time Andrews retired in 1928 the library had amassed more than half a million volumes (19).

Crerar did not specify what kind of library he wanted. Rather he only requested that it maintain "an atmosphere of Christian refinement":

> *I desire that the books and periodicals be selected with a view to create and sustain a healthy*

REPORT OF BOARD MANAGERS, 1893

Illinois Saint Andrew Society
Report of Board of Managers, 1893
From November 3, 1892, to November 2, 1893

Some of the more unusual items included:

Coal supplied to 3 Families ($19.50) in the first quarter
and in the second quarter:
Flour and Oatmeal Supplied to 3 Families ($11.50)
Groceries Supplied to 1 Family ($10)
836 Lodging Tickets Issued ($125.40)
Shoes Supplied to 1 Applicant ($1)
Interments in Burying Ground at Rose Hill Cemetery, 2 Persons ($6.00)

third quarter
Passage Assistance for Old Woman (Widow) to Dundee, Scotland ($21.00)
Rent Paid for 6 Families ($49.00)

Total Disbursement in Charity During the Year ($1,137.19)
Expenses of the Board, Printing 500 Lodging Tickets ($2.75)
Gross Total Expenditures for Year ($1,139,94)

moral and Christian sentiment . . . that all nastiness and immorality be excluded. (10)

In 1963 the Crerar collection was moved to the campus of the Illinois Institute of Technology. In 1984 it moved again, this time to the University of Chicago. Today it is considered the premier science library in the city.

THE FAIR OPENS

The proposal to commemorate the 400th anniversary arrival of Christopher Columbus in the New World had been a matter of discussion for some time prior to 1885 (Pierce 1957, 501). Although other cities vied with Chicago for the opportunity to host the next world's fair—New York, Washington, D.C., and St. Louis—Congress chose the strapping city by the lake. On April 25, 1890, President Benjamin Harrison signed legislation making it official.

The fair opened on May 1, 1893, in Jackson Park when President Grover Cleveland gave the opening address. The grounds were designed by the renowned landscape artist Frederick Law Olmsted under the direction of Chicago's most celebrated architect, Daniel Burnham. Altogether the fair consisted of more than 250,000 exhibits from sixty nations.

Millions of visitors descended upon the city that they had heard so much about, the city that had defied the odds by literally rising anew from the ashes of rubble and ruin to remake itself in its own indomitable image. Cocky and self-assured of its future greatness on the one hand yet eager to please on the other, Chicago was still very much a raw-boned town. Yet within its prairie heart there continued to beat a frontier soul. "Chicago never seems to go to bed," wrote one visitor at the time, "and the streets at night are a blaze of electric light and thronged with people" (Ward 1895, 52).

It also contained an ethnically diverse population as a continuous flood of immigrants arrived to work in the Stock Yards, on the railroads, and in the lumber mills. The elite concentrated their energy on the business of making money, though, caring little with helping the newcomers adapt to their strange new home. These emotionally volatile conditions created the perfect breeding ground for distrust between capital and labor and laid the groundwork for such violent confrontations as the notorious Pullman Railroad strike of 1894. Perhaps, though, the struggle between the haves and have nots—between capitalism and socialism, between WASP and ethnic—had crystallized several years earlier by the Haymarket Affair of 1886. The seeds of discontent that were sowed at Haymarket were still very much alive in 1893.

The months leading up to the world's fair were times of unprecedented levels of unemployment in the city (Hirsch and Goler 1990, 73). Worse, a smallpox epidemic would ultimately claim more than 1,200 lives. Yet the 1880s and 1890s were also a time when many of the best-known and most durable Chicago institutions were established, such as the Fine Arts Building (1886), the Auditorium (1889), and the Art Institute of Chicago (1893).

Despite the problems, Chicagoans were proud of their city, and they wanted to make it better. They had faith, faith that the city would improve, faith in the inevitable pursuit of progress. Nothing was more indicative of this newfound faith and civic consciousness than the Columbian Exposition. With the exposition, growth, progress, and pride all came together. The magic of the fair allowed Chicagoans to forget the troubled times in which they lived. "A visit at night to the fair was a wonderful relief," recalled James B. Forgan (1924, 117), a prominent Scottish-American businessman, in his autobiography, "of which I availed myself as often as possible, frequently going there with my family or other friends to dinner. . . The fair served us in two ways. It helped us out materially with currency through the

money brought into and spent in Chicago by the crowds of visitors, and it relieved us of the nervous and physical strain caused by the panic."

One of the finest sculptures at the Exposition was the work of the Scottish American artist Frederick MacMonnies. MacMonnies's Columbian fountain, Barge of Statue or Triumph of Columbia, was located on the White City's Grand Canal. MacMonnies allegorical salute to America's birth was praised for both its beauty and its inspired vision. Another work, his delightful Storks at Play or The Bates Fountain, is located at the Lincoln Park Conservatory Garden, just east of Stockton Drive.

Perhaps of all the attractions of the fair none captured the public's imagination as much as the Midway Plaisance, a 600-foot strip of land located just west of the main fairgrounds between Washington and Jackson Parks that offered popular exhibits and entertainment. Among its attractions were numerous villages representing countries around the world. It was here that the Ferris wheel—created by engineer George Ferris—made its world debut. The fair's numerous ethnic villages—German, Turkish, Egyptian, Austrian, Lapp, Chinese, the British Building, and so on—proved to be particular favorites of the populace.

The twenty departments of the World's Fair Congress Auxiliary sponsored more than 200 symposiums on different subjects, from religion and literature to medicine and economics, that brought the greatest minds of the day from around the globe (Hirsch and Goler, 1990, 99). The fair attracted

World's Columbian Exposition, 1893 (above). View east of the Court of Honor featuring the fountain designed and sculpted by Frederick MacMonnies, whose family came originally from Dumfries-shire, Scotland.

notable speakers, including Theodore Roosevelt, William Jennings Bryan, Woodrow Wilson, Frederick Douglass, Eugene Debs, Florence Kelley, and Booker T. Washington. Spiritual concerns were also a part of the fair. At the Parliament of Religions, for example, most of the world's major faiths were represented.

Although the fair's 50-cent admission price was prohibitive for many workers—certainly for the city's poor—the fair did regularly offer "nationality days" or theme days, as they were called, to appeal to the city's burgeoning ethnic population.

Harriet Monroe, the official poet laureate of the fair, was commissioned to compose a poem specifically for the occasion. "The Columbian Ode," a salute to America's and Chicago's distinctive roles in its history, brought her to the attention of the general public. She recited the poem at the dedicatory service for the fair buildings on October 21, 1892. Monroe, an art critic for the *Chicago Tribune,* later founded *Poetry Magazine,* the first magazine in the United States devoted exclusively to poetry. *Poetry* was also the first magazine to publish Vachel Lindsay's most famous poem, "General William Booth Enters into Heaven." Lindsay, a native of Springfield, Illinois, was a visionary poet of Scots descent who studied and lived in Chicago for a short time, exerting a considerable presence on the local literary scene.

Monroe was born in Chicago in 1860, the daughter of Harry S. Monroe, a prominent Chicago lawyer of Scots heritage who was also a close friend of Senator Stephen A. Douglas. In her autobiography she recalls her early years.

> *I was born one Sunday morning two days before Christmas of 1860, in the little rapidly growing city of Chicago, even then conscious of its destiny.*

She then goes on to describe her long-held romantic admiration of her Scottish ancestors.

> *Part of me was ranging the Scottish hills with a daredevil highland clan which would later rebel against usurping Hanoverian kings, and, in desperate fealty to the Stuarts, would send three Munro brothers to new colonies across the sea.*
>
> *But half of me was being fashioned by my mothers's tribe, and family tradition tells little about them. Mitchell is a lowland Scotch name, so some adventurous Mitchell must have braved the Atlantic, and I hope there were vagabonds and artists in his progeny. (Monroe 1938, 1–2)*

For a brief period in her life Monroe kept up a correspondence with the Scottish novelist Robert Louis Stevenson. In one letter she described her indebtedness to him as a writer of fiction while managing to gently criticize aspects of his work that, in her opinion, did not quite match his high standards.

About a month after Monroe sent the first letter Stevenson replied, gracefully defending his fictional creations. Then, noticing her name, he couldn't help but wonder if she too were a Scot, "for it is hard to see where Monroe came from, if not from Scotland." He went on to request a photograph.

Monroe eagerly complied, "sending my prettiest picture." Stevenson, in turn, sent his own "shadowy" photograph accompanied by a seven-page letter, which Monroe (64–71) considered to be "the finest ever written, or at least ever published, by one of the great letter writers of our time."

Monroe and Stevenson finally met in 1887 in New York, but for Monroe the encounter was something of a letdown. She was shocked by the sight of this most sickly man of letters—so frail, so haggard was he, his body wasting away, his thin voice barely audible. In a matter of seconds Stevenson

Harriet Monroe (above)

the romantic hero became Stevenson the all-too-human invalid. "[M]y romance collapsed like a house of cards," Monroe confessed (72). They spoke for fifteen minutes about life and art. Stevenson seemed in good humor, and despite Monroe's preoccupation with his wayward appearance, they both enjoyed each other's company. Monroe never heard from the author again, although she always remembered him fondly.

During the run of the fair, various organizations would sponsor numerous events and activities—both ethnic and nonethnic—that were quite separate from the official program. Buffalo Bill's Wild West Show was held outside the fairgrounds, for example. Similarly, "Scottish Week" was sponsored in conjunction with the fair. In June 1893 the Chicago Caledonian Club apparently sponsored a highly successful three-day Highland games that was advertised nationwide and drew participants from throughout the world (Donaldson 1986, 41). The popular tune "The Campbells Are Coming" welcomed the chief of the Clan Maclean to the fair (Berthoff 1953, 10; *Scottish-American* 1893).

During six months in 1893 some 25 million Chicagoans attended this world of wonder, this first international fair ever held in the Midwest (Edelstein 1992, 85). The Columbian Exposition had a long-lasting influence not only on Chicago but also across the nation. The most obvious legacy was the wave of classicism that swept the country in the architecture of public buildings, railroad stations, banks, and churches (Pierce 1957, 511). Indeed, the fair affected national art for decades to come. It also exerted a profound influence on urban planning, spawning the "city beautiful" movement. Probably the biggest legacy of the fair was Daniel Burnham's Chicago Plan of 1909, which included the landscaping of Grant Park, the construction of Northerly Island, the building of the Adler Planetarium, the completion of Navy Pier, the straightening of the south branch of the Chicago River, and the building of Soldier Field (Mayer and Wade 1969, 276). More than anything Burnham's Chicago Plan assured that the legacy of the White City and the city beautiful movement would not be forgotten.

Then it was over. Facades that once thrilled thousands upon thousands were dismantled. Vandalism and fires did the rest. The dream city had vanished, and Chicago had to get back to the very real business of making a living.

Forty-Ninth Anniversary.

HELD AT THE AUDITORIUM HOTEL.

...ANNUAL BANQUET...

—OF THE—

Illinois St. Andrew's Society.

Friday Evening, November 30, 1894.

The Society's annual banquet program 1894 (above)

The first Board of Governors was elected on April 7, 1910. Pictured are Thomas Innes, George Fraser, D.A. Campbell, Joseph Cormack, Dr. John A. McGill, John Williamson, and Alexander Robertson.

FIVE

Home Away from Home

CREATION OF THE SCOTTISH HOME

The need for a home in which elderly men and women of Scottish ancestry could spend their last years in comfort and dignity was recognized long before steps could be taken to make the dream a reality. The uncertainty following the world's fair in 1893, which slowed the Burns Monument, also had a dramatic effect on the construction of a Scottish Old People's Home.

The notion of having a home for needy Scots occurred quite early in the history of the Society, although no actual date can be discovered from the records. We do know that by 1870 the idea was well on its way to completion. The Society most certainly would have been aware of the Old Peoples Home of the City of Chicago, which was founded in 1861 by various Protestant congregations. This home, located on the South Side of the city, was the first institution in Chicago to provide quality health care for elderly women. It is now known as the Admiral and is located at 909 W. Foster Avenue in Chicago.

The Solicitation Committee had started to do its work. It was expected that by May 1871 a proposal would be presented to the Society for ratification. A site already had been selected at the corner of Washington and Desplaines Streets since the committee felt that a central location was very important. The site was apparently owned by a Scot, and, hence, it was felt that a favorable price could be negotiated. Just in case this option was not available, however, the committee also researched the area near Lake and Van Buren Streets and between the Chicago River and Halsted Street.

By this time, the following gifts for appropriation toward the home had been received:

General John McArthur $500
John Alston $500
William Stewart $500
Hugh Ritchie $500
Alexander White $500
John McGlashen $500
Thomas Hastie $500
Solomon McKitchen $500
James Steel $500
Robert Hervey $250
Peter MacFarlane $250

Alexander M. Thomson $125
W. T. Noble $125
George Irons $125
Carlisle Mason $500
Adam L. Robb $500
Hugh Cooper $125
George H. Fergus $125
John McAllister $125
George Anderson $100
James Holton $100
Peter Downey $100
Conklin & Campbell (50,000 bricks) $500
James Thomson (painting and glazing) $500
Joseph Hogan (gas fixtures) $150
Woodruff Raffen $250
Peter Devine (boiler for heating) $200
James Hamilton $125
Nelson Mason $250
John Mohr (ironwork) $250

Two things were to interrupt the project: (1) members were unable to secure the desired location at a favorable cost and (2) the Great Fire would ravage the city. At the anniversary dinner in 1870, a model of the proposed home had been on display, and plans had been drawn. Unfortunately, both the model and the plans were destroyed in the fire.

After the fire, so much energy was consumed in rebuilding lives that little thought was given to establishing a place of charity. Indeed, the idea of creating a Scottish Charitable Home would not surface for another thirty years. Instead, funds of the Society were loaned without interest and directed toward the rebuilding of homes and factories. In the years ahead members would return the money through gifts and contributions. These gifts would then become the foundation of the present Endowment Fund, so important to the Society.

The charitable work of the Society continued in spite of the great losses in the fire. In 1885, for example, seventy-four families were given flour, coal, and help in paying their rent. In addition, seven elderly and sickly persons were returned to Scotland. Five were buried at Rosehill Cemetery. Thirty-six persons were given railroad fares to various parts of the country to help them find work or stay with relatives, and eleven persons were provided with free medical care by Dr. R. D. McArthur. The annual report of 1885 contains the following account:

> *During the past year times have been hard for the new-comers to this country. Hard times in Scotland and the cheap steamship and railway fares tempted old and young to come here. Arriving in New York without money, they were immediately sent to Chicago by agents of the railways for the low fare of one dollar, with nothing but the clothes on their backs and some without a shirt or sound shoes have called on the Society on the coldest days in winter. We were obliged to treat all comers alike, except when in cases of sickness one extra meal ticket per day was given to some persons on the recommendations of Dr. McArthur.*

On November 1, 1890, Jessie McKenzie was sent to the Society by the Chicago Relief and Aid Society. She was eighty-one years of age and had come from New York to live with her granddaughter. When Mrs. McKenzie arrived in Chicago, however, she found that her granddaughter had moved to Grand Rapids. The New York Saint Andrew Society had been helping Mrs. McKenzie for twenty years and had purchased her a railroad ticket to Chicago. Efforts to reach the granddaughter proved fruitless. Without outside assistance, Mrs. McKenzie's fate would have been dire, indeed. The Society that year was also responsible for other indigent Scotsmen and Scotswomen, including George Affleck, seventy-six years old; Nellie Knox, eighty years old; Mrs. Johnson, sixty-three years; and Janet Gunn, eighty-one years.

The World's Columbian Exposition of 1893 occupied the attention of Chicago for several years, both in planning and during the actual year of the celebration. Despite the glamour and excitement associated with the fair, it is easy to forget that the city—indeed the country—was in the throes of a major economic depression. As the charitable work of the Society increased, the necessity for a home became more and more apparent.

A few years earlier in 1889 the minutes of a Governors' meeting indicated that the board was entertaining the idea of a home for aged persons and "strangers in the city destitute of shelter." Several years later, in 1896 at the Fifty-first annual anniversary dinner of the Illinois Saint Andrew Society, the members brought the issue to the surface once again. That year the dinner was held in the Auditorium. As usual, most of the prominent Scots in the city were in attendance, including John Alston and John Sheriffs, at that time the only two surviving charter members of the Society.

On entering the main reception area, the guests were given sprigs of heather. George Anderson's ram's head occupied a prominent position at the head of the table. Soon the skirl of the bagpipes was heard. Pipers Robert Keith and Joseph Cant played "The Campbells Are Comin'." On their heels was the secretary, John F. Holmes, followed by waiters carrying the haggis, Scotland's national dish. As the haggis entered, the members rose to their feet and let out a lusty cheer. Having received the "proper" welcome, the haggis was then placed on the table. The business of eating could now begin.

Since the Society had just celebrated its jubilee, members felt they were on the verge of a new era in the Society's history. At this special dinner a proposal to establish a home for the elderly was again discussed. The program for the evening featured William Rainey Harper, president of the University of Chicago, who examined the defining elements of the Scottish character, Colonel Francis W. Parker spoke on "The Brain and Brawn of Scotland," and the Reverend Dr. H. M. Scott gave his thoughts on "The Land We Left and the Land We Live In." The evening ended with the performance of several popular Scottish songs and the singing in unison of "Auld Lang Syne" (*Scottish-American* 1896).

FINDING A HOME

By 1890 the Society had assumed the complete responsibility and well-being of several individuals. Thus, pressure was mounting for a quick solution. But it would not be until 1901 when the first Scottish Old People's Home would actually begin operation. At that time a two-story brownstone was rented at 547 Bryant Avenue (now Thirty-fifth Street), and the work was begun. The home was located between Martin Luther King, Jr., Drive and Lake Michigan, in close proximity to the Stephen Douglas Monument, also on Thirty-fifth Street.

The district was congested. There was not much open space available for recreational activity. Although it served a useful purpose, the building was old and uncomfortable and proved, if further proof was necessary, of the need for a permanent and better constructed home. At one time sixteen elderly men and women lived in the building. Gradually, the Scottish American community began to look upon the project not as a charity but as a duty.

Housing for the elderly was often formed along ethnic, religious, and fraternal lines, such as the Swedish Home of Mercy, Norwegian Old People's Home, and Home for Aged Colored People. A number of other groups were beginning to start homes for the elderly about the same time and in the same general area on the South Side. The Presbyterian Home, now located in Evanston, began not far from the Bryant Avenue address. The James C. King Home for Old Men was built at Garfield Boulevard and South Parkway, near the University of Chicago. It is also now located in Evanston. The Jewish Home for Aged Men and Women was located on Drexel Avenue—it no longer exists. The Church Home also began on the South Side and is presently situated in Hyde Park. The Chicago Relief Society formed in 1850; the Chicago Home for the Friendless in 1858 (Pierce 1940, 446–47).

The possibility that nursing facilities

could conduct their affairs in a professional manner did occur to the Society. It is clear that the Board of Governors was in contact with similar local institutions based on the following statement that appeared in a Society report dated January 5, 1911:

> *It is our intention to conduct the affairs of the Home in a business-like way. All similar institutions in our city are on this basis, and the first step in this direction was to place the Superintendent in absolute charge of the Institution and to be accountable only to the Board of Governors, and not to any individual.*

In June 1909 President John Williamson announced that a five-acre tract of land had been donated to the Society in Riverside, Illinois (now North Riverside) by Dr. John A. McGill, a wealthy physician who was also prominent in the manufacture of patent medicine. McGill's home at 4938 South Drexel Boulevard was built in 1890, and looking every bit like a French Gothic castle, is still standing. Designed by the noted architect Henry Ives Cobb, McGill's formidable mansion featured hand painted ceilings and walls, a carved staircase, and a spacious and lavishly appointed dining room. (The building was converted to apartments in 1982.) The gift became the impetus for building a full-fledged charitable home for needy Scots—a home away from home.

The gift of land being incentive enough to act, Williamson was instructed to select a committee to raise $100,000—a considerable sum of money in 1909—for the erection and endowment of the home. The burden of raising the funds for construction also fell to Williamson, who was just the kind of man—methodical and efficient—to get the job done. A committee, consisting of James B. Forgan, David R. Forgan, John G. Keith, Daniel R. Cameron, Daniel Campbell, Alexander Robertson, and John Crerar, was appointed to work with him. The home itself was to cost not less than $50,000.

MUNDIE HIRED AS ARCHITECT

Within a year, funds were available. Plans had been drawn up by William Mundie, a Scottish Canadian architect prominent in Chicago and a life member of the Society.

Mundie was born in Hamilton, Ontario,

Drexel Boulevard, circa 1870s (above)

the son of Scottish parents, on April 30, 1863. He was educated in the Hamilton Collegiate Institute, where he trained to be an architect like his father and grandfather before him. He moved to Chicago in 1884 and on his first day in the city he found work in the office of William LeBaron Jenney. Jenney is universally known as the father of the skyscraper. In February 1891 Mundie became a partner at the firm, which then became known as Jenney and Mundie. When Jenney died in 1906, Mundie became the senior partner, and the firm changed its name to Mundie and Jensen.

Mundie not only designed the Scottish Home but also supervised its construction, charging $1,013.72 for his services and then donating the money back to the Society. Among his major commissions were the Horticultural Building at the World's Columbian Exposition, the Union League Boys Club, and Wendell Phillips High School. From 1898 to 1905 Mundie was architect to the board of education.

Mundie was also a member of the Cliff Dwellers Club, the Canadian Club, and the Chicago Architectural Club, among others. He resided at 733 Gordon Terrace (MacDougall 1992, 320). Mundie died in 1939.

THE HOME OPENS

Because of some unforeseen circumstances, the Bryant Avenue home residents were not transferred to the new home in Riverside until October 31, 1910. On September 27 of that year the governors had hired Julia Hunting to be the new superintendent, but she was forced to resign for personal reasons. A Mrs. Dobson, who had served as the matron at 547 Bryant, was retained temporarily until a new superintendent could be found. Finally, on November 24, Cora J. Cummings was hired. Cummings, who lived on the premises, remained superintendent until her death some twenty-five years later.

GEORGE GRANT ELMSLIE

One of the least celebrated Chicago architects of the twentieth century is George Grant Elmslie. Elmslie was a disciple of the renowned Louis Sullivan. He apprenticed under Sullivan, and he did more than anyone to promote the Sullivanesque ideal in architecture.

Elmslie was from the small farming community of Huntly in the northeast of Scotland. Although he emigrated with his family to Chicago in 1884–his father worked for the Armour Meat Company–he always had fond memories of his native land. As early as twelve, Elmslie had displayed "a special flair for drawing." His parents encouraged him to develop this innate talent.

Elmslie and another great American architect, Frank Lloyd Wright, were the principal draftsmen in the firm of Adler and Sullivan. Whereas Wright, the iconoclast, went on to pursue his own individualistic career, Elmslie was more of a team player and throughout most of his professional life labored under the giant shadow of the great Sullivan.

Elmslie worked with Sullivan until 1909. Afterward he formed a partnership with William Purcell, becoming one of the most prolific of the Chicago and prairie school architects in the Midwest during the 1920s.

Several of Elmslie's work can be seen in Chicago and surrounding suburbs, including the Peoples Gas Light and Coke Company at 4839 W. Irving Park Road, Healy Chapel in Aurora, and the First Congregational Church in Western Springs. Perhaps the most Scottish inspired of his buildings though is the Maxwelton Braes resort hotel in Baileys Harbor, Wisconsin, which, appropriately enough, takes its name from the site where the traditional Scottish ballad character Annie Laurie once lived and loved.

Elmslie believed architecture should be regional and personal; he had no patience for the international style, which he considered sterile and cold. He died in 1952 and is buried in Graceland Cemetery along with his mentor, Louis Sullivan (Zabel 1991, 1–41).

The home's groundbreaking ceremony was held on March 23, 1910, and the cornerstone was laid on May 21. The first Home Committee was elected on April 4. Finally, in October the Bryant Avenue residents were moved into their new home in Riverside. The home was officially dedicated on November 5, 1910, with elaborate ceremonies. Several hundred people attended. At that time, James B. Forgan turned over the home to the Saint Andrew Society, and "a Scottish boys' band" provided the music. There was also sword dancing and costume dances by a group of young Scottish girls. The entire Scottish community had contributed to the building of the home, and it became an object of pride within the community. Indeed, the home continues to be the most visible aspect of Scottish culture in the city.

The first eleven residents who entered the home in the fall of that year were George McPherson, Emma Jane Lasco, Mary Jane DeWolf Stewart, Isabella Hope, Alexander Fraser, John Louis Ramsay, John H. Carson, Margaret Holder, Robert Forsythe, Andrew Minto, and Dr. David Buchanan. Eight of the eleven were native-born Scots, one was born in New York, another in India, and still another in Belfast of Scottish parents. A number of these residents are buried in the Society's grounds at Rosehill Cemetery. Indeed, Rosehill has become somewhat of a major landmark within the Scottish community. People from all over Scotland are buried there: Aberdeen, Glasgow, Edinburgh, Dumfries-shire, Inverness, Fort William, Caithness, Lewis, and North Uist.

Probably no one had done more for both the home and the Society than John Williamson, who remained a beloved figure in the Scottish community. Born in Dundee, Scotland, he was a highly respected vice pres-

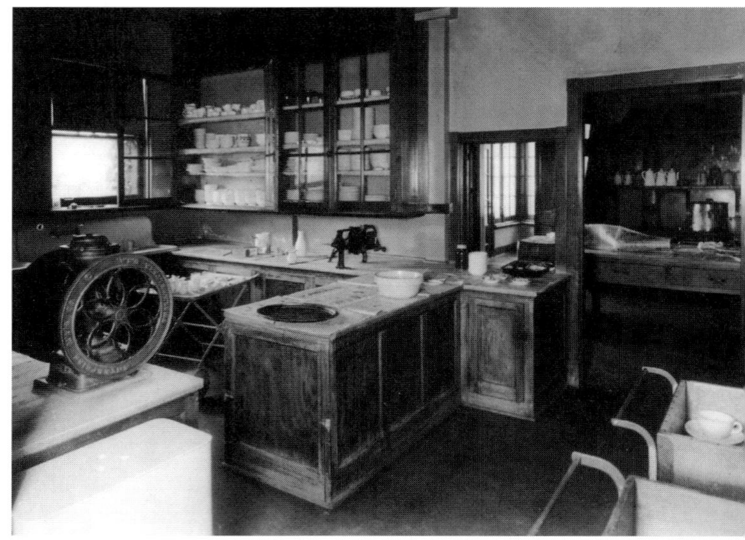

Scottish Old People's Home under construction, 1910 (above)
Kitchen at the Scottish Home, 1920s (above, right)

ident of the Peoples Gas Light and Coke Company. On April 6, 1912, a dinner was given in his honor at the Auditorium Hotel. At that point, the Scottish Home had been open for two years in its new Riverside location. Williamson had used every means possible—his time, money, and influence—to complete the home. The invocation at the dinner was given by the Reverend James MacLagan, pastor of the Scotch Presbyterian Church. Professor David McKinley presented the main address. The young dancers

were Bella Sellars, Dorothy Grant, Alexander Sim, and Robert Soutar. The pipers were Donald Forbes and Alexander Sim. The Fosolona's Orchestra played and closed the evening with a rendition of "Auld Lang Syne."

HOME DESTROYED BY FIRE

On March 26, 1917, the Scottish Home was destroyed by an early Sunday morning blaze that reduced the two-story red brick structure to ashes and rubble. Sadly, four of the thirty-eight residents perished. The evening had begun innocently enough.

The residents of the home had enjoyed a pleasant Saturday night's worth of entertainment by the Fuller Sisters, who sang Scots and English folk songs. Cora J. Cummings, administrator of the home, recalled their joyous mood: "They came out to divert the old people, and their people were enthusiastic in their applause and praise, and, as the sisters kindly responded to their pressing appeals for encores, were kept up later than usual." As the residents were retiring that night, they could not have imagined the terrible tragedy that would befall them before morning.

At approximately 12:30 a.m. a small fire began in the basement. (Crossed electrical wires were later blamed for the accident.) Shortly after one o'clock Cummings was awakened by the barking at her bedside of two of the home's dogs, Topsy, a collie, and McDougal, a Scotch terrier. Cummings and her sister alerted the residents and summoned the local fire department. Many of the residents were in their night clothes and remained calm. The Riverside, Cicero, and Berwyn fire departments answered the distress call. Topsy escaped the ordeal unscathed, but little McDougal lost his life in the flames. Yet, the dogs, by their quick

Residents of the first Scottish Home (above)
Cora J. Cummings, superintendent of the Scottish Home (above, right)

action, had saved many lives.

"There were no loud outcries nor shrieks of terror as the work of rescue went on," a reporter in the *Western British American* newspaper observed. "The discipline of the Home was wonderfully maintained and the aged men and women kept their heads like veterans in battle."

Flames quickly engulfed the entire building and, tragically, water to fight the fire was not readily available. The building, valued at $40,000, was gutted. Residents were unable to save any of their personal belongings—everything was destroyed. Worse, four of the thirty-eight residents perished in the raging fire: seventy-five-year-old Jeanette Greenock, ninety-two-year-old George McPherson, eighty-year-old William Robertson, and seventy-six-year-old Thomas Louttit. Funeral services for three of the victims were held at the Scotch Presbyterian Church, conducted by the Reverend James MacLagan, pastor, who also served the Society as chaplain. Greenock and Louttit were buried at Rosehill and McPherson at Forest Home. A diligent search of the ruins failed to recover the body of William Robertson.

REBUILDING

The Scottish Home was a total loss. Temporary quarters were rented until a new structure was completed. Donations from the residents were taken at the Riverside Town Hall within hours of the fire. Upon hearing of the tragedy, John Williamson hurried from his home at 1441 Washington Boulevard in Chicago. As one of the first to arrive on the scene, he must have been shattered by the sight of such destruction. Only a few walls remained standing, and the ruins were still smoldering. The sickening smell of smoke and charred matter settled for days over the village of Riverside and wafted innocently across the Des Plaines River.

As word of the disaster spread from person to person, many flocked to view the ruins, mourn the loss of life, and talk of the future.

Throughout the following day, a Sunday, members of the Society arrived to survey the terrible scene. Among them were James B. Forgan, John G. Keith, Daniel Ross Cameron, Thomas Innes, Daniel Campbell, Alexander Robertson, Hugh Richie, Robert Falconer, W. B. Mundie, the Reverend James MacLagan, James Glass, and John Crerar.

The first concern of everyone was naturally the condition of the "inmates," as the residents were then called. Temporary shelter was found for the remaining residents in the home's hospital. Several of the governors took residents into their own homes. Those who could stayed with relatives and neighbors, and the rest were housed in rented quarters. The people of Riverside donated clothing, furniture, food, and other items to benefit the displaced residents. In a special tribute to the generous residents of Riverside, the *Western British American* newspaper wrote: "None was Scottish; but each was a rare example of that rarest of blessings—the friend in need."

Almost immediately, subscriptions to the rebuilding of a new home had begun. Scots from around the country offered their generosity. William Scott of New York City, for example, wired his deep sympathy to John Williamson and gave a donation of $3,000 while fellow New Yorker William B. Walker offered $500. Even non-Scots were touched

John D. Williamson (above)
After the fire of March 26, 1917 (right)

by the tragedy. E. G. Elcock enclosed a check for $1,000. Williamson, McGill, and Forgan themselves also contributed $1,000 each. The current Society president Joseph Cormack gave $500, as did treasurer Alexander Robertson and another Society member Charles M. MacFarlane.

On Monday, March 27, 1917, a few days after the fire, Williamson called an emergency session of the Board of Governors. His office was located in the recently constructed People's Gas Building, which still stands at the corner of Adams and Michigan. The building, designed by Daniel H. Burnham, was lavishly furnished with mahogany from East India and marble from Greece. Here, amidst the splendor of this historic edifice, they made a bold decision: The Scottish Home would be rebuilt immediately.

In 1910 these same men had raised the funds to build the first Scottish Old People's Home. Now they faced the prospect of starting over. This time, however, the cost would double. Other challenges also awaited them. In 1910 there had been a united effort among all the Scottish people in Chicago to establish an institution that would care for the elderly among them. The various Scottish societies in the city organized under the name of the United Scottish Societies for the purpose of centering their activities on the home. This time, though, there would

were available for rental. Pipe bands came to perform, picnics were held, and children played games with the elderly. The Scottish Home was a wonderful place to visit, a bucolic retreat from the bustle of city life.

In 1924 Cora J. Cummings addressed the Chicago Council of Social Agencies, of which the Scottish Home was a member. She discussed the home's history and its policy. Admission to the home, she indicated, was restricted to persons of "Scottish birth, or wife, widow, child or grandchild of a native of Scotland." Men had to be at least sixty-five years of age and women sixty. All prospective residents were required to have been residents of Cook County for at least one year. Also, according to Cummings, "it must appear that the applicant is unable to provide for himself a home of his own. Applicants must be free from any contagious or infectious disease (including tuberculosis), from insanity, paralysis, epilepsy or feeble-mindless, and must not be a helpless cripple or suffering from any chronic or acute disease requiring hospital care."

There was no admission fee, but if an applicant had the means or the property it was to be transferred to the Society prior to admission. Each applicant was admitted on a six-month probationary period and was required to have approval of the home's physician before becoming a permanent resident.

In 1924 the home had one nurse, a cook, a janitor, two housemaids, and two dining room maids. The assistant superintendent also served as housekeeper. The daily routine consisted of an early rising gong at 6:45 a.m. and a breakfast gong at 7 a.m. Following breakfast, said Cummings, "the family gathers in the living room where a short service of Scripture reading followed by a repetition of the Lord's prayer is held." Each "member of the family" was required to attend the

be no such concerted effort. The members of the Society would have to accomplish the feat alone. In addition the threat of war increased the urgency of the project; it was imperative that the work be started and finished quickly.

William B. Mundie was asked once again to serve as the architect, only now he was requested to design a fireproof building to ensure that such a tragedy would never be repeated. The exterior would remain largely the same, but Mundie planned many improvements to the interior. Within two weeks, all the money was raised and within six months the building was completed. Shortly after, a resolution by the Board of Governors changed the designation "inmate" to the more soothing "resident."

A SOURCE OF PRIDE

From 1910 to 1917 the home was a source of great pride in the Scottish community. Nothing like it existed in the entire country. It was the center of activity for clans, concerts, and other Scottish organizations. With its close proximity to the Des Plaines River, the grounds became a popular gathering place during the summer months. Canoes

Off to church on a Sunday morning, 1928. The Studebaker was donated by John T. Cunningham. (left) Scottish Home bedroom (above)

religious service. After the service, the "family" gathers the mail together. But the "real event of the day" was "seeing the old gentleman off for the village where he walks the two miles every day, rain or shine, winter or summer." The old gentleman, unnamed, was eighty-eight years old.

Then the daily newspapers were read in the living room. "The majority of the women do a great deal toward keeping their clothes in order, making over garments that are sent in, and many do this for those unable to sew for themselves." Some of the ladies crocheted and knitted. If they could sell any items that they made, they were allowed to keep the money.

Dinner, or lunch, was served at noon. Afterward, the men gathered in the smoking room, and the women took naps to ensure they were properly refreshed for any possible visitors they might receive between the usual visiting hours of 2 to 4 p.m. daily except Monday. Supper, or tea as it was called, was served at 5:30 p.m. In the evening members sang or played for the family, or residents gathered for a game of cards or checkers or listened to the radio. Unless there was some special entertainment, the residents were required to go to their rooms by 9 p.m. Lights were out at 9:30 p.m. Religious services were conducted each Sunday afternoon between three and four o'clock.

"During the years many entertainments are given at the Home by various Scottish societies," continued Cummings, "and as we have the piano, the Victrola and now the radio, time passes very pleasantly. We have on the whole a very happy and contented family with little discord when one considers the great age and the great differences in temperament and disposition. We try to maintain the Home atmosphere and a family spirit as far as possible and find that the same gentle firmness in discipline required as in a small family."

By modern standards the rooms were small, but there was no central heat or air conditioning. Some heat was provided by a coal furnace, which proved inadequate during the cold winter months. For many years the fireplace in the living room was a primary source of heat. Water came from a well located at the rear of the home. A large garden, tended by the residents, furnished much of the food. The surplus was canned and used during the winter months. Pigs were kept and fed the leftovers from the kitchen. They were butchered in the fall, the meat cured and salted for later use. Chickens were raised on the property and supplied both meat and eggs. By 1912 a number of fruit trees had been planted. In later years, sheep would graze inside the fenced-off area. Thus, the Scottish Home became self-sufficient, quite distinctive from the teeming metropolis to the east. It was a peaceful and safe haven for those who lived there.

But the world outside was rapidly changing. Soon World War I would envelop the United States, changing forever the Scottish community in Chicago. While their activities flourished during the next decade, the feeling of combined unity–of one for all–was diminished. After the war, there was a large influx of people from Scotland. Many arrived by way of Canada, others through Ellis Island. They crossed the ocean on ships named the *Saturnia, Letisia,* and *Cameronia.* They came, like others before and since, hoping to improve their lot in a strange new land.

Ivy-covered Scottish Home, late 1920s

SILVERMAN'S BANK

SIX

An Emerging Maturity

The Scottish community, like the city itself, was exhibiting undeniable signs of maturity. Scots founded their own churches, their own newspapers, and their own businesses. Long apolitical, they even began to get involved in the sensitive quagmire of Chicago politics. Although Scots were scattered throughout Chicago and its environs, many wealthy second and third generation Scots in the late 1890s lived along the city's fashionable avenues, such as Prairie Avenue or Drexel Boulevard. During the 1920s and 1930s numerous Scottish concerts were held on the South Side in places like Prospect Hall and the Masonic Temple.

Visitors found much to admire in the Chicago of the 1890s. Wrote a visiting Scottish journalist, William Archer, in 1898 about the city: "It is the young giant among the cities of the earth, and it stands but on the threshold of its destiny" (Ebner 1988, 49).

As always the Scots were vastly outnumbered by other ethnic groups, and many foreign languages were heard on the city streets. Indeed, by the turn of the century German remained the dominant foreign tongue in the city with approximately 500,000 speakers. Other major languages represented included Polish with 125,000, Swedish with 100,000, Bohemian with 90,000, and Norwegian and Yiddish with 50,000 speakers each. The Celtic languages were also present although in considerably smaller quantities. Thus, in 1903, according to the same study, Irish speakers numbered around 10,000, Welsh from 1,000 to 2,000, and Scots Gaelic around 500 (Hirsch and Goler, 1990, 27).

The turn of the century witnessed the construction of dank and dark tenements. Three or four stories high, these tower ghettoes were the municipal response to overcrowding in the inner city and the subsequent need for low-cost housing. Horror stories about life in these slums abound, of a dozen people occupying three-room apartments, of rooms where the sun never shined, or of poorly constructed buildings with primitive sanitation. Robert Hunter, an Indiana sociologist of Scots descent who spent some time at Hull-House, the pioneering social settlement, concluded that these tenements make for the "worse possible dwellings for human beings." In 1904 Hunter published *Poverty,* a classic study of social conditions in America during the early years of the twentieth century.

Dearborn and Washington, 1890 (left)

DIRECTORY

—OF THE—

First Scotch Presbyterian Church

OF CHICAGO:

Containing the Reports for the Year 1875, a Complete List of the Membership, alphabetically arranged, a Short Sketch of the Church, a List of all the Presbyterian Churches of the City, and other matters of interest.

JAMES BARNET, PRINTER AND PUBLISHER,

160 NEWBERRY AVENUE, COR. W. 14TH ST.

MARCH, 1876.

THE SCOTTISH CHURCH

Like most immigrants, the Scots too created their own church that was both Scottish in name and membership. Most of the immigrants from Scotland were Presbyterians or a variation thereof. Hence, from the urban setting of Chicago to rural settlements in Argyle, Caledonia, or Elmira, Illinois, the Presbyterian Church formed the focal point of the community, creating a sense of stability and common purpose.

THE SCOTCH PRESBYTERIAN CHURCH

The vast majority of the people who settled in Chicago in the first half of the nineteenth century belonged to predominantly Protestant denominations, whether Presbyterian, Methodist, Baptist, Episcopalian, or Lutheran. The Protestant stronghold, however, would not last through the end of the century, for by the 1890s mass influxes of Irish and German Catholics soon outnumbered the Protestant contingents (31).

In the 1860s the First Scotch Presbyterian Church was established. Originally under the wing of the Canada presbytery, it eventually withdrew and sought admission into the Chicago presbytery. At first the effort to unite with the United Presbyterian Church of the United States was thwarted because the church membership could not garner the necessary required majority (Directory 1876, 34). The change was ultimately made, however, and in August 1874 the First Scotch Presbyterian Church was admitted to the Chicago presbytery.

The congregation was organized in a room on Monroe Street on July 8, 1866 by the Reverend John Proudfoot of London, Ontario, with forty-six people enrolled as members. The following individuals were appointed to the provisional committee:

George McPherson, chairman
Andrew Drysdale
James F. Mackie
Peter McEwan
Alexander Barnet
James Symington
James Mowat, secretary

McPherson, Drysdale, Barnet, and Robert Watson were elected elders. For more than eighteen months services were held in St. George's Hall on South Clark Street near Jackson Boulevard. The Reverend R. F. Burns of St. Catherines, Ontario, was asked to be pastor. He accepted, and his induction took place on March 20, 1867, in the Music Hall on State Street. In the evening a celebration was held in his honor. The following lines were written as the welcoming address:

Let's welcome him! the choice of all,
Who far has come at duty's call,
To hasten here the Lord's good time
For those who hail from Scotia's clime.

The little congregation grew. Since St. George's Hall was too small to accommodate the crowds, services were moved to the Metropolitan Hall, at Randolph and LaSalle Streets, until the congregation was able to secure its own building at the corner of Sangamon and Adams. On August 16, 1868, the dedication of the church building took place (29–30).

Dr. Burns was pastor for three years before returning to Canada (32). For two years the congregation had no minister. Finally, in June 1872 the Reverend James MacLagan, who had also been ministering in Canada, accepted the invitation to come to Chicago. On July 11 he became the church's new minister (32). MacLagan was an important figure in the Scottish commu-

The First Scotch Presbyterian Church (left) as it would have appeared in 1876. The congregation met at various locations during its exsitence. Rev. James MacLagan, pastor, Scotch Presbyterian Church (above).

nity for many years, both in Chicago and elsewhere. In addition to the Scotch Presbyterian Church on the North Side, he was also the minister of the Brighton Park Presbyterian Church and, later, of the Willow Creek Church in Argyle, Illinois (MacMillan 1919, 37).

OTHER PRESBYTERIAN CHURCHES

Other Protestant churches had Scottish associations. As early as 1833 twenty or so Presbyterians met at Fort Dearborn in a primitive cabin on Wolf Point. A forty-by-twenty-five- foot frame building near the southwest corner of Lake and Clark Streets was built the following year. In 1835 the congregation was incorporated as the First Presbyterian Church and Society of Chicago (Frueh and Frueh 1988, 10). Later, the building was enlarged and relocated near Clark and Washington Streets.

In 1842 the church was split apart by the controversial slavery issue. Those who advocated immediate abolition of slavery remained with the First Church. Others who felt that slaves should be granted freedom only after their "future welfare was assured" formed the Second Presbyterian Church. Members of this group held services on the third floor of the Saloon Building at Clark and Lake Streets.

The present church located on South Michigan Avenue was completed in 1874 (an earlier church, the famous Spotted Church, was destroyed in the Great Fire of 1871). The Second Presbyterian Church is the work of James Renwick, of Scots descent and one of the best-known American architects of his day. The beautiful interior incorporates elements of the arts and crafts style as well as contains twenty-two stained glass windows. Fourteen of those windows are by Louis C. Tiffany; two were designed by the English painter Sir Edward Burne-Jones and executed by the William Morris firm. Many of Chicago's leading merchants and industrialists, who lived on nearby Indiana and Prairie Avenues, attended the church in its heyday. Abraham Lincoln's son, Robert Todd Lincoln, for example, was a church trustee from 1879 to 1889 (9–10). Years later, after another fire destroyed most of the nave and the entire roof in 1900, the membership chose fellow member and socially prominent architect Howard Van Doren Shaw, of Scottish descent, to rebuild the nave (14).

Shaw was greatly influenced by the English arts and crafts movement. He transformed the formerly neo-Gothic nave into one of the finest example of arts and crafts style in the city. The church is also rich in imagery and iconography. Liturgical symbols are scattered throughout the nave as well as olive branches, fruit trees, roses, and even the Scottish thistle (17). A bronze Celtic cross from the isle of Iona was given to the church by Pastor Ernest R. Ackerman in 1957 (20). Of the many beautiful stained glass windows, "The Five Scourges," which symbolizes Christ's torments, was installed around 1919 and commemorates the friendship between Timothy P. Blackstone, president of the Chicago and Alton Railroad, and

ST. MARGARET OF SCOTLAND CHURCH

St. Margaret is one of the patron saints of Scotland. The church that bears her name at Ninety-ninth and Throop on the South Side was established in 1874 to serve Catholic families living in what was then the suburb of Washington Heights. Despite its Scottish name, early parish members came from Prussia, Westphalia, Luxembourg, and Bavaria. It later became an Irish parish. The present building dates from 1928. Today St. Margaret of Scotland serves a predominantly African American congregation (Koenig 1980, 560–63).

the Scottish American philanthropist John Crerar (34). The church was designated a national landmark in 1974.

More recently, the Reverend J. Laing Burns was pastor of Second Presbyterian Church from 1990 to his death in October 1993. Most of his career, however, was spent as pastor of North Riverside Community Presbyterian. He was also an associate pastor at Yorkfield Presbyterian in Elmhurst and head of Willow Springs Presbyterian. Born in England of Scottish ancestry, Reverend Burns immigrated to the United States with his family in 1921. From 1947 to 1970 he was pastor of various churches in Ohio and Wisconsin before moving to Illinois.

The Fourth Presbyterian Church, a magnificent neo-Gothic structure on North Michigan Avenue, has had a volatile history in its own right. Although known for its stable leadership, the church has been graced with the presence of passionate pastors, committed both to the church itself and to the greater metropolitan community. In 1985 the Reverend John Buchanan, a Scottish American, replaced the Welsh-born Elam Davies.

THE SCOTTISH BUSINESS COMMUNITY

Many Scots fared well in the Chicago business community, especially within the banking and commercial industries. One of the most outstanding figures in banking was James Berwick Forgan, a Scottish-born member and one-time president of the Illinois Saint Andrew Society.

Forgan was born April 11, 1852, in St. Andrews, Scotland, the capital of the golfing world. "I left St. Andrews, Scotland, which was the home of my boyhood, before I attained my majority," he recalls in the opening pages of his autobiography (Forgan 1924, 17). His father, Robert Forgan, manufactured golf balls and golf clubs in St. Andrews.

Forgan became an apprentice banker at the Royal Bank of Scotland. He found a position with the British Bank of North America in London and in 1872 was sent to Montreal, then to New York, and finally to Halifax. Promotions came quickly. When he was thirty-three he was assigned to establish an American branch of the Canadian Bank in Minneapolis. While there, Chicago banker Lyman J. Gage had heard of Forgan's talents and offered him the position of vice president at the First National Bank of Chicago. In 1900 Forgan became president. He retained that position until 1916. From 1914 to 1916 he was also a director of the Federal Reserve Bank of Chicago.

Upon arriving in Chicago Forgan wasted no time in becoming a member of the Illinois Saint Andrew Society. In 1916 he was elected president. During his term as president he presided over two major changes in the Society's policy. Since 1846 the Society had sponsored an annual celebration that

SCOTS AND AMERICAN PRESBYTERIANISM

That the Scottish influence on American Presbyterianism has been considerable since colonial days is of no surprise. What is surprising, or at least curious, are the various Protestant sects with Scottish roots that either made their way across the Atlantic or bore fruit in American soil. The MacDonaldites, for example, originated in Prince Edward Island before making converts in Boston while their rival, the Campbellites and their society called the Disciples of Christ, established by an Ulster Scot, Alexander Campbell, found their most ardent supporters in the prairie states of the Midwest. Illinois prairie poet Vachel Lindsay was a devout believer. Certainly the most controversial of the Scottish-influenced group's was John Alexander Dowie's Christian Catholic Apostolic Church in Zion.

was exclusively for men where the "water of life" was served free. Under a resolution that was previously adopted by the Society, women were allowed to attend the banquet, and the serving of whisky and other strong drinks was reduced. A strict Presbyterian, Forgan encouraged the men to be on their best behavior in deference to the ladies. Orchestral music and dancing were added to the programs. Overall, the result was a "greatly improved" social atmosphere (232–33).

Forgan, a North Sider who lived at 1415 North Dearborn, was an active member of the Scottish American community. Among his many responsibilities, he was a governing

Kirkin' O the Tartan, a twentieth-century Scottish American tradition at the Second Presbyterian Church of Evanston, January 26, 1964 (above).

member of the Art Institute, life member of the Field Museum, member of the British Empire Association, and member of the English Speaking Union. He also played an important role within a number of local philanthropic organizations—as treasurer of the Chicago Federation of Aged and Adult Charities, advisory board member of the Chicago Home for the Friendless, and sustaining member of the Presbyterian Home (239). He was also a member of the Fourth Presbyterian Church. Forgan died on October 28, 1924.

JAMES SIMPSON

As president of Marshall Field and Company and chairman of the Chicago Plan commission, James Simpson was one of the most influential—if little known—Scots in the city's history. "It is inevitable as death or taxes," he once said, "that Chicago is destined to become the greatest city in the world."

Born in Glasgow, Scotland, on January 26, 1874, Simpson was brought to America by his parents William Simpson and Isabella Brechlin in 1880. He received his education in the Chicago public school system, and in 1891 he became a cashier clerk at Marshall Field and Company.

Simpson moved quickly up the corporate ladder. He had vision. He was quick and intelligent, polite and energetic. When Marshall Field died in 1906, Simpson was made second vice president and assistant to the president. In 1923 he attained the title of president.

When Charles Wacker resigned as head of the Chicago Plan commission, Simpson was chosen to be his replacement. The Chicago Plan was nothing less than the apotheosis of the "city beautiful" concept and, as such, involved the beautification of the city's boulevards, museums, and lakefront. Simpson was also instrumental in the organization of the Merchandise Mart and was a director of the Federal Reserve Bank and of Commonwealth Edison. Further, he played a role in the straightening of the Chicago River, the building of Union Station, the completion of Lake Shore Drive, and the creation of the Shedd Aquarium. He was also a big supporter of "A Century of Progress," Chicago's world's fair of 1933.

Another president of Field's, John McKinlay, was born in Greenock, Scotland, just fifty miles from Simpson's place of birth.

A number of Chicago businesses, including some of the best-known institutions in the city, have Scottish roots.

ENCYCLOPAEDIA BRITANNICA

The oldest continuously published reference work in the English language, *Encyclopaedia Britannica*, was founded in 1768 in Edinburgh, Scotland, by Colin Macfarquhar, a printer and bookseller, and Andrew Bell, an engraver. The first editor

BIRTHPLACE OF SOME OF THE SOCIETY'S REGULAR MEMBERS, C. 1895

John J. Badenoch, Aberdeen
Daniel R. Cameron, Glengarry County, Ontario
Joseph Cormack, Banff
James B. Forgan, St. Andrews
William Gardner, Kilmarnock
Robert Hervey, Glasgow
John F. Holmes, Edinburgh
Thomas MacLagan, New Scone, Perth
Charles MacFarlane, Glasgow
John McArthur, Erskine, Renfrew
James McGill, Glasgow
John C. Pirie, Rhynie, Aberdeenshire
James Steel, Kilmaurs, Ayr
Andrew Wallace, Stranraer

was twenty-eight-year-old William Smellie. The three-volume first edition was completed in 1771 and contained 2,659 quarto-pages and 160 copper-plate engravings by Bell (Hasser n.d., 3–4).

The first non-Scottish editor of *Britannica* was an English-born Shakespearean scholar named Thomas Spencer Baynes, who had been professor of logic at St. Andrews University and editor of the *Edinburgh Guardian*. He also edited the Ninth Edition. The Ninth was important for a number of reasons, not the least of which that it was the first Britannica to appear in an authorized printing in the United States.

Around the turn of the century the company moved to London. In 1902 an American corporation, the Encyclopaedia Britannica Company, was formed. The Eleventh Edition was printed at Chicago's R. R. Donnelley and Sons plant. The Chicago ties became even stronger when in 1920 Sears, Roebuck, and Company purchased the firm. The relationship between the giant mail order firm and the encyclopedia was rocky at best. In 1941 William Benton, a University of Chicago vice president, convinced Sears' president General Robert E. Wood to give the publication to the university as a gift. After all, who had ever heard of a mail order firm owning an encyclopedia. Wood agreed.

Yet the university declined the offer for a second time. Finally, Benton put up his own money and agreed to take over the company himself. The university though did receive a one-third interest and royalties on sales. Benton was *Britannica's* publisher for thirty years. The firm celebrated its bicentennial in 1968 with the inauguration of the Britannica Lecture at the University of Edinburgh.

The list of contributors over the centuries has been impressive: Sir Walter Scott, Thomas Henry Huxley, Matthew Arnold, Robert Louis Stevenson, Harry Houdini, Marie Curie, Leon Trotsky, among many others.

Despite some serious financial problems, the now Swiss-owned *Britannica* remains a major part of Chicago's business and literary landscape. The Scottish thistle continues to be the company's familiar and enduring symbol.

CARSON PIRIE SCOTT AND COMPANY

Few companies are as strongly associated with Chicago as the department store of Carson Pirie Scott and Company.

In 1904 two businessmen from Germany, Leopold Schlesinger and Daniel Mayer, sold their interest in the department store that stood at the corner of State and Madison for more than thirty years to Carson Pirie Scott and Company. But the Scottish roots of the company are far older.

John T. Pirie was born in Scotland in 1827. He left his homeland to work in his uncle's dry-goods store in Ireland at the age of fifteen. There he met another young man, Samuel Carson. They decided to move to Belfast to try their hand at bigger plans. They didn't stay in Belfast long, however, for they soon learned of a flourishing business in the thriving Illinois river town of Peru. They decided to emigrate to America, and in 1855 they established a store in nearby LaSalle, Illinois. They prospered and soon opened up other stores.

John T. Pirie (above)

Looking for better and bigger opportunities, they directed their attention to the rough-and-ready frontier town of Chicago. George and Robert Scott had already operated the downstate outlets. Soon they too came to Chicago, and the firm of Carson Pirie Scott and Company was born.

The success of the firm was due largely to the business acumen and stolid determination of a somber Scotsman named Andrew MacLeish. Born in Glasgow in June 1838, Andrew MacLeish was the second son of Archibald MacLeish. The family originally hailed from Lochwinnoch in the Scottish Highlands.

MacLeish arrived in Chicago when he was eighteen with a fellow Scot named Edward Couper. On their first evening in the rough town, they enjoyed a walk out to the "boundless prairie" at Union Park.

MacLeish worked for numerous dry-goods stores without much success until 1867, when Samuel Carson invited him to join Carson and Pirie, a wholesaler, as a junior partner. His assignment? To develop a retail store in Chicago. With MacLeish at the helm as the new store's founder and manager, business blossomed. By the mid-1870s the newly named Carson Pirie Scott and Company had become one of the city's leading department stores (Donaldson 1992, 4–5).

Years later, more than 120 Carson executives gathered on the eighth floor of the store to honor Bruce MacLeish, the seventy-four-year-old chairman as he completed his fiftieth year with the company that was founded by his father, Andrew, in 1867. A young Scottish American dancer Margaret Baikie played the pipes.

Archibald MacLeish, Andrew's famous poet son, later described his father as a reserved man who spoke very little:

> *My father came from a very old country in the north and far away, and he belonged to an old strange race, the race older than any other. He did not talk of his country but he sang bits of old songs with words that he said no one could understand any more. (Donaldson 1992, 2)*

When his parents moved to Glencoe, Illinois, in 1889, they named their home Craigie Lea, after the words to a Scottish ballad.

STEWART TEA COMPANY

In 1913 William A. Stewart, born of a Scottish family, founded a tiny coffee roasting plant in Chicago. Within fifteen years Stewarts Private Blend Coffee was the preferred choice for many of Chicago's hotels, clubs, and restaurants. In 1925 Stewart moved into a five-story building on West Washington Boulevard and changed the name to Stewart and Ashby Coffee Company. During the Century of Progress of 1933 Stewart's was selected as the "official world's fair coffee."

Stewart, being the good Scot that he was, always appreciated a proper cup of tea. But he couldn't find any in Chicago. He then introduced his Private Blend tea to add to his coffee products. Today the family owned company still offers coffee, tea, and related specialty food items. William A. Stewart, grandson of the founder, has served as president since 1975. Stewarts Private Blend Foods, located at 4110 W. Wrightwood Avenue, is reportedly Chicago's last family owned coffee business.

ERNST AND YOUNG

The accounting firm of Ernst and Young started as Arthur Young and Company. Young, a Glasgow-born Scot, was probably the most influential accountant in the city's history. Although he entered accounting when the profession was still in its infancy, he managed to turn the public accounting firm that he founded into one of the largest accounting firms in the country and a member of the "Big Eight."

Born in Glasgow, the son of a shipbuilder, Young was educated at the prestigious Glasgow Academy. He received a master's degree from Glasgow University in 1883 and a law degree in 1887.

Young emigrated to America in 1890 and found work at an international banking firm in New York that was run by fellow Scots. Deciding to not only change residences but also professions, Young moved to Chicago four years later and started his own public accounting firm with Charles W. Stuart in a one-room office in the Monadnock Building. Young became one of the first certified public accountants in Illinois.

In 1906 the Scotsman founded Arthur Young and Company and moved into larger quarters in the Borland Building on South LaSalle Street. Since accounting was such a new profession in the United States, Young felt he had no alternative but to recruit accountants in Scotland. Among the most important of Young's clients included Swift and Company, William Wrigley, Jr., Company, Montgomery Ward and Company, Encyclopaedia Britannica, and Rand McNally.

Young died on April 3, 1948. In June 1989 Arthur Young and Company merged with Ernst and Whinney to form Ernst and Young and become, in the process, the top-ranking accounting firm in the city, edging out the historic leader and long-time rival, Arthur Andersen and Company. Arthur Young was an active member of the Illinois Saint Andrew Society (Sawyers 1991, 278–79).

MACARTHUR FOUNDATION

All too few people realize that the MacArthur Foundation, the nation's sixth largest foundation, is based in Chicago. Although the philanthropic company contributes to research in mental health, the environment, world peace, and other social issues, the lion's share of public attention is given to the foundation's fellows program, the so-called genius grants. Winning a prestigious MacArthur fellowship is a godsend for many creative people trying to make a living in an increasingly business-oriented world.

The MacArthur Foundation is the brainchild of the late John D. MacArthur. MacArthur made his fortune in the insurance industry with Bankers Life and Casualty Company and in shrewd real estate investments. According to one account, MacArthur had a suspicion of inherited wealth and a strong dislike of the Internal Revenue Service. When he died in 1978, he left most of his vast estate to establish a nonprofit charitable foundation in his name and that of his second wife, Catherine T. (Pick 1995, 24). As far as how his fortune should be used, he left it to the discretion of his board of directors.

John Donald MacArthur was born in 1897, the youngest of seven children in the coal mining community of eastern Pennsylvania. His father, William T.

John D. MacArthur (above)

MacArthur, was a strict Baptist preacher of the hellfire-and-brimstone variety. Around the turn of the century the family moved to Illinois, but in 1910 they moved back east to Nyack, New York, where John attended the Wilson Academy. A bright but mischievous youngster, John had no patience for schooling—he got mostly D's and F's—and dropped out in the eighth grade.

As a young man, he moved to Chicago, where his brothers were already meeting with much success, including the journalist Charles MacArthur. John tried to follow Charlie's footsteps—he was a cub reporter for the *Chicago Herald and Examiner,* but he decided journalism was not for him. He had reportedly told his father, "Charles is out there in the wicked city of Chicago. I'd better go out there and see what he's doing, so I can give you a report."

During World War I he joined the navy and served in the Royal Canadian Air Force as a pilot. Before the war John had worked as a door-to-door salesman in his brother Alfred's insurance company. It was in the insurance industry where he would find his true calling in life. (*John T. MacArthur* n.d., 3–4).

During the Depression he bought the financially troubled Bankers Life and Casualty Company. Working from his kitchen table, he laid the foundation for what would become a hugely successful profit-making venture. He experimented with the at that time innovative idea of selling insurance by mail. In this way, he sold hundreds of thousands of low-cost policies to people across the country (8).

MacArthur became a millionaire by the time he was forty-five. He reached billionaire status in his late seventies.

MacArthur lived up to his reputation as a thrifty Scot. Never much for pretense or showiness, for many years he conducted business from a rear table in the coffee shop of the aging Colannades Beach Hotel that he owned in Palm Beach Shores, Florida (10). He had no interest in creature comforts and he was known to be notoriously tight with his wallet. It was said that he loved having other people pick up the tab for a meal and turned off the air conditioning in his coffee shop "office" when no one was present to save on the bills.

The MacArthur clan achieved prominence in many professions. In addition to his Pulitzer Prize–winning playwright and journalist brother, General Douglas MacArthur was a cousin.

Other Chicago businesses with Scottish roots or Scottish connections include the advertising firm of Ogilvy and Mather, the pharmaceuticals company Littlejohn and Littlejohn, the Wrigleyville coffeehouse Uncommon Ground, and the Hyde Park bookshop O'Gara and Wilson. Gaelic Imports, owned by Dick and Cathie Mulholland since 1971, has been a Chicago fixture for years. Originally opened in 1957 on North Avenue as White Heather Imports by Cathie's brother George Hudson, Gaelic Imports moved to its present location near the corner of Austin and Lawrence in the Jefferson Park neighborhood more than a decade ago. George, who was the host of a popular Scottish radio show some years back, runs Hudson Holidays in Elmwood Park.

THE SCOTTISH PRESS

Typically the ethnic press of most immigrant groups mixed news of the ethnic community with news from similar communities across the country. Scottish ethnic publications, especially newspapers, usually contained reports from Canada, since a large Scottish population resided there, as well as news from the homeland itself.

THE SCOTTISH ETHNIC PRESS

The mainstream press could not hope to cover the Scottish community in the way that the ethnic press could—no matter how many Scots were staff members. For that,

Scots in America turned to such publications as the *Western British American*, the *British-American*, the *Scottish-American*, and the *Highlander.*

The *British-American* was established in the 1880s and was published by the British American Company, with offices in the Pontiac Building at 542 S. Dearborn Street. The editor was James C. McNally. In 1932 the paper celebrated its forty-fourth year, quite a remarkable achievement for an ethnic publication. The *British-American* published news from and about the larger British communities in Chicago and around the world. A typical issue would feature football match reports, a British American Societies column, news from Britain, and news from the city's various Scottish organizations, such as the Orkney and Shetland Society, Daughters of the Empire, and others.

Social events received prominent play, such as the time when the Waverly Social Club announced that their dance party was to be held at Elmore's Hall, 6319 S. Ashland Avenue, where one could "[d]ance to the strains of Scottie Hepburn and his melody men." An accompanying advertisement called them "Chicago's best Scotch Orchestra" (*British-American* 1932, 5).

The club's debating team raised some rather unusual issues, such as the February 30 meeting, which was determined to answer the question: "Is it cheaper to build a wall around Aberdeen than build an asylum in it? Aberdonians please note this date" (ibid).

The newspaper also published selections of original poetry, "Doings in the Dominion," Chicago Football News, British Football News, and a column about Chicago cricket. There were at least three cricket teams in the metropolitan area in 1932, including the Oak Park Cricket Club, the Lincoln Park Cricket Club, and Argyle Cricket Club.

Probably the most important Scottish periodical in the country, however, was the weekly New York–based *Scottish-American Journal.* Operated by Archibald M. Stewart from 1857 to 1919, it contained items of interest from Scottish communities around the country, including Chicago. (After 1886 it was known simply as the *Scottish-American.)* It ended its almost continuous run in 1925. During its heyday the journal had as many as 15,000 subscribers in the country. The present Barrington, Illinois–based magazine *Highlander* dates from 1962 (Berthoff 1953, n. 49). Its founder and a former president of the Illinois Saint Andrew Society, Angus J. Ray, died at the age of eighty in 1992.

Other Scottish newspapers around the country included another New York publication, the *Scotsman,* John Adamson's *Boston Scotsman,* and a literary monthly established in 1901 by the Gaelic scholar and Reverend Donald MacDougall called the *Caledonian.*

CHARLES H. KERR

Charles H. Kerr and Company is reportedly the oldest publisher of socialist books in the United States. Founded in 1886 during the height of the city's labor woes, the company was established by Charles Hope Kerr, the son of Alexander and Katharine Brown Kerr, abolitionists and Congregational liberals. Alexander Kerr was born in Scotland in 1828 and immigrated with his family to Illinois in 1838. Charles was born in 1860 in LaGrange, Georgia. Following the outbreak

Charles H. Kerr (above)

of the Civil War, the couple fled with their infant son to Illinois. Charles spent his childhood in Rockford and Beloit, Wisconsin (Ruff 1986, 19–20).

Kerr graduated from the University of Wisconsin at Madison in 1881 and then decided to pursue a career as a journalist and publisher in Chicago. At that time, Chicago had earned a reputation as the radical capital of the United States.

Kerr found work as a clerk and sales agent for James Colegrove, an independent publisher who specialized in the writings of the radical wing of the Western Unitarian Conference (20). By the time Kerr founded his own publishing company a few years later, he began to publish populist tracts, utopian novels, and similar works. One of Kerr's best-known and most enduring books, *The Pullman Strike,* by Reverend William H. Carwardine, examined the Pullman community and its problems from the viewpoint of a sympathetic Protestant minister.

In 1901 Kerr and his wife, the former May Walden, joined the Chicago branch of the Socialist Party of America (23). The couple lived in the small community of Glen Ellyn, west of Chicago, where they helped to establish a socialist workers' school, Ruskin College. Kerr also taught at the school (Maass 1986, 30). Ruskin College was founded in Ruskin, Tennessee, moved to Missouri, and then to Glen Ellyn. Among the many activities associated with the college were Ruskin Sanitarium, Ruskin University Press, Ruskin Industrial Guild, and Ruskin Cooperative Association.

Public support for the institution was

Charles H. Kerr house, Glen Ellyn (above)

always minimal at best. Eventually the building that housed the college was sold to Jacob Winnen. Winnen had plans to open it as a first-class summer hotel when it was struck by lightning and burned to the ground (Harmon 1928, 86). Ruskin College may be a remnant of the past, but the house that Charles H. Kerr once lived in still stands. Today the Kerr house is a local historical and cultural landmark as well as one of the oldest houses in the community.

The Kerr Company printed the first complete text of Karl Marx's *Das Capital* in English in 1909 as well as the early works of Jack London and Carl Sandburg, including Sandburg's poem "Billy Sunday." Other writers published by Kerr included Eugene Debs, "Big Bill" Haywood, Mother Jones, Mary Marcy, and Upton Sinclair as well as such international socialists and anarchists as Lenin, Trotsky, and James Connolly. In 1887 the company published a series by the then little-known lawyer Clarence Darrow. By the end of the decade Kerr had turned his small venture into the nation's largest publisher of reform material. The company became a cooperative in 1893 and within less than a decade began to specifically concentrate on labor and socialist works. At the turn of the century Kerr published the monthly *International Socialist Review,* then considered the most important socialist publication in the country. The company also published political and scientific books and journals, novels, and even socialist playing cards (20).

Charles MacArthur

Kerr divorced his wife in 1908 and in 1928 retired and moved to Los Angeles. Scottish-born John Keracher took over. Keracher, a resident of Detroit, reportedly sold his shoe store in order to buy out Kerr's stock (31). Kerr himself died in 1944.

Keracher was the leader of an obscure political group called the Proletarian Party. He wrote various short pamphlets, including *Crime: Its Causes and Consequences, Wages & the Working Day, Frederick Engels,* and his critique of the mass media, *The Head-Fixing Industry.* Keracher died in 1958.

Since the mid-1970s Charles H. Kerr & Company has been under the watchful eye of Franklin and Penelope Rosemont. Recent titles include *The Autobiography of Mother Jones;* a Sixties Series (including The Port Huron Statement, considered by many to be the single most influential document in the early history of the American New Left); *Rebel Voices: An IWW Anthology; Haymarket Scrapbook;* and *Lucy Parsons: American Revolutionary.*

JOURNALISM

During the early 1850s seven daily newspapers were published in Chicago (Pierce 1940, 416). It was a great town for an ambitious scribe with a flair for the dramatic. Journalism nourished many a latent novelist's heart while offering a living wage. Hence, the idiosyncrasies of creative minds were not only tolerated but also indulged. Many Scots played a vital force in journalism, both here and throughout the country. After all, one of the giants of twentieth-century journalism, James "Scotty" Reston, was a Scot. Born in Clydebank, Scotland, the legendary Pulitzer Prize–winning *New York Times* columnist died in December 1995 after a lifetime reporting the news. Chicago, too, had its fair share of Scottish American newshounds. In the days before the Great Fire of 1871, for example, James Chisholm, writing under the pseudonym of "John Barleycorn," was the drama critic for the *Chicago Inter-*

Ocean. (MacMillan 1919, 27) while George Sutherland worked for the *Western British American*.

Thomas C. MacMillan was editor of the *Inter-Ocean* from 1873 to 1895. Born in Stranraer, Scotland, in 1850, he came to the United States with his parents in 1857. He was educated in the Chicago public school system and attended the old University of Chicago. MacMillan also spent many years as a public servant. In December 1895 he was named clerk of the U.S. district court, Northern District of Illinois. He also served six years in the Illinois state legislature—in the House of Representatives from 1885 to 1889 and in the Senate from 1889 to 1891. He was a member of the committee that drafted the Chicago Sanitary District and was chairman of the State Senate Committee on the World's Columbian Exposition of 1893. In addition, he was a member of the Cook County Board of Education and director of the Chicago Public Library from 1882 to 1887. A member of the Illinois Saint Andrew Society, Macmillan was president of the Society from 1906 to 1908 (MacDougall 304–5).

During the controversy surrounding the Kansas-Nebraska Act when civil unrest threatened to bring the city to its knees, a young Scot named James Redpath was writing some of the most volatile and vivid prose to ever appear in the pages of the *Chicago Tribune*. The twenty-year-old Redpath reportedly even invented the phrase "border ruffians" to describe the violent activities of proslavery supporters (Wendt 1979, 65).

Another talented journalist was David Henderson, a Scot who emigrated to America in 1868. He was drama critic of the *Inter-Ocean,* the *Chicago Tribune,* and the *Herald,* and later managing editor of the *Daily News*. He later left journalism altogether to become a theater manager.

In later years Charles MacArthur—one-half of the Front Page Era partnership with Ben Hecht—was probably the best-known Scottish American journalist to work in the city.

MacArthur, brother of the equally flamboyant John D. MacArthur, began his journalism career as a reporter with the *Oak Leaves* in Oak Park. He paid his dues at the *Chicago Herald Examiner* before jumping to the *Chicago Tribune*. There his cynical gallows humor matched perfectly the flippant mood of Chicago journalism. With colleague Ben Hecht, he wrote the plays *The Front Page* and *The Twentieth Century*. He also co-wrote screenplays with Hecht, including *The Scoundrel, Barbary Coast, Gunga Din,* and *Wuthering Heights*. He was married to the first lady of American theater, Helen Hayes.

Robert R. McCormick, publisher of the *Chicago Tribune* and king of hyperbole, often claimed to have royal Scottish blood running through his veins. In more recent times, the versatile Paul Galloway, a long-time *Tribune* feature reporter who recently served a short stint as the *Tribune's* religion editor, continues in the grand Chicago journalism tradition. Always an astute observer of the local scene, Galloway is both tough and compassionate, combining the accuracy and clear prose of a reporter with the storytelling talent of a novelist. For many years, John Maclean, the son of writer Norman Maclean, was a financial reporter for the *Tribune*.

Trade journals were also published. The most important labor newspaper in town was the controversial *Workingman's Advocate,* published from 1864 to 1877 (Pierce 1940, 420; Berthoff 1953, 99, 217) and edited by the Berwick-born printer Andrew Carr Cameron.

Andrew and his brother Daniel were the sons of Daniel Cameron, a printer and devout friend of labor, who emigrated to Cook County in 1851 (Gottlieb 1978, 403n. 13). Andrew Cameron had significant influence with miners on both sides of the Atlantic.

The leader of the Scottish miners in Scotland, Alexander MacDonald, for example, made numerous trips to the United States, including a visit in 1867 and again in

1869 to Braidwood (Gottlieb 1978, 400). The Illinois towns of Braidwood and Streator were important centers of trade union activity with the immigrant miners, maintaining close ties with union leaders in both Scotland and England (399).

In 1869, following a mining disaster in Pennsylvania, MacDonald accompanied Cameron from Chicago to Braidwood to discuss with the miners what measures could be taken to avoid a similar tragedy in their mines (403).

POLITICS

Unlike the Irish, Italians, Scandinavians, Polish, African Americans, or other such ethnic groups across the country, Scottish Americans were never politically cohesive enough to form a voting bloc. For this reason, issues that were of concern to the Scottish community were usually neglected. Indeed, a large number of Scottish immigrants never bothered to even become American citizens, choosing instead to remain in a political limbo for the rest of their lives.

Contrast this situation with the Irish, who, for the most part, became citizens as soon as they were legally able and, once doing so, wasted no time in entering the rough-and-tumble world of Chicago politics. Mention Chicago politics and such quintessential Irish names as Edward Kelly, Johnny Powers, Martin Kennelly, Jane Byrne, Richard J. and Richard M. Daley almost instantly come to mind. With the possible exception of Governor Richard Ogilvie, or Senator Adlai Stevenson, very few Americans of Scottish descent rose to prominence within the local political arena.

The Irish wanted desperately to belong. Feeling oppressed and impotent in their native land, they welcomed the opportunity to become full participants in the democratic process. The Scots, on the other hand, especially Lowlanders, emigrated primarily for economic reasons and, hence, did not harbor the same sense of urgency or angry feelings. The passion to become fully Americanized simply was not as strong a motivating factor.

During the 1870s and 1880s, in particular, Irish Americans began to flex their political muscles. Although British Americans—that is, English, Scots, and Welsh as well as Canadians of Scottish, English, and Welsh heritage—matched the Irish in population, they lacked the unity and the voting power necessary to compete against the ambitious and numerous Irish. Political reality also played a role. While Great Britain may have been a political unit across the Atlantic, in the United States each group tended to adhere to their separate national identities. Hence, Scots joined Scottish societies, Welsh joined Welsh societies, and English joined English societies. Like their Scandinavian counterparts, there was no strong incentive to join pan-British organizations. An incident that occurred in Boston, however, helped galvanize all elements of the heretofore separated British American community across the country (with the possible exception of the Welsh) into a unifying force.

In 1887 British immigrants throughout the United States celebrated Queen Victoria's Golden Jubilee. The English and Scottish societies of Boston were granted permission from a local British-born alderman to use Faneuil Hall for a banquet. Almost immediately an Irish priest protested, charging that to hold such a meeting would be a desecration to his fellow compatriots, especially those who were oppressed under various English and later British regimes. Even so, the meeting went on as planned. On the night of the event, the 400 celebrants were met by a mob of some 15,000 angry Irish. Several hundred people were able to keep order inside the hall while the Irish heckled loudly throughout the speeches. Significantly, none of the invited members of the city, state, and federal officials attended (197).

Within a few weeks, members of the Jubilee banquet committee formed the British American Association and urged all British immigrants who were eligible to obtain their naturalization papers (198). Before the year ended, British American organizations were formed in New York, Pennsylvania, and Illinois. A few years later in Chicago, the weekly newspaper *British-American* was launched. As late as 1896, the Victoria Club of Chicago encouraged hundreds of Britons to become citizens. Since most Irish were Democrats, the British tended to vote Republican (201–2).

Several years earlier, on May 12, 1937, members of the British community in Chicago came together to celebrate the coronation of King George and Queen Elizabeth on Coronation-Empire Day. A commemorative banquet and dance was held under the auspices of the United British Societies of Illinois in the Grand Ballroom of the Stevens Hotel. The net proceeds went to the British Charities in Illinois. The societies included the United British Societies of Illinois, such as the British American League of Women, British and Colonial Veterans, British and Colonial Veterans (Women's Auxiliary), British Empire Association, British Old People's Home, and Daughters of the British Empire; strictly English groups as the Daughters of St. George and Sons of St. George; strictly Scottish groups as the Illinois Saint Andrew Society, Chicago Scottish Choral Society, Daughters of Scotia, Orkney and Shetland Society, and Scottish Old People's Home (Ladies Auxiliary); as well as Welsh (Chicago Welsh Male Choir, Chicago Welsh Woman's Club, Kymry Society) and Manx groups (Chicago Manx Society).

Part of this British American unity was due in no small measure to the fear of Catholicism. As the Catholic population of the country increased, more and more native-born Americans and foreign-born Protestants began to work together, including Scots and other members of the British community, to combat the so-called Catholic menace. Supporters of this mindset even formed a short-lived political party, the Know-Nothing Party, which looked upon the growing number of immigrants—read Catholics—as a threat to its vision of a "pure" Anglo-Saxon or northern Protestant European America. Hence, Americanism or nativism became irretrievably linked with Protestantism.

The underlying animosity toward Britain resurfaced again during the 1927 reelection campaign of Chicago Mayor William Hale Thompson. Proclaiming an "America First" platform, Thompson accused the city's school superintendent William McAndrews of being a "stool pigeon of King George V." To prove his patriotism, Thompson then threatened to "swat" the king on the "snoot." Fortunately, the hot-tempered mayor never got the opportunity.

In 1907 three Scottish American physicians named Alexander A. Whamond, Fred G. Whamond, and Joseph Mills founded the Robert Burns Hospital at 3807 W. Washington Boulevard. The hospital opened its doors on July 15 of that year and had a capacity of twenty-five beds.

SEVEN

A New Wave of Emigration and Another Fair

The end of World War I and the onslaught of the 1920s ushered in a decade of extraordinary growth and prosperity. Chicago grew up and upward. The rise of the automobile created the growth of the suburbs and increased mobility. The development of the lakefront, improvements in streets and parks, the building of new bridges, and a burgeoning commercial and industrial infrastructure all pointed to bigger and better things. Municipal Pier (later Navy Pier) was completed in 1916, the Field Museum of Natural History opened in 1919, and the Shedd Aquarium opened in 1929.

The 1920s brought a new wave of Scottish emigration, too. According to the 1920 census, 254,570 inhabitants of the United States were born in Scotland. Indeed, the greatest decade of Scottish emigration to the United States occurred during this period, consisting mostly of unemployed Lowlanders. What's more, an additional 300,000 emigrated to America during the ten-year period from 1920 to 1930 (Graham 1956, 182).However, by the 1930s and 1940s, the Great Depression and the outbreak of World War II virtually brought emigration from Britain to a standstill. During the postwar era, most of the newcomers were war brides (Berthoff 1953, 209). In fact, British brides accounted for the largest single group of female immigrants to the United States in the 1940s—some 70,000 women (Virden 1996, 1).

In October 1929 the glamorous world of the 1920s came crashing down with the collapse of Wall Street. Almost overnight, everything changed. It was a whole new world. Squatters built makeshift houses of cardboard and scrap lumber—anything they could find—and lived in "Hoovervilles" on vacant lands and near railroad yards scattered throughout the city. Mayer and Wade (1969, 358) called them "villages of the unemployed."

THE SCOTTISH COMMUNITY TAKES STOCK

A changing of the guard took place too within the Scottish community. On April 1, 1922, John Williamson, the great Scot who did so much for the residents of the Scottish Home during the ordeal of the tragic fire, died. For thirty-five years he had been a leader among the Scots of Chicago, serving on the Board of Governors for more than fifteen years. The governors, in their tribute to him, said, "His devotion to the interests of the Home, his kindness to and consideration for the old people in it, and their loving regard for him were outstanding features of his exemplary and successful life."

Williamson imbued his family of five children with his love for all things Scottish. His oldest son was a member of the choir that sang at the dedication of the Robert Burns Monument. His grandchild unveiled the cornerstone at the dedication of the Scottish Home in 1910. For twenty-five years, the family prepared and served Thanksgiving dinner to the residents, a practice that continued long after his death. The iron fence around the home was a gift from the family in honor of their father. His son, John A. Williamson, following in his father's path, was president of the Saint Andrew Society in 1931.

Now, individuals with names like Glass, Black, Lister, Alexander, and Cunningham enthusiastically took on the responsibility of overseeing the operation of the Scottish Home. It was a busy and active decade interrupted by the shock of the Great Depression. Meanwhile, George Buik, a native of Dundee, organized a Robert Burns Society in Chicago, and a number of the clans remained active. Professor DeWar taught Highland dancing. The Ladies of Clan McDuff were formed, and new leaders for the Society emerged.

The Scottish Home always maintained a small infirmary of six beds. It served more as an area to quarantine those who became ill, for there were no nurses at the home at that time. If a resident became seriously ill, he or she was sent to the hospital. The Presbyterian Hospital often extended free care to the residents, as did the Robert Burns Hospital on Washington Boulevard. The physicians also served without remuneration. Dr. R. D. McArthur helped the Scottish community for more than fifty years without pay, and Dr. Albert Hall and Dr. Arthur MacNeal volunteered their services to the Scottish Home for more than twenty-five years. In 1926 Dr. Hall and Dr. MacNeal founded MacNeal Hospital in Berwyn. After the death of John Williamson's wife in 1924, the family set up a renewable fund to hire the home's first professional nursing personnel.

SURVIVING THE DEPRESSION

The years of the Great Depression were times of significant stress and sacrifice. This was especially true of the Society and the operation of the Scottish Home. It was a constant struggle to pay the bills and care for the residents without endangering the small, but growing, endowment fund. The home was made as self-sufficient as possible. The residents maintained a garden and tended chickens and pigs. Sheep grazed inside the iron fence. Residents were required to help with the chores as they were able. Cora J. Cummings served as administrator for twenty-five years, living on the premises and working as a staff member. Her salary was reduced from $100 to $50 a month at the height of the depression, and yet she continued to serve unselfishly.

William Cameron, a native of Scotland, was owner and president of the Cameron Can Company. Cameron was president of the Society in 1934 and died on Christmas Day at his home in River Forest that same year. Unlike Williamson, Cameron had failed to place the home in his will. Even so, his family responded with a memorial to honor him when his son, Allan M. Cameron, presented the Board of Governors with a check for $10,000. It was the miracle so desperately needed, enabling the Scottish Home to survive the years of the Great Depression.

The residents of the home received a well-deserved lift in 1932 when Queen Mary—grandmother of the present Queen Elizabeth—sent a cordial letter to the home. Cora Cummings apparently had sent photographs of the home and a clipping from a Scottish newspaper telling about the facility to the queen. The monarch responded, through Lady Cynthia Colville, in a letter dated January 29, 1932:

> *The Queen is always interested to hear what is being done abroad for British people and not least for those from the country of Holyrood and Balmoral, and this Old People's Home at Riverside looks very charming in the photographs—a home in every sense of the word.*
>
> *The Queen very much appreciates Mrs. Cummings' kind thought in acquainting Her Majesty with this interesting and attractive piece of work that is carried on by the Illinois St. Andrew Society, and wishes every success to its continuance. It has given the Queen very real pleasure to learn something of the purpose and scope of an organization of this kind. (British-American 1932, 6)*

The anniversary dinners continued to grow and increase in attendance each year. In 1933 the dinner was scheduled to be held at the Stevens Hotel. There was great concern, however, about the attendance because of the severe financial crisis. Despite the worry, some 1,000 people—a record figure—paid $5 each to enjoy the evening. In 1936 CBS broadcast the dinner from coast to coast, reportedly the first national broadcast of such an event. Several years later, in 1940, the largest attendance of any anniversary dinner took place with 1,470 guests.

In the same year the Illinois Saint Andrew Society raised $779 for the British War Relief Society. The membership was reported at 333, and the Endowment Fund had nearly reached the $300,000 mark. The Streeter Estate then contributed $200,000 to the Scottish Home. But on December 7, 1941, Japan bombed Pearl Harbor, and everything changed. The United States was once again at war. The world, and the Scottish community of Chicago, would never be the same.

A CENTURY OF PROGRESS

In Washington, D.C., President Franklin Delano Roosevelt had just promised a New Deal for everyone. In Europe few people understood the menace beginning to emerge in Germany as the Nazi Party solidified its first year in power. While in Chicago, the opening of the city's second world's fair, "A Century of Progress," captured the imagination of the general public.

The depression had taken a heavy toll on the people of Chicago. By 1930 the city was officially bankrupt. There was no money to pay civil servants—no funds in the city's tills for police officers, firefighters, or school teachers (Dedmon 1983, 335). Despite these considerable hurdles, Chicago became even more determined to launch "A Century of Progress" in celebration of the 100th anniversary of the incorporation of the city as a village.

A corporation was established for this purpose. The organizers boasted that the fair would be built without any governmental subsidies or taxes. On the contrary, Chicago's business community would assume full responsibility. The site of the fair was to be located on more than 400 acres of artificially created landfill on the city's lakefront.

This new fair, which opened on April 29, 1933, shared several similarities with the earlier World's Columbian Exposition of 1893. The secretary of "A Century of Progress" was Daniel H. Burnham, Jr., son of the famed architect and mastermind of the 1893 exposition. Unlike the neoclassical architecture that dominated the earlier fair, though, "A Century of Progress" celebrated modern architecture, much it of with geometric angles, soaring towers, and brightly colored buildings. It was, quite simply, a paean to the wonders of science.

Other similarities to the World's Columbian Exposition included the inclusion of Midwaylike villages, such as the partial reconstruction of a walled city in China and a teahouse from Japan. Also featured were a diamond mine and a mechanical robot who lectured on proper nutrition (336–37). The "Streets of Paris" replaced the exposition's "Streets of Cairo." The sensation of the fair was an unemployed silent film actress named Sally Rand, who flaunted convention and decorum by riding nude upon a white horse like a latter-day Lady Godiva.

By the end of the summer of 1933 more than 22 million people had attended the fair. In fact the fair was so successful that the organizers decided to continue its run into the following year. Thus, another 16 million attended the 1934 fair (339). Daily attendance averaged more than 100,000 people. By October 1934 almost 40 million people had attended the city's second world's fair (Mayer and Wade 1969, 364).

SCOTLAND DAY AT THE FAIR

Ethnic days were popular features of "A Century of Progress." In September 1933 the Scottish people of Chicago had their own special day. Contemporary newspaper accounts reported that 40,000 Scots "mingled with the other visitors to make the Fairgrounds a surging sea of color." Other reports cited full attendance figures during Scotland Day at an estimated 180,000.

The Stock Yard Kilty Band opened the Scotland Day ceremonies while the Canadian Essex Scottish Regiment, which consisted of 50 officers, 250 men, a pipe band, and a brass band, marched and played in observation of Canadian Week. Encamping in Soldier Field, the bands gave concerts at the Hall of Science Court that afternoon. Principal speakers of the day were Bishop George Craig Stewart, Gilbert Alexander, president of the Illinois Saint Andrew Society, and Alexander Mackenzie, president of the United Scottish Societies of Illinois.

Various Scottish events took place in the weeks and months leading up to the Scotland Day extravaganza. On June 19, 1933, for example, members of the Chicago branch of the Order of Scottish Clans sent delegates and friends to the Royal Clan Convention held at the Stevens Hotel. The Chicago Highlanders Pipe Band and the Stockyards Post Highland Band performed as did the Charleston dancers and pupils of dancing teachers Nettie MacPherson, George Hendry, and John Dewar. There were also Scottish songs by Mary Dingwall and May Bailey Isles, tunes by Duncan and John MacNeill, and comic songs by Sam Galbraith. Galbraith was known for his wicked impersonations of the Scots comic Sir Harry Lauder. In September the Daughters of Scotia held their annual convention, also at the Stevens Hotel.

QUEEN FOR A DAY

Scotland Day required the crowning of a queen. On September 29 Margaret Baikie, a sixteen-year-old Chicago girl of Orcadian ancestry, was chosen Queen for a Day. Baikie was the granddaughter of Maggie Petrie of Stromness, Orkney. Dancing since the age of five, Baikie learned to play the pipes when she was just twelve. Thus she was not only an accomplished piper but also owned literally hundreds of dancing medals and trophies.

In addition to representing Scotland at the fair, Baikie also worked at the Merrie Old England village (Scotland didn't have its own exhibit). During the second year of the fair, she participated in the Scottish portions of the "Pageant of the Celt," a pan-Celtic entertainment extravaganza staged in 1934.

Margaret Baikie was active in the Scottish community for many decades as both a piper and a dancer. She was the official piper of the Orkney and Shetland Society. As early as July 4, 1929, she won first prize in competitive dancing at a Scots picnic. This picnic is worthy since it was reportedly the occasion of the first joint picnic of all the Chicago clans and was called by one reporter, in typical hyperbole, "an epoch-making day in the history of the Chicago Clans and their asso-

SCOTLAND DAY

Saturday, September 30, 1933
Hall of Science Court — 2 to 6 p.m.

Part One

1. "Star Spangled Banner" — Choir and Audience
2. Introduction of Chairman — William Lister, L.L.B.
3. Address of Welcome — Robert Black, General Chairman
4. Introduction of Colonel Walter Scott, Honorary Chairman, Past Royal Chief, Order of Scottish Clans of America; Gilbert Alexander, President Illinois St. Andrew Society; Alexander McKenzie, President United Scottish Societies
5. Selections by Stockyards Post 333 Kilty Band — Robert Sim, Pipe Major
6. Dance — Highland Fling — Massed Dancers
7. Song — "The Border Ballad" — The Chicago Scottish Choir; Captain George Calder, Conductor
8. Introduction of Speaker by Reverend Allison A. McCracken
9. Address Right Reverend George Craig Stewart
10. Scottish Comedy — "Just for Fun" — Jamie Shepherd
11. Instrumental Selections by Michigan City Boys' Kilty Band — E. M. McLundie, conductor
12. Songs — "Hail Caledonia" "MacGregor's Gathering" — Cameron McLean
13. Dance: a. Shean Truibhais — Jessie Charleston b. Sword Dance — Ruby Lennox, Marion Gourlay, Julia Steven, James Jamieson; Pipers — Pipe Majors Norman Dewar and John MacPhail

Ten Minute Intermission

Part Two

14. Selections by Essex Scottish Highlanders Military Band, Windsor, Ontario, Canada
15. "Afton Water" — Chicago Scottish Choir
16. Selections — Essex Scottish Highlanders Pipe Band
17. Songs — a. "Where Hath Scotland Found Her Fame?" — Dorothy Marwick; b. "Lochnagar"
18. Highland Fling — Adeline McKenna, Robert Sim, Pipe Major
19. Song — "A Man's a Man For A' That" — Chicago Scottish Choir
20. Duet: a. "The Crookit Bawbee" — Dorothy Marwick and Cameron McLean; b. "Come Under My Plaidie"
21. Selections — Curtiss Kilties Band, John MacPhail, Pipe Major
22. Dance — Scottish Reels
23. a. Psalm 24 (Tune St. George's Edinburgh) — Chicago Scottish Choir; b. "Scots Wha Hae"
24. "Auld Lang Syne" — Choir and Audience; Accompanists: Gene Melvin, Maybelle Howe Mable, Lyman E. Goss
26. Retreat — Essex Scottish Highlanders Band

Margaret Baikie, "Queen for a Day" at the 1933 Century of Progress

ciated lodges of the Daughters of Scotia, also the Thistle Football Club." The picnic was notable too for its the rather unusual award categories. Recognition was given, for example, to the largest Scottish family on the grounds, the oldest Scotswoman, and the oldest Scotsman.

Baikie's husband, Angus Macdonald, was a member of the Stock Yard Kilty Band. Macdonald, a native of Stornoway on the island of Lewis, had labored on his father's sheep ranch before emigrating to America. When Margaret was a mere lass of ten, her father, William, who was president of the Caledonian Society of Chicago, invited Angus to the house to teach his precocious daughter to play the pipes. Angus drifted out of Margaret's life until a number of years later, when a friend invited him to attend her surprise seventeenth birthday party. From that point forward, they were smitten with each other.

The couple got married at Drexel Park Presbyterian Church at Sixty-fourth Street and Marshfield Avenue on the South Side. Macdonald worked at the Carnegie-Illinois Steel Company at the time while Baikie took dictation at Darling and Company, a packing firm in the Stock Yards district. Margaret Baikie, who is now in her nineties, is a life member of the Illinois Saint Andrew Society.

SCOTTISH CLUBS AND ORGANIZATIONS

Like immigrants everywhere, Scots established social and cultural clubs and organizations from Burns clubs to Gaelic clubs, thistle clubs to county clubs, nurturing their own culture and continuing their own customs. "In Boston, New York, Detroit, and Chicago," writes Rowland Berthoff (1953, 7), "people from more than twenty towns and districts from Dumfries to Lerwick had their special societies." The Order of Scottish Clans, a national fraternal order, had been founded in St. Louis in 1878 and its female counterpart, the Daughters of Scotia, in 1895 (7, 181). These clans, or local lodges, held annual games and, says Berthoff, "commemorated epic battles like Largs and Bannockburn."

Some overlapping among the various organizations and clubs within the Scottish community in Chicago is apparent. Saint Andrew Society members Walter S. Bogle and John F. Holmes, for example, were also closely involved with the Scottish Musical Club (SMC). In 1865 the president of SMC was Robert Hervey, who, at various times, had also been president of the Illinois Saint Andrew Society. Another Saint Andrew member, John McGlashan, was president of the SMC a few years later in 1869.

Today, according to Jim Hewitson and Michael Brander (1993, 274; 1996), there are more than 200 clan societies and family associations in the United States, as well as 100 Scottish societies and 125 pipe bands, in addition to cultural organizations, Burns clubs, country dance groups, Highland games, and import and craft shops.

A description of some of the more historically significant Scottish social clubs in Chicago follows.

CHICAGO CALEDONIAN CLUB

The Chicago Caledonian Club was instituted on December 19, 1865, and incorporated on February 21, 1867. The objects of the club were (1) "the preservation of the Ancient Literature and Costumes, and the encouragement and practice of the ancient Games of Scotland"; (2) "the establishment of a Library and Gymnasium, and employment of Lecturers before the Association"; and (3) "charity, which, in its amount, character, and mode of distribution, shall be dependent on the will of the majority of its members" *(Constitution and By-Laws of the Chicago Caledonian Club* 1872).

The Caledonian Club membership seemed to appeal more to working-class Scots, such as David Johnston. Johnston came to Chicago from Wisconsin in 1860. Within a few years he joined the Illinois Saint Andrew Society. But he came to consider the Society apparently too elite for his own tastes and hence supported a club that catered more to the wages of the working man. "My business at that time," he wrote, "carried me among the machine shops, in which many Scotchman were employed, who nearly to a man were ready to argue against the propriety of becoming members thereof, on the ground chiefly of exclusiveness." He concluded, "Five dollars for the annual dinner was too steep for a workingman."

Johnston became chief of the Caledonian Club in 1873 and began unsuccessfully to try to establish a "healthful retreat" to be called Chicago Caledonian Park, but the idea apparently never got off the ground since the Chicago, Milwaukee, and St. Paul Railway—which apparently owned the property—never really took the plan seriously, or, as Johnston says, they rendered the idea "nugatory" (Johnston 1885, 204).

During the club's early years it apparently met with "the most unexampled success." Like most social clubs of a national nature, the Chicago Caledonian Club encouraged its members to behave with dignity and to honor both the land left behind and one's adopted country "and thus tend to render us good citizens of the land of our adoption, by upholding in our characters the dignity of the dear native land that we left." (*Constitution and By-Laws of the Chicago Caledonian Club* 1872).

By early 1868 the members were able to procure "a handsome suit of rooms" at 101 Washington Street, which apparently included a reading room and library, "where our countrymen can get all current news from Scotland, Canada, and the United States, and be enabled to store their minds with the best literature of Europe and America." Indeed, Bessie Louise Pierce (1949, 27) says the Caledonian Club had a library of several hundred volumes in 1869 "providing reading materials in a day when there was no public library."

Regular meetings were held the first Tuesday of every month; an annual meeting for the election of officers was held on the first Tuesday in October. In order to perpetuate the romantic image of Scotland, the officers went by titles such as "Chief" for president, "First Chieftain" for vice president, "Second Chieftain" for treasurer, "Third Chieftain" for financial and recording secretary, and "Fourth Chieftain" for corresponding secretary.

"None but Scotsmen, the sons of Scotsmen, or the sons of members" were eligible to become members. (Honorary members were allowed if elected by two-thirds of the members present.) Activities included a semiannual gathering during the summer and winter "to celebrate and compete in the Scottish Games, as practised in Scotland." The games were to be public and held in the open air.

Unfortunately the Great Fire of 1871 destroyed the cub's possessions and property and left many members "for a time homeless and desolute." Yet, despite the tragedy, the club continued to live up to its high standards. The members wasted no time, for example, in starting a new library and established temporary meeting quarters at the Scotch Presbyterian Church. They became even more determined to "keep fresh and green the memories of 'auld lang synge' " (*Constitution and By-Laws of the Chicago Caledonian Club* 1872).

CALEDONIAN SOCIETY OF CHICAGO

Another important Scottish organization was the Caledonian Society of Chicago. Founded on June 8, 1884, its objects were

1. the cultivation of friendship and sociability among Scots, and their children, resident in this locality;

2. the encouragement of the Scottish national costume;

3. the perpetuation of Scottish music, history, and poetry.

The club achieved these goals through such annual celebrations as Burns's anniversary supper, the Caledonian games, and Halloween activities. In addition monthly socials, usually of a literary nature, were presented during the winter months. Business meetings were held on the second Thursday of the month at their 45 E. Randolph Street location.

The Caledonian Society of Chicago held its annual picnic and games at such places as Riverview Park at Belmont and Western Avenues. Race, football matches, and competition and ballroom dancing were common activities.

In April 1896 the members proposed that a union of Scottish societies in Chicago take place or, at the very least, that the various societies sponsor national celebrations, events, picnics, and so on jointly. Both the Orkney and Shetland Society and the Caithness Association tentatively approved the idea in principle. Other organizations, however, such as the Scottish Assembly, did not express much enthusiasm for the proposal. At least one editorial writer, though, thought the idea a good one: "There is no city in the country in a better position than Chicago to have a really good Scottish organization of some kind" (*Scottish-American* 1896).

In February 1934 the Caledonian Society of Chicago celebrated its fiftieth anniversary with a concert and dance at the Auditorium Hotel.

ORKNEY AND SHETLAND SOCIETY

The Orkney and Shetland Society had its origins in John Harper's tailor shop in 1885 when a handful of members met at 199 S. Clark Street. They published a monthly journal, the *Orkney & Shetland American,* edited by Magnus Flaws, which was "devoted to the social and commercial interests of Orcadians and Shetlanders abroad." In addition to literary and social events, they also sponsored occasional festivals, such as a local version of the Up-Helly-Aa Viking fire festival, which is still held each January in the harbor town of Lerwick, Shetland. The *Western British American* (1914) refers to a reception and dance sponsored by the association. John Williamson, one-time president of the Illinois Saint Andrew Society, played a crucial role in the proceedings:

The feature of the evening was the reception of the Shetland "Guizers." J. D. Williamson as chief "guizer" at the head of his squad of "monks," led the "guizers'" grand march which

SCOTTISH ORGANIZATIONS IN 1934

The United Scottish Societies of Illinois
Caledonian Society
Clan Campbell
Lady Campbell Lodge
Clan MacDonald
Lady MacDonald Lodge
C. G. Mitchell Lodge
Clan MacDuff
Lady MacDuff Lodge
Lady Rob Roy Lodge
Clan Scott
Lady E. Scott Lodge
Englewood Scottish Club
Evanston and North Shore Scottish Society
The Highland Society
Illinois Saint Andrew Society
John O'Groats Caithness Society
Orkney and Shetland Society

was followed by an excellent exhibition of the Shetland Reel by a squad of "guizers" in appropriate suits.

The president of the Saint Andrew Society discussed the original Up-Helly-Aa festival in Lerwick as well as its Norse origins. The Lerwick festival is always held on the last Tuesday in January. After a day of feasting and a torchlight procession through the streets of the town, the celebration ends with the ritualized burning of a Viking longship on the grounds of a large playing field. The first Up-Helly-Aa fire festival took place in 1881 (Irvine 1982, 12–15). Guizing, or masquerading, is a very old Shetland custom and refers to "the disguising, the visiting of friends' houses, the play-acting, the eventual unmasking to reveal true identities" (62).

Over the years the group has held its anniversary meetings in different locales. The fiftieth anniversary banquet, for example, took place in the Crystal Room of the Great Northern Hotel, at Dearborn and Jackson on January 19, 1935; its sixty-first banquet on March 9, 1946, at the Graemere Hotel, 113 N. Homan Avenue; and its eightieth anniversary on September 18, 1965, at the Austin YMCA. Margaret Baikie, that fine daughter of Orkney, played the pipes at the latter celebration.

ELGIN SCOTTISH SOCIETY

In January 1904 a group of friends met in the home of Dr. Anne W. Martin on Chicago Street in Elgin to celebrate Robert Burns's birthday. From this small gathering came the idea to form the Elgin Scottish Society. Within three months a constitution and bylaws had been drawn up and the purpose of the society determined, which included "the mutual well-being, engagement and entertainment of its members by social gatherings at the houses of its members or other public places as deemed expedient by the Society and to study and be familiar with Scottish history." Over the years the society has participated in parades, Highland games, ethnic fairs, picnics, potluck dinners, Scottish country dances, and parties.

SCOTTISH CULTURAL SOCIETY

In 1977 a dozen Scottish enthusiasts formed a social club devoted to the music, arts, literature, and crafts of Scotland. Past meetings have tackled such topics as the poetry of Robert Burns, the writings of Sir Walter Scott, genealogy, Scottish movies, Scottish history, country dance lessons, the art of proper Highland dress, solo bagpipe concerts, and other activities. For a number of years the society held an annual Tartan Ball and the indoor Scottish Fair. They also publish *The Celtic Knot* newsletter.

OTHER SPECIAL EVENTS

Social functions were always popular within the Scottish community. During the first few decades of the twentieth century Mrs. James Waldie presided over the annual "Scotch Soiree" at Englewood Presbyterian Church at Yale Avenue and Sixty-fourth Street. She had started these annual gatherings "for loyal Scotch" in 1904.

Traditionally, the biggest holiday of the Scottish social year is Hogmanay, the Scottish New Year's Eve. In 1929 the Englewood Scottish Club presented its "Annual Hogmanay Concert and Dance" at Prospect Hall, Sixty-fourth Street and Ashland Avenue. The festivities included bagpipe selections by Murdo Mathieson, Jessie E. Charleston's juvenile pipe band, and Scottish dances.

Another regular event was the annual Burns concert sponsored by Clan Scott and

Magnus Flaws of the Orkney and Shetland Society (above)

Lady Edith Scott. In the 1940s, Clan Scott met in Anderson's Hall at Sixty-ninth Street and Halsted Avenue on the first and third Mondays of the month. Clan Scott was founded in 1924 and in August of the same year became affiliated with the United Scottish Societies. In 1944 the clan published a souvenir booklet celebrating its twentieth anniversary. Lady Edith Scott met in the same hall on the second and fourth Mondays of each month.

Both Clan Scott and Lady Edith Scott members formed a choir. Their first concert was held in April 1928. But they did more than just sponsor concerts. Philanthropic deeds were also part of their mission. In January 1930 they sent donations to the Scottish Naval and Military Veterans Home in Edinburgh. During World War II they participated with other Chicago clans in the Tartan Ball, which resulted in $6,000 being sent to Glasgow for the British war relief effort. In March 1935 the clan won the basketball championship of the Chicago Clans, under manager Bill Angus.

Other Scottish organizations over the years have included the Scotch Thistle Club, the Highland Association, and the Heather Club (Pierce 1957, 32n. 37).

BURNS CLUBS

No literary figure in Scottish history is as beloved as Robert Burns, the Ayrshire lad who took Edinburgh and the rest of the world by storm with his simple yet immensely profound and deeply human poems and love songs. Burns societies have existed wherever Scots have congregated from New York to Moscow. The first Burns club is said to have started in New York in 1847 (Hewitson 1993, 127). Chicago's Burns Society was incorporated in the summer of 1950 as a nonprofit corporation "to celebrate the natal day of 'Auld Scotia's Bard'—to commemorate and revere his memory by the spoken word and song." The following year the Burns Concert and Tartan Ball was held at the Stevens Hotel, January 18, 1951.

But there had been Burns celebrations in Chicago much earlier. On January 24, 1936, for example, the Burns Anniversary Celebration Concert and Dance was held under the auspices of the Past Chiefs and Chiefs Association, O.S.C. and the Chicago Scottish Choral Society at the Masonic Temple at 32 W. Randolph Street.

Traditionally, Burns suppers are held on the Saturday closest to the bard's January 25 birthday.

Today several organizations come together once a year to celebrate the spirit of the bard. The Elgin Scottish Society has been celebrating Burns's birthday for more than ninety years. For the past twenty years or so their annual Burns Supper has been held at the St. Andrews Country Club in West Chicago. There are also Burns clubs in South Holland, Rockford, and Barrington. The Robbie Burns Irregulars have been recreating the old country atmosphere of the traditional Burns suppers since 1986.

Scottish social and literary clubs, benevolent associations, tartan balls, and concerts all helped to encourage a spirit of camaraderie among Scots and Scottish Americans, instilling a feeling of national pride in both one's country and one's heritage. But probably no Scottish activity stirred the blood as much as the sound of the bagpipes playing in the open air. For these, the Scots turned to their most popular pastime of all—the Highland games.

Program from the annual Scotch Soiree at Englewood Presbyterian Church (above)

Caledonian Society
OF CHICAGO.

Fourth of July Celebration.

FIFTH .. AND . ANNUAL

GAMES PICNIC

WEDNESDAY, JULY 4TH, 1888,

ON THE GROUNDS OF THE

Chicago . Amateur . Athletic . Association,

12th and 13th Sts., Lincoln and Robey Sts

CHICAGO.

Tickets, = Fifty Cents.

EIGHT

Fun and Games

The Illinois Saint Andrew Society has been sponsoring the modern version of the Highland games since 1986. For several years prior to 1987, the games were held in Grant Park. Indeed the 1984 games, sponsored by PipeFest U.S.A., attracted as many as 35,000 people to the park, according to some accounts (Viallet 1985). When it became apparent that the nonprofit organization running the games would not hold them in 1987, it appeared that the event would die. Donald A. Gillies, president of the Society at the time, made a decision, which the Board of Governors later ratified, that the games were too important not to continue. Gillies prevailed on Edward C. Rorison to organize the games. Because decisions had to be made quickly, the games were moved to the grounds of the Scottish Home in North Riverside. Using the surrounding forest preserves to good advantage, they were held there for two consecutive years.

As the attendance continued to grow, it became necessary to move the games to a larger location. Lacking a permanent facility, the games have been held in Glendale Heights, Downers Grove, Oak Brook, and Grant Park. The long-range plan of some Society members is to obtain property in the greater Chicago area and give the Highland games a permanent home. All proceeds of the games benefit and support the Scottish Home.

To understand the significance of the games on the Scottish mentality, it is important to understand the role that the games have played in the fabric of Scottish American life.

THIS SPORTING LIFE

THE HIGHLAND GAMES

The Highland games in Chicago—indeed America—have had a rich history. Although Scottish societies usually included Burns clubs, Caledonian clubs, Saint Andrew's societies, and similar organizations, the activities that probably garnered the most public attention were—and continue to be—the Highland games. The games, usually called Caledonian games in the nineteenth century, consisted of various athletic contests as well as Scottish dancing and music. Some historians believe that the Highland games inspired modern track and field American athletics (Redmond 1971, 20). Whatever their ultimate influence, the games were evidence not only of the growth of elite and mid-

Caledonian Society games program (left)

CATEGORIES OF THE MODERN GAMES

Modern games have much in common with their predecessors. Such Scottish events as the caber toss, sheaf toss, hammer throw, and stone put have been accompanied by the javelin throw and wrestling. Trophies and medals continue to be awarded.

In addition to piping competitions, the games also feature mini-golf, lectures and storytelling, vendors and exhibitors, food and beverages, and musical entertainment.

Ian Baker (above, left), a young Scot at the games. Competition is not taken lightly at the games. (right)

dle-class voluntary sports associations but also of ethnic athletic clubs in nineteenth-century America.

The first reference to the Highland games in the United States refers to a gathering that took place in 1836 by the Highland Society of New York when it held its first "Sportive Meeting" in the Elysian Fields, Hoboken, New Jersey (Donaldson 1986, 12–13). However, most historians believe that the first traditional games in the United States were started by Boston Scots in 1853 (Redmond 1971, 15). A few years later, the New York Caledonian Club, one of the most successful of the country's Scottish clubs, held its first games in 1857 (40). It is generally agreed that the Caledonian games enjoyed their heyday in the post–Civil War era with as many as more than 100 cities and towns in America holding their own games and at times attracting as many as 20,000 people (38).

The awarding of prize money at the games was common. In fact, the games were such an important part of the Scottish community in America that veterans of the Highland games in Scotland eagerly competed at stateside events (Berthoff 1953, 151). Games committees encouraged professional athletes to participate since known commodities usually attracted bigger crowds. The greatest of the Scottish athletes were Donald Dinnie and James Fleming. Dinnie was in a class by himself. During his nearly sixty-year career, Dinnie won more than 11,000 sporting contests (Donaldson 1986, 15).

The games were staged in major cities throughout the country. According to Gerald Redmond, Highland games were taking place in Chicago as early as 1869 as well as in San Francisco, Cincinnati, Detroit, Milwaukee, and Cleveland (Redmond 1971, 43). Activities included such contests as tossing the caber, putting the stone, and tug of war. Americans were always made to feel welcome at the games and indeed proved to be loyal supporters for many years.

The games were so numerous that an organization to regulate them was established in the post–Civil War era. In 1866 representatives from Scottish clubs in both the United States and Canada met at the New York Caledonian Club to discuss the matter at length. Consequently, on July 1, 1867, the first International Highland Games was held in New York City (Donaldson 1986, 37). Three years later a convention was held to discuss the standardization of rules. From this convention emerged the North American United Caledonian Association (NAUCA), governing body for the games in both the United States and Canada.

The Caledonian Society of Chicago sponsored its own games in the 1880s. The July 4, 1888, games were held on the grounds of the Chicago Amateur Athletic Association at Twelfth and Thirteenth Streets and Lincoln and Robey (Damen) Streets. Judges of the various events included a Dr. L. D. McMichael from Buffalo, New York; John Ramsay, chief of Clan McDuff; and Mayor William Steen, the Scottish-born mayor of south suburban Braidwood, Illinois.

The program consisted of twenty-nine events from the peculiarly Scottish putting the heavy shot, throwing the heavy hammer, and tossing the caber to the Americanized track and field activities, such as running the high jump and tug of war. There were also bicycle team races and a potato race as well as a Highland fling dance and a broadsword dance. And just for fun anyone could participate in the Best Dressed Highlander category.

In the second half of the nineteenth century, American sports began to take on national characteristics. During this time the Highland games entered a gradual period of decline. Various reasons have been cited, including the rise in the popularity of track and field, the availability of other sporting activities, and the appeal of amateur sport. Homegrown sports like baseball, American football, and basketball eventually were preferred over such "foreign" substitutes as cricket and rugby. The games fell prey to this nationalistic backlash. Instead of building on their initial popularity, the games would eventually become little more than the ethnic tradition of a minority immigrant group.

The games entered a transitional phase. Ironically, as interest waned sponsors began to stage more elaborate and more expensive events. The attempt to make the games a larger-than-life extravaganza were woefully inadequate. Faced with dwindling receipts, the smaller clubs collapsed. Even the New York Caledonian Club, one of the country's largest and wealthiest clubs, could not continue to sponsor the games during the Great Depression (41). Some clubs felt that the only way to survive was to return to their Scottish roots and to exclude outsiders from competition altogether.

The 1920s and 1930s saw a gradual rekindling of interest in the games but it wasn't until the founding of the Grandfather Mountain Games in North Carolina in 1956 that the modern-day revival can said to have begun. In the 1960s more and more Scots felt the urge to start their own clan gathering while the 1970s and 1980s saw a virtual explosion. In the Chicago area communities such as Midlothian and Elgin have sponsored their own version of the games. Today the games show no sign of abating.

But there was more to Scottish athletic events than just the Highland games. Curling was a popular winter sport, for example. Still the sporting activities that garnered the most loyalty were soccer and golf.

SOCCER

Rugby and British-style football, or soccer, teams first played in the United States in the 1870s. Soccer was especially popular among the immigrant working class in the nation's industrial cities. Communities with large Scottish populations, such as Braidwood, Illinois, had their own soccer teams, for example. Chicago itself had teams with such Scottish-sounding names as the Chicago Thistle and the Chicago Colhours. Throughout the country, other cities—including Pittsburgh, St. Louis, Denver, San Francisco, Seattle, Tacoma, New York, and Philadelphia—also had teams with Scottish connections (Hewitson 1993, 219–20). So popular was the sport that an American Football Association was formed, and an annual championship game established (Berthoff 1953, 150).

Apparently the Americans of 1890 did not fully appreciate the complexity of the game, however, for the *Scottish-American* (1890) contained a report anticipating the arrival of a Scottish football team to the United States, proclaiming: "They will give an exhibition which will demonstrate the science and beauty of the game, and not the rough and tumble game played by athletes here." Unfortunately, the team was unable to complete its journey.

In 1890s Chicago there were numerous Scottish football teams or, at least, teams with a significant number of Scottish players on the roster. The *Scottish-American* (1894, 1891) refers to Primrose, Thistle, and Gaelic football clubs as well as the existence of a Scottish Athletic Club that included both football and cricket teams. In 1905 the Chicago League of Association Football—soccer—was formed with eleven team members (*Scottish-American* 1905). Four years later, in 1909, there were about ten soccer clubs operating in the Chicago area, many with Scottish connections, such as the Campbell Rovers, the Scottish Americans, and the Coal City Football Club. Around this time Peter J. Peel and a number of others got together and established the Peel Cup Commission and the Peel Challenge Cup Competition. Chicago's premier soccer trophy was known locally as the "Peel Cup."

Sports teams helped to promote a sense of community. A growing middle-class interest in sports was a result of the improved economic conditions of the cities, a rising urban population, more leisure time among nonfactory workers, the rise of middle-class voluntary organizations, and so on (Riess 1989, 47).

Indeed, sports—whether it be a team sport or a manifestation of the Highland games—was also a form of assimilation and, at the same time, a source of ethnic pride. It not only helped immigrants adjust to American life but also it helped to maintain Old World ties. Members of the Caledonian Society of Chicago, for example, were held up to the highest possible standards and were expected to conduct themselves accordingly or face the possibility of expulsion or, worse, a loss of respect. They were constantly being reminded that they were continuing important traditions by participating in the "ancient and honorable" games of the homeland. To many Americans, sports and morality were irretrievably linked. It's not surprising then to read a report in the *Scottish-American* (1890) denouncing football playing on Sunday. Here, the spiritual significance of sports is clearly shown.

Native-born Americans particularly were impressed with what they considered the more acceptable sporting activities of the English, Scottish, and German immigrants rather than the so-called blood sports—such as wrestling—of the Irish (Riess 1989, 21). Soccer required considerable skill and technical expertise. In general, then, English and Scots immigrants faced little cultural shock and little discrimination, and this was reflected in their choice of sporting activities.

In recent years, professional soccer franchises in Chicago have met with mixed results. In the 1970s and 1980s, a native-born Scot, Derek Spalding, played for the Chicago Sting, the city's most successful professional soccer team, in the now defunct North American Soccer League. Spalding had played for the Hibernian Football Club in Scotland before being signed in late 1977 and played for the Sting until 1983. In 1990 he became head coach for the Chicago Power of the American Indoor Soccer Association. That league also folded.

GOLF

Probably no one is more important to the history of golf in Chicago than Charles Blair Macdonald. Macdonald was a wealthy man who had fallen in love with the game as a teenager when his father sent him to finish his studies in the old university town of St. Andrews, Scotland. It was there that his grandfather introduced young Charles to some of the game's great champions. The charm of the old gray town had its affect on the young man. More important, though, the game itself cast its spell on him.

Macdonald returned to Chicago in 1875, but to his dismay golf had not caught on yet in the United States. Indeed, he would have to wait until 1888 for the first permanent golf club in the country, the St. Andrew's Golf Club in Yonkers, New York, to be established (Wind 1975–76, 246).

Yet Macdonald, then a broker on the Chicago Board of Trade, was a very patient, persuasive, and determined man. His love and devotion to the game knew no limits. He persuaded twenty or thirty members of the socially prominent Chicago Club to contribute $10 each to acquire land on a farm located some twenty-four miles west of Chicago. An abandoned railway company served as the clubhouse (Forgan 1924, 118), and nine holes were built on it. The following spring he added nine more holes, and in July 1893 the Chicago Golf Club was incorporated.

The layout was said to be comparable in many ways to the Old Course that Macdonald loved so much back in St. Andrews (Wind 1975–76, 246). James B. Forgan, a lifetime member of the Illinois Saint Andrew Society and its president in 1916, was one of the seven men who organized the club. Forgan, a lover of both the game and his adopted city, believed that the fate of the two were intertwined. "The development of the game of golf has kept pace with the development of the city, both of which are almost inconceivable," he recalled (Forgan 1924, 118).

Macdonald had started a trend. By the turn of the century Chicago had some twenty-six golf clubs, including Glen View in Golf, Illinois, founded in 1897 and site of the U.S. Amateur in 1902, and Midlothian founded in 1898 (Wind 1975–76, 249). The Glen View Club, in particular, has a number of very strong Scottish connections.

Glen View Club was the idea of a Scot named William Caldwell, who was a professor of sociology at Northwestern University. Caldwell had longed for a private club that was fairly close to the university yet outside the boundaries of its four-mile limit. The infamous four-mile limit warning was contained in the university charter, adopted in 1855, which stated, "No spiritous, vinous, or fermented liquors shall be sold under license, or otherwise, without four miles of the location of the said University, except for medicinal, mechanical, or sacramental purposes" (Ebner 1988, 25). The Methodists had established Northwestern University, and the people of Evanston were forever mindful of their community's noble origins.

Caldwell suggested the idea to his friend Hugh R. Wilson. Wilson, in turn, discussed the subject with his neighbors William H. Bartlett and Frank P. Frazier. Daniel Burnham is credited with finding the site, according to some accounts. Others say the spot was discovered by Wilson, Bartlett, and Frazier during a leisurely drive one particular Saturday afternoon (Fyfe 1971, 45).

The property was purchased from the John Dewes family—the log cabin that Dewes built still stands on the grounds of the club. Then on March 29, 1897, the Glen View Club and Polo Club was incorporated. Polo was short-lived, however, and in 1900 the name was changed to simply the Glen View Club (43).

Several Scots held positions as the club professional. Richard Leslie not only served as the club's first professional but also served as the greenskeeper and clubmaker. Lawrence (Laurie) Auchterlonie, a native of St. Andrews, took over in 1901. He was succeeded by James A. Donaldson from Aberdeen in 1911 and by Jock Hutchison, also of St. Andrews, in 1918. Hutchison, considered the dean of Chicago area golf professionals, retired in 1953 after serving more than thirty years. He was winner of the Western Open in 1920 and 1923 and winner of the British Open in St. Andrews, becoming the first American citizen to win the coveted title. Hutchison was inducted into the Illinois PGA Hall of Fame in 1990.

Golfing and songs soon became intertwined at Glen View. Indeed, Glen View inspired a number of songs in its day, most of them composed by club member Angus Hibbard, including "Auchterlonie," dedicated to Laurie Auchterlonie, "the brawny Scotchman who came sailing o'er the sea"

HARRY LAUDER IN CHICAGO

Harry Lauder was warmly received whenever he came to Chicago. In April 1918, for example, he played a week's engagement before a capacity crowd at the Auditorium Theatre. Lauder's presence during this visit was quite conspicuous. He received military honors by the British Canadian recruiting mission; he made an appearance at a concert and ball at the West Side Masonic Temple at Oakley and Madison sponsored by Clan MacDuff No. 16, Order of Scottish Clans; and he performed for sailors at the Great Lakes Naval Training Station. Sir Harry made frequent stopover trips to Chicago on his way to somewhere else such as the time in August 1929 when the Chicago Highlanders Pipe Band gave him a hearty welcome when he and his entourage stopped off the train at the Chicago and North Western Station.

and "Twa Days," saluting the annual member-guest tournament held each July that is still going strong (Hibbard 1934, 14).

Hibbard found a willing music-making partner in Dave Noyes. "He liked my songs and I liked him and the way he sang them," recalled Hibbard (n.d., 26). "So together, in 1898, we started golfing songs." Hibbard set the tune of Sir Harry Lauder's "Scotch Blue Bell" to new verses and a chorus and retitled it "Golf Is a Grand Old Game."

In November 1914 Hibbard got word that Lauder, the great Scots entertainer, was in town. Glen View's golf professional, James Donaldson, and Lauder were old friends, and Donaldson arranged for Lauder to play nine holes at the club. It was a raw and blustery November day when Lauder, Donaldson, Hibbard, and Hibbard's daughter, Janet, ventured out to the course to brave the dreadful weather. Before long, though, they returned to the warmth of the club's blazing fire. At lunch Hibbard asked the Scotsman to write a song for the club. "When?" he asked. "Now," Hibbard replied. Within a few minutes, Lauder had scribbled on the back of a restaurant order blank the following words:

Ode to "Glen View"

I'm going away but I'd like to stay,
Here at "Glen View"

This is the place you'll always meet,
Friends so true;

Old friends are best friends
In sunshine or rain;

Some day we may,
Meet at "Glen View" again

(28)

The club's motto was—and still is—"Laigh and Lang" ("Low and Long"), referring to a favorite golfing technique. The village of Golf's post office and headquarters still house the offices of the Western Golf Association and the Evans Scholars Foundation.

CULTURAL AND SOCIAL LIFE

Scottish residents of Chicago enjoyed a rich social life that was quite separate from the activity associated with the clans and other specifically ethnic organizations. A number of Scottish Americans added immeasurably to the cultural life of the city.

LITERARY

MARGARET ANDERSON

Margaret Anderson was a free spirit, an enigma. She established one of the most important literary publications of this century at the age of twenty-one. *The Little*

JOHNNY "RED" KERR

A prominent Scottish American in the sports arena is Johnny "Red" Kerr. Kerr's father was born in Glasgow. Sports personality and television sports commentator, Johnny "Red" Kerr is president of Kerr Financial Services and author of *Bull Session.* Kerr played professional basketball for the Syracuse, Philadelphia, and Baltimore teams. He was the first coach of the Chicago Bulls during their inaugural 1966–67 season and led the team to the playoffs, earning the title of the NBA's Coach of the Year.

John Kerr (above)

Review, she promised, would be "the most interesting magazine that had ever been launched" (Dedmon 1983, 277). She kept her word. Contributors included Sherwood Anderson, Malcolm Cowley, Gertrude Stein, Hart Crane, T. S. Eliot, Aldous Huxley, Marianne Moore, Vachel Lindsay, Amy Lowell, Emma Goldman, and a young writer from west suburban Oak Park named Ernest Hemingway.

Margaret Anderson on Chicago

"Chicago: enchanted ground to me from the moment Lake Michigan entered the train windows. I would make my beautiful life here. A city without a lake wouldn't have done."

(Anderson 1930, 13)

Anderson was born in Indianapolis, the daughter of Arthur Aubrey Anderson, a Presbyterian of Scottish descent. Always in search of freedom, she left home for Chicago in 1908, accompanied by her sister Lois. In Chicago she wrote book reviews for a religious publication and worked as a bookstore clerk for Francis Fisher Browne in the Fine Arts Building before joining the staff of *The Dial* magazine and, soon thereafter, establishing her own magazine, *The Little Review.*

That she managed to publish such a magazine was impressive in its own right, but that she did it with no reliable source of funding is even more remarkable. In 1915 she was living in a large rented house in Lake Bluff for $25 a month. When she couldn't afford to meet the payments, Margaret, her sister Lois, and her sister's two children, Tom and Fritz, a cook named Clara and her son Johnny, and a friend, Harriet Dean, decided to look for better and more satisfying living conditions. They found it near a stretch of empty beach near Ravinia, a short walk from the Braeside train station. Here, on a cold April morning, they loaded their belongings onto a rickety wagon, pitched a few tents, and spent the summer, "living like gypsies and roasting corn over the campfire and baking potatoes in its ashes" (Anderson 1930, 278; Hansen 1923, 105–6). "What was to prevent our putting up tents and living the pristine life of nomads?" Anderson (86) asked. The tents were simply furnished, nothing more than a cot, a deck chair, and an oriental rug. "We dined under the evening sky and slept under the stars, " Anderson (89) recalled.

In 1917 Anderson moved *The Little Review* to New York. The magazine gained its greatest notoriety by serializing installments of James Joyce's *Ulysses* over a three-year period. In late 1920 the editors of the magazine, including Anderson, faced an obscenity trial, and in early 1921 they were convicted and fined. The magazine struggled along for close to a decade before its final issue was published in 1929 (1930).

THE SALON ON GROVELAND

From 1913 to 1928, Harriet Moody, wife of poet William Vaughn Moody, played host to the finest poets, musicians, and artists in the country in her three-story red brick house on South Groveland Avenue (now South Ellis). In 1915 Scottish folk song collector Marjory Kennedy-Fraser and her daughter Patuffa were on an American tour, offering a series of recitals on the folk songs of the Hebrides. Mother and daughter stayed briefly at South Groveland and established a close friendship with Moody that lasted many years (Dunbar 1947, 130).

Margaret Anderson (above)

ARCHIBALD MACLEISH

Born in Glencoe, Illinois, Archibald MacLeish grew up to be the unofficial poet laureate of the United States as well as a dedicated public servant. He has written some of the finest poetry of the twentieth century, "Ars poetica," "The End of the World," and "You, Andrew Marvell" perhaps being the best known. He was also an early editor of *Fortune* magazine, librarian of Congress under Franklin Delano Roosevelt, assistant secretary of state, and for nearly fifteen years Boylston Professor at Harvard University. He won three Pulitzer prizes.

Wherever he went and whatever he accomplished, MacLeish's Scottish heritage was never far behind. He often expressed pride in the contributions that his fellow Scots made to the "strength, character, and well-being" of the United States (Donaldson 1992, 12). His father, the Scottish-born Andrew MacLeish, was president of Carson Pirie Scott and Company. Although a remote presence during his formative years, MacLeish would later remark that "Father was more of a man than I am or ever have been" (3).

Glencoe and the manor house called Craigie Lea that he grew up in figure prominently in a number of his poems, including "Cook County," "Ancestral," "Eleven," and "Photograph Album." The thirty-room mansion was completed in 1891 and was named Craigie Lea after Robert Tannahill's song "Thou Bonnie Wood of Craigie Lea" (Drury 1948, 147). In 1910 the MacLeish's returned to their roots with visits to Edinburgh, Glasgow, Loch Lomond, Oban, and Iona. The latter had great significance for the family for it was on Iona where reportedly the name MacLeish originated (Donaldson 1992, 43). Years later, in the spring of 1969, Archie and his son Kenneth, a *National Geographic* editor, took a trip together to Barra in the Outer Hebrides. The account of the journey appeared in the May 1970 issue of the magazine.

Archie's beloved brother, Kenneth MacLeish, was killed in combat over Belgium during World War I. His brother's untimely death haunted Archie for the rest of his life. He dedicated the poem "Kenneth" and, later, "Memorial Rain for Kenneth MacLeish" to his memory. There were other memorials. The First Baptist Church of Evanston—the family church where Archie had been baptized—named an addition the Kenneth MacLeish Hall and a naval destroyer was christened *USS MacLeish* at Philadelphia in 1919 (99).

In 1971 MacLeish was honored by the American-Scottish Foundation for his many contributions to society—both American and elsewhere. It was an opportunity for him to ponder what it meant to be Scottish. He concluded that the Scots "were true to themselves as human beings—put their humanity first—their responsibility to the world and to the word and to each other" (496).

NORMAN MACLEAN

After enjoying a long and successful career as an English professor at the University of Chicago, Norman Maclean published his first book of short stories at the age of seventy-three. It proved to be a smashing debut. *A River Runs Through It and Other Stories* sold, largely through word of mouth, more than 160,000 copies even before the 1992 film version by Robert Redford had been considered (McFarland and Nichols 1988, 1). Born in Clarinda, Iowa, in 1902, Maclean grew up in Missoula, Montana. He was the William Rainey Harper Professor of English at the University of Chicago until his retirement in 1973.

Maclean's father was a Presbyterian minister and a considerable influence on Norman's life. He recalls his father's origins:

> *My father was all Scotch and came from Nova Scotia, from a large family that was on poor land. His great belief was in all men being equal under God. . . .*
>
> *My father loved America so much that, although he had a rather heavy Scottish burr*

when he came to this country, by the time I was born, it was all gone. He regarded it as his American duty to get rid of it. He despised Scotch Presbyterian ministers who went heavy on their Scotch burr. He put a terrific commitment on me to be an American. I, the eldest son, was expected to complete the job.

He told me I had to learn the American language. He spoke beautifully, but he didn't have the American idioms. He kept me home until I was ten and a half to teach me. He taught me how to write American. (McFarland and Nichols 1988, 11)

Maclean, a member of the Illinois Saint Andrew Society, later recalled his father's practice of preaching two "very good sermons" on Sundays and baptizing, marrying, and burying "the local Americans of Scotch descent on weekdays" (14).

WILLIAM MAXWELL

Writer and editor William Maxwell was born in Lincoln, Illinois, in 1908, but moved with his family to Chicago when he was fourteen. He received his education at the University of Illinois at Urbana and did some graduate work at Harvard. For forty years he was fiction editor at the *New Yorker*, but he has also written novels, including perhaps his best known, *So Long, See You Tomorrow*, as well as short fiction, a collection of literary essays, and children's books.

Maxwell came from a family of lawyers. He was a descendant of Henry Maxwell, who was born in Scotland around 1730. In *Ancestors: A Family History*, Maxwell muses about distant ancestors in faraway countries and about the world of nineteenth-century midwestern landscapes that later ancestors would come to intimately know. Maxwell is a Lowland name, he tells us, "common in Dumfriesshire but not limited to it":

I have always liked my name. . . . William Maxwell . . . is not a common name and neither is it exactly uncommon. It turns up in the Waverley *novels, in Scottish and English and American history, in the juvenilia of Charlotte Bronte, in all sorts of places. When Boswell has*

SCOTS IN BROADCASTING

Dave Garroway, the first host of the popular *Today* program, got his start as a staff announcer on WMAQ radio in Chicago. David Cunningham Garroway was born in Schenectady, New York. His father was of Scots descent.

In January 1946 he hosted the 11:60 Club, a midnight radio program that allowed him the freedom to play "pure" jazz and comment on whatever he liked. Garroway became so popular that by fall 1947 he added a daily show and a Sunday night variety show to his schedule.

The anything-goes atmosphere of the radio format was transferred to television in 1949 with *Garroway at Large,* a variety program that was known for its innovative camera techniques and Garroway's casual yet intimate style of delivery. Along with *Stud's Place and Kukla, Fran & Ollie,* Garroway's show came to epitomize what came to be known as the Chicago School of Television. With his horn-rimmed glasses and tweed suits, Garroway projected a cultured, urbane image. He proved that talent and imagination were more important than big budgets and famous guests.

Another WMAQ alumni was Bill Hay, a native of Dumfries in the Scottish Lowlands, who served as the radio station's sales director and chief announcer. He was the announcer for the *Amos 'n Andy* and *The Goldbergs* programs. He also hosted his own show, *Auld Sandy,* on Sunday nights.

Other Scots who have made an impact in Chicago broadcasting include the Scots Canadian WBBM-TV news anchor Linda MacLennan and, also at the same station, veteran reporter John Drummond.

supper with his cousin, Sir William Maxwell, at Howell's in Half Moon Street, I know that it is not me, that it has nothing to do with me, but, irrationally, I am pleased.

Or perhaps the real reason I like my name is that it is Scottish. When I was six years old my mother took me to Bloomington, thirty miles away, to hear Harry Lauder. And when we arrived at the theater there were two bagpipers—huge men, over six feet—in kilts, walking up and down and making those squealing noises and my heart began to pound with excitement. Since that moment everything Scottish—kilts, plaid, bagpipe music, the accent, the coloring—produces a mysterious, un-thinking pleasure in me. (Maxwell 1971, 20)

Other Scots who have contributed to the literary landscape of Chicago include Neil Henderson, a writer of charming poetry, much of it written in the urban patois of his native Glasgow. Douglas Macdonald, a poet who has published a number of small chapbooks, is the nephew of Angus Macdonald, president of the Society in 1970-72. For several years the younger Macdonald ran a bookshop on Halsted Street called The Stone Circle.

MUSIC

MARY GARDEN

One of the most outrageous individuals in Chicago history was the Scots-born Mary Garden, the grand dame of Chicago opera. Garden's controversial performance of Strauss's *Salome* in 1910 raised a raucous that echoed throughout the city from Prairie Avenue mansions to pulpits to street corners. The credit for bringing opera to Chicago, however, must go to Harold McCormick and his wife, Edith Rockefeller. From their graystone mansion at 1000 Lake Shore Drive, they directed the fortunes of culture in Chicago.

On the verge of financial ruin due to the loss of its brilliant director, Cleofonte Campanini, McCormick in 1921 asked Garden to become the director of the Chicago Opera Company. "We want to go out in a blaze of glory," he reportedly said to her, "and we need your name" (Dedmon 1983, 309).

As expected, Garden's season was wracked with feuds; both glorious and messy. She signed up so many artists but ran out of time for them to perform. Since she didn't have a business mind, she couldn't confirm or deny published reports that she had spent lavishly or that the company lost $1 million during her season. "If it cost a million dollars, I'm sure it was worth it," she said, by way of explanation (310).

Garden was a dificult personality and stubborn to the bone. While temperamental outbursts would eventually take their toll, there was no denying that she brought high standards and great enthusiasm to the position. She left by mutual consent, explaining, "I am an artist and my place is with the artists."

DAVE TOUGH

Small, wiry, and intense, Dave Tough (born David Jarvis) was the son of Scottish immigrants and considered by some to be the best white jazz drummer of his generation. Tough attended Oak Park High School and was a member of the famous Austin High Group, which included Benny Goodman and Bud Freeman. Troubled and sensitive, he was the band's resident intellectual. In the late 1920s he moved to Paris before eventually returning to New York, a brokenhearted alcoholic, hurt by both life and love. He also played with Tommy Dorsey, Artie Shaw, and Woody Herman. He died in New Jersey in 1948 from head injuries received in a fall (Collier 1989, 224–25).

Mary Garden (above)

SCOTTISH MUSICAL CLUB OF CHICAGO

The Scottish Musical Club of Chicago was organized at the January 1905 meeting of the Illinois Saint Andrew Society. According to program notes, the club intended to offer two concerts each year, "one purely Scotch, and the other Oratorio."

On the evening of May 4, 1905, the club presented a "Grand Scottish Concert" at Orchestra Hall. Under the direction of Charles E. Allum, a doctor of music from Trinity College, Dublin, a 100-member chorus presented a program of Scottish ballads. The singers consisted of baritone William Beard, tenor George L. Tenney, and soprano Madame Schelke.

The material consisted of typically romantic fare from classic Robert Burns ("Ae Fond Kiss," "Whistle and I'll Come Tae Ye My Lad," "Ye Banks and Braes," "The Deil's Awa' wi' the Exciseman"), Lady Nairne ("Caller Herrin"), patriotic hymns ("Scots Wha Hae"), and a Jacobite rallying song ("Wha'll Be King But Charlie?"). Madame Schelke performed an aria from Donizetti's *Lucia de Lammermoor.* The program ended on an appropriately patriotic mood with versions of both the "Star Spangled Banner" and "Auld Lang Syne."

TRADITIONAL SCOTTISH MUSICIANS

Although traditional Irish musicians received the lion's share of attention in Chicago, there were certainly a number of Scottish traditional musicians in the city too. Highland piper William McLean, for example, was born in Ross-shire in the Scottish Highlands before emigrating to America. By 1875 he was considered an expert performer on the Highland war pipes. And, it was said, he could play Irish dance tunes just as well. Traditional Irish music collector Francis O'Neill recalled the times when McLean would play for hours in the evening in a large room in a building at the corner of Clark and Jackson Streets (O'Neill 1987, 350).

Another famous Highland piper was Joseph Cant, a native of Inverness and one of Chicago's earliest settlers. A carpenter and cabinetmaker by trade, Cant was familiar with the classic repertoire of the Highland bagpipe. He won first prize at the Illinois Saint Andrew Society games at Chicago's Dexter Park in 1877 and at various other games, including the games of the Highland Society of Chicago in 1888 (352).

Daniel O'Keeffe was an expert on the Highland pipes even though he hailed from County Kerry. O'Keeffe came to Chicago in the late 1860s and, like many a native of Ireland and Scotland before and since, opened a saloon on Kinzie Street. O'Keeffe's saloon was a boisterous kind of place made even more distinctive by the large sign that swung over the door, "on which was painted a Highland piper in full costume, playing the pipes and dancing to his own music." According to the sign, free drinks for a week were offered to anyone who could beat O'Keeffe in dancing a jig, reel, hornpipe, or Highland fling (349).

PIPE BANDS

Pipe bands have played an important role in the perpetuation of traditional Scottish music in Chicago. In 1896 the Chicago Scots Guards, formerly the Royal Scots of Chicago, were an active part of the city's musical community (*Scottish-American* 1896, 8). Three years

Robert H. Sim (above). From 1923-63 Sim was the official piper at the Society's annual banquet.

earlier, though, saw the formation of the pipe and drum band of the First Regiment of Royal Scots, which Dr. Rowland Berthoff calls the first regularly organized band of its kind in the United States.

One of the best-known pipers in Chicago was the late Robert H. Sim. In 1921 Pipe Major Sim and his brother Drum Sergeant James H. Sim founded the Chicago Stock Yard Kilty Band (SYKB).

Robert H. Sim was born in 1895 in Aberdeenshire. He joined the Gordon Highlanders and served in France during 1914–17 and was wounded at the Battle of Ypres. While recuperating he met Henry Forsythe, the king's piper. Sim came to the United States in 1920 and formed the British Legion Band in 1921, which later became the Chicago Stock Yard Kilty Band. He was considered a great teacher of the pipes. Among

Stock Yard Kilty Band (above). Robert H. Sim is in the second row.

his students is Will Norman, still active today. A baker by trade, Sim worked for the Quaker Oats Company in Chicago. He died in 1968.

In 1926 the Kilty Band became affiliated with Stock Yards Post #333, thereby becoming the first pipe band in American Legion history. It also served as the official pipe band of the Illinois Saint Andrew Society.

Sim also played with the Billy Caldwell Pipe Band, originally organized as the Chicago Highlanders in July 1931. Most of the band members were war veterans, many with famous Scottish regiments, such as the Argyle and Sutherland Highlanders. Nettie MacPherson, its only woman piper, was also the band's manager.

From 1921 to 1976 the Stock Yard Kilty Band practiced at the Stock Yard Inn free of charge. The band's final ceilidh took place there in October 1976. With it went a tradition "that has been the center of Chicago's Scottish community," said David McKee, pipe major of the band (Currie 1976).

On September 14, 1994, Alderman Patrick M. Huels, on behalf of the residents of Chicago, extended to the Sims family the city's "heartiest congratulations and sincerest appreciation for over fifty years of traditional Scottish bagpipe music."

Other predominantly Scottish pipe bands or bands with strong Scottish roots in the Chicago metropolitan area include the Rampant Lion of Illinois Pipe Band, the Royal Chicago Scots & Juniors, the University of Chicago Alumni Association Pipe Band (formerly Invermich Gaelic Society Pipe Band), the Chicago Highlanders Pipe Band, the Chicago Metropolitan Pipe Band, the Fort Dearborn Highlanders, Medinah Highlanders, Tunes

Chicago Highlanders Pipe Band (above). A young Robert H. Sim is in the first row.

of Glory, and probably the most highly acclaimed pipe band in the area, the Midlothian Scottish Pipe Band, led by pipe major Ian Swinton. In 1983 Midlothian competed at the World's Pipe Band Championships in Glasgow, where they won the Best Overseas Band trophy.

GEORGE ARMSTRONG

An illustrator by profession, George Armstrong was best remembered as a fine traditional folk singer, a radio host, a teller of tales, and, most of all, a bagpiper. For thirty years Armstrong opened the annual University of Chicago Folk Festival with a blast of the pipes. And when illness forced him to stop, his daughter Jenny carried on the family tradition in 1991.

The Armstrong clan has often been called the first family of Chicago folk. George Armstrong's wife, Gerry, is a singer, storyteller, and writer while his two daughters, Jenny and Rebecca, are also singers and musicians.

Armstrong was always proud of his Border Scots heritage. He learned to play the pipes when he was twelve, playing in both the Chicago Stock Yard Kilty Band and the Fort Dearborn Highlanders. He was stationed in Austria during World War II, where he managed to find the time to assemble a pipe band.

In the early 1950s he met Gerry at a live taping of WFMT's *Midnight Special* radio program, reportedly carrying his pipes and wearing his kilt. In the late 1970s he hosted a weekly radio program, *The Wandering Folksong,* on the station. He also had close ties with the Old Town School of Folk Music—he played the pipes at the school's opening day on December 1, 1957.

During the 1960s the Armstrongs invited a

The Illinois Saint Andrew Society Pipe Band (above). The ubiquitous Robert H. Sim is in the second row, second from the right.

number of folk musicians to their Wilmette home. The group that gathered came to be known as the Golden Ring. Norm Pelligrini, former program director of WFMT, made some of the early recordings in the Armstrong living room and additional sessions at the WFMT studios.

In addition, Gerry wrote and George illustrated several Celtic-themed children's books, including the Scottish *The Magic Bagpipe* in 1964, the Cornish *The Boat On the Hill* in 1967, and the Irish *The Fairy Thorn* in 1969. The Armstrongs also made several recordings: *Simple Gifts* (Folkways), *The Golden Ring* (Folk Legacy), and the two-volume *Five Days Singing* (Folk Legacy). In 1992 *The Wheel of the Year: Thirty Years with the Armstrong Family* (Flying Fish) was released. It contained a compilation of tunes, Child ballads, May Day songs, and medieval carols that were recorded at WFMT between 1959 and 1985.

In recent years, Jenny Armstrong enjoyed much success with her one-woman autobiographical show, *WomanSong*. The sound of the bagpipes is the thread that holds the show together. "They're a very organic instrument," she once said. "When you're playing, it feels as if they are an extension of your body, because you're breathing through them" (Van Matre 1992).

George Armstrong, the patriarch of the Armstrong clan, died at age sixty-six on July 5, 1993. Fittingly, the last tune that Armstrong was able to play on the pipes was "The Green Hills of Tyrol," better known as "The Scottish Soldier."

SCOTTISH DANCE

There were several Scottish dance schools in Chicago or at least studios where Scottish dance was taught in the 1920s and 1930s. Jessie E. Charleston had a school of dance at 710 W. Sixty-ninth Street, where she taught "Scotch, Fancy, Character, Acrobatic, Tap and Toe Dancing." Piper and dancer Margaret Baikie was among her students.

Pupils of Charleston held their first annual recital and dance at Barbee's Masonic Hall at the northeast corner of Sixty-ninth and Wentworth on Saturday, May 26, 1923. The

Curtiss Kilties (above). Even local companies were known to have their pipe band, such as the Curtiss Candy Company, maker of Baby Ruth.

program included a bagpipe selection, highland fling, sword dance, and Harry Lauder impersonations by Sam Galbraith.

The ninth annual program was held in 1930 at the Englewood Masonic Temple, at Sixty-eighth and Yale. By that time the Charleston school was located on the second floor of a building at 6932 S. Halsted Street. Charleston was a member of the Chicago Association of Dancing Masters and the Dancing Masters of America.

Another dancing school with Scottish connections was the MacPherson-Hendry School of Dancing at 1607 W. Sixty-fourth Street, near Ashland Avenue, run by Nettie MacPherson and George Hendry. MacPherson and Hendry also sponsored special dance programs, such as their revue in June 1932 at the South Side Masonic Temple, Sixty-fourth and Green Streets.

SCOTTISH COUNTRY DANCING

Scottish dance is generally divided into two main categories: Highland dancing and Scottish country dancing. Highland dancing developed in the Highlands in the eleventh century. The sword dance and the Highland fling are probably two of the best-known examples. According to tradition, these dances were originally the province of men and were performed before a battle to ensure good luck. The sword dance was said to be performed on the eve of battle by men who used their sword in the form of a cross to mark the spot of the dance. If the warrior danced without touching the sword with his feet this was considered lucky and brought good fortune in battle. During the seventeenth century the influence of the Presbyterian Church effectively stamped out dancing in most of its forms. It wasn't until the early eighteenth century that dancing became socially acceptable again in Scotland.

Scottish country dancing is more recent, probably dating back to the sixteenth or seventeenth centuries and, according to some accounts, was brought over to Scotland from France. Indeed, its steps are said to have their origins in the French ballet. Initially they were performed at court but soon spread to the countryside. Scots added their own qualities, such as the use of the stately strathspey rhythm, which gave it a distinctive Scottish touch. It is the ballroom dancing equivalent of Scotland.

After World War I the popularity of Scottish country dancing was on the wane, as jazz and modern dance took its place. In the early 1920s, however, two Scots established the Scottish Country Dance Society in Glasgow.

In recent years Scottish country dancing has caught on in Chicago, too. In 1980 the Loch Michigan Scottish Country Dancers were organized, and in 1987 the Chicago branch of the Royal Scottish Country Dance Society came into being.

Today the Gillan School of Highland Dance, founded by the Dundee-born Frances Gillan, the McGladdery Highland Dancers, founded by Nancy Strolle, and the Evanston Scottish Country Dancers continue the dancing traditions of Scotland through classes, demonstrations, and performances.

Jessie E. Charleston, Scottish dance teacher. Program for the first annual recital and dance given by the pupils of Barbee's Masonic Hall, 69th and Wentworth, 1923. (above)

The Illinois Saint Andrew Society
100th Anniversary
The Oldest Charitable and Philanthropic Organization in Illinois
1845
1945
Scottish Old People's Home
Riverside . . . Illinois

NINE

A Changing Society

During the many years of its existence, the Illinois Saint Andrew Society has survived seven wars: the Civil War, the Spanish-American War, World War I, World War II, the Korean War, the Vietnam War, and, most recently, the Gulf War. The valor of Scottish men and women has been evident in every one of these conflicts.

The Civil War was the most personal, of course, since its bloody battles were fought on native soil. Chicago was smaller then with more of a hometown flavor than can be imagined today. One man was quoted as saying there was "hardly a house that did not display the black flag of death." More than 200,000 men volunteered from Illinois. So many Society members fought in the war that its influence was felt for many years upon the membership. General Daniel Cameron, General John McArthur, and Colonel R. Biddle Roberts all served as presidents of the Society following the war. Roberts was the last of the three, serving in 1882.

America's entrance into World War II began on December 7, 1941, with the bombing of Pearl Harbor and ended with the surrender of Japan in 1945. Unlike the Civil War, the effects of this conflict on the Society were measured not so much in personalities as in the changes it brought to Chicago. During the postwar era, for example, many Chicagoans made a mass exodus to the suburbs. By 1960 the metropolitan population was 6,794,461 while the population of Chicago was 3,550,404, an actual decline from the previous census.

This migration had a dramatic effect on the Society, scattering the membership over the greater metropolitan area. Previously, all Society activities—board meetings, quarterly meetings, and special events—were conducted downtown. But the popularity of the suburbs and the "age of the automobile" brought its own divisions to the organization. Scottish events long held in the Loop became more and more difficult to sustain as the postwar generation pursued the possibilities of obtaining an education and raising families. The Society was no longer a close-knit group whose members lived in a confined area. Two decades of good fortune and growth changed the interests of Scottish people, and it became increasingly difficult to find common goals. In truth, members displayed less interest in the Society and their Scottish heritage. Prosperity led many to believe that "the distressed" no longer existed and, if they did exist, the government should care for them.

During this period most of the clan societies ceased to meet on a regular basis. A list of some of the clans and organizations that no longer

The Society's 100th anniversary program (left)

exist include the following: Caledonian Society of Chicago, Orkney and Shetland Society, John O'Groats Caithness Association, Clan MacDuff of Chicago, Clan Campbell of Chicago, South Chicago Caledonian Club, Englewood Scottish Club, Scottish Highlanders of Chicago, Carlyle Club of Chicago, the Highland Pipe Band, the Robert Burns Society, and Clan McKenzie. These highly active groups had met monthly, offering entertainment and social activities to their members.

The last citywide tattoo was held on August 21, 1954, at the International Amphitheater with George C. Buik, Sr., serving as general chairman and featuring the champion pipe bands of Canada and the United States, notable among them the Chicago Stock Yard Kilty Band, Billy Caldwell Pipe Band, Pipes and Drums of 48th (Sault Ste. Marie), Toronto Scottish Pipe Band, Grove City Pennsylvania Highland Band, Georgetown Girls Pipe Band, Heather Highlanders Pipe Band (Youngstown, Ohio), Mohammed Kiltie Band (Peoria, Illinois), and the City of Winnipeg Police Pipe Band.

No longer did the familiar sound of Scottish concerts resound in the opera halls of Chicago as the population continued to move outward in ever widening circles. The last of the White Heather concerts was held on October 23, 1963, at the Arie Crown Theater. For six consecutive years, these concerts had given Chicago a taste of Scottish talent. For this final concert, the late Andy Stewart of "The Scottish Soldier" fame brought a troupe of entertainers that included Jill Howard, Dixie Ingram, Jimmy Neil, Dennis Clancy, Arthur Spink, and Harry Carmichael. The Chicago Highlanders Pipe Band played during the intermission.

The one unifying force for the Society during this period proved to be the Scottish Home. It offered the Society a strong and unified purpose. The building demanded attention, and the residents needed care. The Scots who lived in the home thus became the very heartbeat of the Society. Without the home, it is very likely that the Society would have disappeared along with the many other Scottish organizations that had

From the White Heather concert program, 1961 (above)

once prospered in Chicago. The home provided the Society with the impetus to fulfill its original mission: "Relieve the distressed."

From 1945 to 1970 the anniversary dinners continued as usual; however, during World War II the dinners were moved to the Palmer House since the government had taken control of the Stevens Hotel. Obviously, attendance declined during the war years, and the shipments of the traditional haggis from Scotland ceased, but the dinners were always held, becoming, in fact, the major annual effort for members of the Society. Eight committees were always appointed—Decorations, Greetings, Hotel, Reception, Entertainment, Publicity, Speakers, and Tickets—actively engaging some sixty members each year. For several years, attendance varied between 1,200 and 1,400 people.

In 1945 the Society celebrated its 100th anniversary. The Great War had just ended and the entire population rested from the strain of the conflict. The anniversary dinner was once again held at the Stevens Hotel, and the haggis arrived from Scotland. The pipe major was Robert H. Sim and the dancing was led by Margaret Baikie Macdonald. The toastmaster was James G. McMillan. Dr. William A. Irwin of New York City gave the address on the topic of "The Land We Live In" while Colonel George C. D. Kilpatrick, director of army education for Canada, spoke about "The Land We Left." The main address was given by Field Marshal Sir Henry Maitland Wilson, the Supreme Allied Commander in the Mediterranean in 1944. In honor of this

Arrival of the haggis aboard a Great Lakes ship in 1947. Robert Black (second from left) accepts while the pipers play on. (above)

Listening to the piping of Marilyn Petersen, a member of the University of Iowa all-girls pipe band, are Right Honorable James Miller (left), Lord Provost of Edinburgh, and Hughston McBain, chairman of the board of Marshall Field and Company and president of the Illinois Saint Andrew Society. December 6, 1952.

historic and poignant occasion, two large monuments were placed on the burial grounds at Rosehill Cemetery. In 1955 the first Society office was established in Chicago at 134 S. LaSalle Street in room 1515.

In 1963 retired Marshall Field Company chairman of the board Hughston McBain assumed the leadership of the Society. As president, McBain began immediately to revitalize the organization. The central office was moved to 25 E. Washington Street, room 1122. Dues were increased. Every event sponsored by the Society was promoted with an enthusiastic publicity campaign. Under McBain's leadership, a new health care wing was constructed at the Scottish Home, the first construction in more than fifty years. The major contributor was James G. McMillan, president of the Wander Corporation, the makers of Ovaltine. "No man has made a greater contribution to the Society and the Home for more than a decade," said McBain of McMillan. The fourteen-bed James G. McMillan Infirmary Wing was completed and dedicated on April 20, 1964. As pipers James Mooney and David Pryde played, Margaret McBain Haynes christened the building with a bottle containing water from Loch Ness in the Highlands of Scotland. Sadly, James G. McMillan had died shortly before the dedication.

The creative leadership begun by McBain continued into the presidency of Angus J. Ray. Under his direction, the Board of Governors enlarged the small rooms, which contained neither a bathroom nor closet. This problem was remedied, and central air conditioning was also installed.

At a quarterly meeting in 1968, the membership approved a twofold program: the modernization as outlined by the Board of Governors, and the construction of a new two-story residential wing, the cost not to exceed $950,000. The new wing would be located west of the existing wing and would have an elevator to provide access to the home's basement, offering indoor recreation space in the event of inclement weather. The groundbreaking ceremony was held on Saturday, April 12, 1969, with an invocation by the Reverend James W. McGlathery. The speaker was past president Edmund L. McGibbon and closing remarks were given by Robert Crawford.

From 1970 to 1995, much progress and growth occurred. The Highland games of 1995, for example, were again held in Grant Park after an absence there of almost ten years. A renewed emphasis on publicity brought the Society to the attention of the general public. Chicago is now much more aware of the Society as the oldest charitable organization in Illinois.

The role of women in the Society has improved tremendously during the past twenty-five years, too. Although Nancy LeNoble Strolle was the first and only woman in 150 years to serve as president of the Society, women have always played a significant role from the earliest times, as they ministered to the needy women and children of the Scottish American population. Today, women function at every level of the Society.

In 1970 the construction of a new two-story addition to the Scottish Home and a major renovation of the older building was begun. The total cost was $1 million, and the capacity of the home was increased by 30 percent. The Board of Governors proudly proclaimed, "The Scottish Home is now one of the outstanding old peoples homes in the nation. It is attractive, comfortable, and offers the finest in geriatric care. If those early Scots of Chicago could be with us today, they would be well pleased at the way we are following through to fulfill their dreams." In 1974 the kitchen was modernized and the air conditioning system was completed.

The final phase of construction during this period occurred in 1984, when the "Shetlands" was added to the health care wing. This large, airy room provides the residents with a central dining room and much needed activity area. The major donors for the Shetlands were Pete Georgeson and his wife. The room was named for Georgeson, who came from the Shetland Islands.

In the 1970s James C. Thomson began working on an idea that soon developed into the Scottish-American Hall of Fame, located in the basement of the home. Thomson, who died in December 1994, researched and wrote the 120 biographical plaques. (More will be added.) The carved heading of the Hall was the work of the late George M. Wood, Clansman of the Year in 1991.

DWINDLING NUMBERS

"Since the Second World War, the numbers of Scots emigrating to the United States have been relatively small—a total of 22,471 from 1951 to 1957 and some 3,000 to 4,000 in each year since," according to Gordon Donaldson (1966, 196). Others say the annual migration from Scotland to the United States is no more than 8,000 (Brander 1982, 110).

For many years the children and grandchildren of the Scottish emigrants made little effort to carry on the traditions brought over by their parents or grandparents. Rowland Berthoff makes a persuasive case that among "British Americans" there was no second generation. The children became simply Americans, no longer hyphenated Americans. He cites the example of a young schoolboy and his conversation with his father who hailed from Yorkshire about the Revolutionary War: "You had the king's army, and we were only a lot of farmers, but we thrashed you" (Berthoff 1953, 210). Already it was a case of we against you.

With a decrease in emigration and the rapid assimilation of immigrant children into American society, it didn't take long for the Scottish American community to become weakened. The *Scottish-American Journal* expired in 1925, and many of the local societies also fell on hard times. Yet as late as the 1940s there was enough of a Scottish presence in the city to hold a Scottish-American Night at Chicago's Free Fair at Forty-seventy and Damen. Today the Illinois Saint Andrew Society, with its over 1,000 members, continues to uphold the traditions started by earlier generations of Chicago Scots.

OUTREACH

In recent years the Illinois Saint Andrew Society has been doing its best to keep the Scottish American community of Chicago informed about not only its own events but also of other items of interest to the Scottish community at large. The Society has been doing this in various ways from the publication of a newsletter, the *Tartan Times,* to the sponsorship of History Club tours and a History Club newsletter as well as various events and programs.

The highlight of the Society's social year is the annual Anniversary Dinner. The program consists of pipe bands, Highland dancing, entertainers, and, of course, the serving of the traditional haggis. It is at this event that the Society presents its annual awards, the Distinguished Citizen, Clanswoman of the Year, Clansman of the Year, and the crowning of the "Heather Queen."

ILLINOIS SAINT ANDREW SOCIETY TARTAN

In 1992 the Illinois Saint Andrew Society approved a red, white, and blue tartan. In the same year the Society adopted a new symbol to mark its 150th anniversary: the lion rampant of Scotland and the thirteen red and white stripes of the American flag, symbolic of the flags of the United States, Scotland, and Great Britain.

SCOTTISH AMERICAN HALL OF FAME

Located in the basement of the Scottish Home, the Scottish American Hall of Fame honors the lives and work of prominent native Scots, Scottish Americans, and Ulster Scots from the pre-Revolutionary War era to the present day.

Inventors

Bell, Alexander Graham
Inventor of the telephone

Edison, Thomas Alva
Inventor of the electric light bulb

Fulton, Robert
Inventor of the steamboat

Henry, Joseph
America's greatest early scientist

Military

Clark, George Rogers
Frontier hero of the Revolutionary War

Jackson, Stonewall
Confederate general

Johnston, Joseph E
Confederate general

Knox, Henry
General, aide to General Washington

Logan, John
General, founder of Memorial Day

MacArthur, Arthur
Army general, father of Douglas

MacArthur, Douglas
World War II general

McClellan, George B.
U.S. Civil War general

Macomb, Alexander
General, hero, War of 1812

McPherson, James B.
Civil War general

Mitchell, William (Billy)
Air power advocate

Moultrie, William
Revolutionary War general

Patton, George S.
World War II general

Scott, Winfield
Chief of staff during Mexican War

Stuart, J. E. B.
Confederate calvary general

Boone, Daniel
Frontiersman, Indian fighter

Carson, Christopher "Kit"
Frontiersmen, explorer

Clark, William
Explorer with Meriwether Lewis

Crockett, Davy
Frontiersman, died at the Alamo

Naval

Farragut, David Glasgow
Civil War naval hero

Jones, John Paul
Revolutionary War naval hero

Religion

Campbell, Alexander
Founder, Church of Christ

Makemie, Reverend Francis
Advocate of religious freedom

Marshall, Peter
World War II U.S. Senate chaplain

Sports

Naismith, James, M.D.
Originator of basketball

Reid, John
Started first golf club in United States

Science

Carothers, Wallace H.
Developed first synthetic fibers

Fleming, Williamina P.
Leading woman astronomer

Langmuir, Irving
Nobel Prize winner in physics

McClure, William
Scientist

Millikin, Robert
Physicist

U.S. Presidents

Arthur, Chester

Buchanan, James

Grant, Ulysses S.

Hayes, Rutherford B.

Jackson, Andrew

McKinley, William

Monroe, James

Polk, James K.

Wilson, Woodrow

Founding Fathers

Dallas, Alexander
Secretary of the Treasury

Hamilton, Alexander
First Secretary of the Treasury

SCOTTISH AMERICAN HALL OF FAME (CONTINUED)

Hamilton, Andrew
Lawyer

Henry, Patrick
Orator, colonial statesman

Thomson, Charles
Secretary, Continental Congress

Wilson, James D.
Signer, Declaration of Independence

Witherspoon, Reverend John
Only clergyman to sign Declaration of Independence, founder of Princeton University

Business

Cargill, William W.
Founder, Cargill, Inc.

Crerar, John
Businessman, philanthropist

Dollar, Robert
Ocean shipping tycoon

Hill, James J.
Railroad builder, developer

Legge, Alexander
President of International Harvester

Mellon, Andrew
Banker, Secretary of Treasury

Oliver, James
American inventor and manufacturer

Stewart, Alexander Turney
Marketing innovator

Strong, Henry
Railroad builder and administrator

Wallace, Henry Agard
Agricultural scientist, Secretary of Agriculture, Vice President

Industry

Armour, Philip D.
Businessman, meatpacker

Burden, Henry
Colonial industrialist

Carnegie, Andrew
Industrialist, philanthropist

Cooper, Peter
Industrialist, inventor

Douglas, Donald W.
Founder of Douglas Aircraft

McCormick, Cyrus H.
Industrialist

McDonnell, James
Plane designer, industrialist

Literature

Caldwell, Erskine
Author

Garland, Hamlin
Author

Irving, Washington
First internationally recognized U.S. author

Lindsay, Vachel
Illinois poet

Melville, Herman
Author

Wallace, Lila Bell
Cofounder, *Readers Digest*

Wallace, Lew
General, author of *Ben-Hur*

Media

Bennett, James Gordon
Prominent newspaper editor, publisher

Forbes, Bertie
Founder, *Forbes Magazine*

Greeley, Horace
Influential newspaper editor

Medill, Joseph
Editor of *Chicago Tribune,* mayor of Chicago

Scripps, Edwin W.
Newspaper chain publisher

Wallace, DeWitt
Cofounder, *Readers Digest*

Education

Blair, Reverend James
Founder, College of William and Mary

Cameron, Andrew C.
Editor, labor leader

McGuffey, William Holmes
Educator, author of *McGuffey Reader*

MacLeish, Archibald
Poet, archivist, politician

Art/Design

Carmichael, Hoagy
Songwriter, composer

Duncan, Isadora
Dancer

Garden, Mary
Opera singer, actress

Garden, Alexander
Civil War photographer

SCOTTISH AMERICAN HALL OF FAME (CONTINUED)

MacDowell, Edward A.
Music composer

McKay, Donald
Designer and builder of clipper ships

Phyffe, Duncan
Furniture designer

Robertson, Anna Mary (Grandma Moses)
Primitive painter

Stuart, Gilbert
Portrait painter

Whistler, James McNeill
Painter

Biologists

Corbett, Elizabeth Wiley
First U.S. woman doctor

Douglas, David
Botanist, Douglas fir named in his honor

Gray, Asa
Early U.S. botanist

McDowell, Ephraim, M.D.
Performed first abdominal surgery

Mercer, Hugh, M.D.
Revolutionary War general

Morton, William T.
First to use ether as anesthetic

Wilson, Alexander
Pioneer ornithologist

Politics

Calhoun, John C.
Southern statesman

Cameron, Simon
Political leader in Lincoln's Cabinet

Dallas, George M.
Vice President, promoted Manifest Destiny; Dallas, Texas, named for him

Davis, Jefferson
President of the Confederacy

Douglas, Stephen A.
U.S. Senator from Illinois

Douglas, William O.
U.S. Supreme Court justice

Houston, Sam
Father of Texas

Wiley, Harvey
Father of U.S. Pure Food Act

Wilson, Henry
Vice President, abolitionist

Wilson, James
Secretary of Agriculture

Wilson, William B.
First Secretary of Labor

Miscellaneous

Kinzie, John
First white settler in Chicago

McCullum, Daniel
Ran railroads for North during Civil War

Muir, John
Author, conservationist

Pinkerton, Allan
Founded detective agency

Americans of Scottish Ancestry Who Signed the Declaration of Independence

Thomas McKeon
Matthew Thornton
James Smith
Philip Livingston
George Taylor
George Ross
John Witherspoon
Thomas Nelson
James Wilson
William Hooper

CONTEMPORARY SCOTTISH CULTURE IN CHICAGO

In recent years many Scots have traveled through town:

Writers

James Kelman at Waterstone's

Alasdair Gray at Barbara's Bookstore

Margot Livesey at Women and Children First

Scots Canadian short story writer Alice Munro at Barbara's Bookstore

Music

Rock

Del Amitri at the Vic

Texas at Metro

Simple Minds at Poplar Creek

Roddy Frame at Metro

Proclaimers at Metro and the Vic

Traditional

Jean Redpath

Silly Wizard

Andy M. Stewart

Eric Bogle

Capercaillie

Dougie Maclean

Classical

Sir Peter Maxwell Davies's opera *The Lighthouse* by Chicago Opera Company and his own conducting of *An Orkney Wedding, with Sunrise* at Orchestra Hall

Percussionist Evelyn Glennie at Orchestra Hall

Theater

Pop singer Sheena Easton opposite Raul Julia in *Man of La Mancha* at the Auditorium Theatre

Art

"Scottish Expressionism 1984" at the Dart Gallery, 212 W. Superior Street, July–August 1984; artists included Steven Campbell, June Redfern, Graham Durward, Andrew Williams

Exchange between the Edinburgh-based 369 Gallery and East-West Gallery, 356 W. Huron, September 1988; artists included Graham Durward, Ian Hughes, Andrew Williams, Fionna Carlisle, Caroline McNairn, Donald McFadyen

"The New British Painting" at the Chicago Cultural Center and the Gallery at 333 N. Wacker Drive, January–March 1989; artists included Steven Campbell, Stephen Conroy, Ken Currie, Peter Howson, Jock McFadyen

Peter Howson, first solo exhibition in America at the Lannon-Cole Gallery, 365 W. Chicago Avenue, April–May 1991

"Scotland Exchange Show," exchange between Glasgow-based cooperative Transmission Gallery and Artemisia Gallery, 700 N. Carpenter, November 1993; included Mary Burke, Carolyn Giles, Craig Richardson, and a lecture series at the University of Illinois at Chicago.

Duke of Perth, Clark near Diversey. An authentic Scottish pub and the place for haggis wings, the William Wallace cheeseburger, the Robert the Bruce burger, the Sean Connery burger, and the Rob Roy shepherds pie. Pub owner, Colin Cameron, a former police officer, hails from Forfar in the northeast of Scotland.

The Scottish Home continues to be the heart and soul of the Society. Many believe firmly that there would have been no 150th anniversary without the home as its anchor. While most other Scottish organizations formed in the early history of Chicago have gone by the wayside, the Illinois Saint Andrew Society survives.

TOWARD THE FUTURE

As the Society enters the twenty-first century, it is being reborn. It has adopted an innovative mission statement that says that the Society will "nourish the Scottish identity through the celebration of culture and traditions, fellowship and service." A campaign, under the direction of Robert Bruce Graham, seeks to raise $7 million to enlarge the McMillan Wing and make other improvements to the Scottish Home. The present kitchen will be enlarged and the older portion of the building will be modernized with new windows and extensive masonry work.

In addition to improvements in the Home, the Society has other goals it wishes to meet in the years ahead; namely, to bolster its endowment for educational programs; remodel the basement, or Undercroft as it is called, to accommodate an enlarged Scottish American Hall of Fame and to better house a growing collection of artifacts, which include old Gaelic bibles and rare editions of Robert Burns's poetry; offer financial aid for education and scholarships for study in Scotland and the United States; expand the Highland Games; open a research and genealogy center; and develop cultural outreach programs.

Creating a higher profile for Scots and Scottish Americans within the city's business infrastructure is also part of the Society's larger plan. In 1996, for example, the Society, along with prominent members of the Scottish American business community, established the Scottish Business Forum. The Forum's mission is to create a Chicago-based network for those who either have or seek to have a business or professional connection with Scotland.

In these and countless other ways, the good works of the original founders, the rich traditions of the Society, and, indeed, the deep-rooted values of Scottish culture itself will be preserved and maintained for the benefit of future generations of "dispossessed" Illinois Scots.

Scotch settlement marker, Argyle

TEN

Historic Scottish Communities in Illinois

Scots settled throughout the prairie state. Indeed communities with Scottish place names range from Inverness to Dundee, Bannockburn to Midlothian. The following are brief sketches of some of the more prominent Scottish American communities in northern Illinois.

ARGYLE

Most of the Scots who settled in Argyle in northern Illinois came from Argyllshire. There were various reasons for the Argyllshire Scots to emigrate, but poor crops and high rents were among the most pressing ones.

Some called the area Scotch Grove or simply the "Scotch" community. The heart of the community was the Willow Creek Scotch Presbyterian Church in Argyle.

The early pioneers came from Kintyre, Argyllshire, in southwestern Scotland. The first to leave the Kintyre peninsula were John and George Armour and their cousin James Armour, who came to Ottawa, Illinois, in 1834. They were not farmers; rather they were tradespeople or mechanics. James Armour, a shoemaker by trade who was living in Ottawa, began looking what is now Argyle, Illinois. He claimed some prairie land that was located on Willow Creek on the Boone and Winnebago County lines, which would eventually be called Scotch Grove.

James Armour eventually gave up his claim to his cousins, John and George. In turn they built a log cabin on the claim site, north and west of the grove. Eventually the Armours would return to Ottawa. Years later, though, George Armour became a very wealthy man as a merchant. He contributed hundreds of dollars to the building of the Willow Creek Church.

John Greenlee, however, is considered the true founder of Argyle since Greenlee and his family became the first Scots to permanently settle in the area. A bust of Greenlee is located in the Willow Creek Church. Their early years were difficult, threatened, as they were, by packs of wild wolves and troubled by a lack of food. Gradually, though, they were joined by more and more Scots so that by 1844 there were more than fifty-one charter members of the Willow Creek Presbyterian Church. The church also served as a school.

Greenlee was born August 16, 1791, at Southend, Argyllshire, Scotland, and died at Belvidere, Illinois, in 1882 (Harvey 1924, 15). The

SCOTTISH PLACE NAMES AND SITES IN ILLINOIS

A rectangle indicates a Scottish connection.

Most places were either founded by Scots or Scottish Americans or were named after sites in Scotland. Several sites, though, require further explanation.

Monmouth College in Monmouth was founded by Scots; Onarga was the former site of Allan Pinkerton's home; Prairie du Rocher was the site of John Law's Company of the West; Virgil was the site of John Regan's homestead, circa 1840s.

Greenlees emigrated to America in 1836 and settled in Ottawa. John Greenlee was the uncle of the Armour boys. Greenlee and John Armour then built a log cabin on the north side of the grove that summer, before returning to Ottawa in the winter. In the winter of 1836 Greenlee worked as a stonemason on the Illinois and Michigan Canal at Ottawa (30). The following spring the Greenlees returned to the cabin, and by the summer Greenlee was ready to claim his own piece of land.

The little community was growing. By 1841 fifteen families from Scotland had settled in the vicinity of the original Armour family homestead: George Picken, Robert Howie, Andrew Giffen, Alexander Macdonald, William Ferguson, James Picken, John Andrew, Alexander Reid, Robert Armour, Samuel Howie, William Harvey, John McEachran, John Picken, Gavin Ralston, and David Ralston (Harrison 1995, 8). The Ralstons owned the land where the present-day village of Caledonia–a few miles east of Argyle–now stands (Harvey 1924, 36), and it was Gavin Ralston who gave the village its name (90). Ralston Brothers built its grain elevator in Caledonia in 1880 (91).

In 1842 a log school house was built on Robert Howie's farm, south and west of where the Willow Creek Church now stands. The building was used for a day school, Sunday school, and church service for a number of years. It was here that the Willow Creek Church was organized in December 1844 by the Reverend Norton with fifty-one members (Harvey 1924, 38, 53; Harrison 1995, 9). The first elders of the church were Greenlee, Daniel Smith, and James Montgomery (Harvey 1924, 55). The church was built in 1849. It had walnut pews, and at the west end, on an elevated platform, stood the enclosed pulpit. In 1858 a frame addition was erected.

Caledonia Church, Caledonia (above, left)

Willow Creek Church, Argyle (above, right)

Years later, the Reverend Matthew Howie described the interior of the church, capturing its somber mood and insular quality:

> *It had walnut pews with doors to them, so that when all the family got in they latched the door and shut out all intruders. At the west, on an elevated platform, was an enclosed box pulpit, also with doors, so that when the preacher got inside he was secure against all inquisitive eyes and could take a pinch of snuff and curl his hair or adjust his white necktie, without any one being the wiser for it.*
>
> *Just in front of the pulpit on a less elevated platform stood the presenter, George Greenlee, who led the singing in Rouse's version of the Psalms. . . . No instruments were used, but he use a tuning fork to get the pitch and catch the mysterious spirit of the hymn. (Harrison 1995, 11)*

By 1858 the community had increased so much that the church could not hold the congregation. A frame building was added and served the town for twenty years until the current building was dedicated on February 7, 1878 (Harvey 1924, 60). In 1859 the Scottish Cemetery at Willow Creek was organized.

Scottish preachers served the Willow Creek Church community off and on over the years. The Reverend Thomas Baxter, a crowd-pleasing Scottish-born minister, was pastor from 1929 to 1936.

In 1914 the church steeple blew down during a bad storm. It was not replaced for many years. On November 8, 1936, John W. Thompson presented his play *The Builders* in celebration of the 100th anniversary of the founding of the "Scotch" settlement. Many in the cast were descendants of the early pioneers (Harrison 1995, 25).

Today Argyle is a prosperous and close-knit community. Scottish street names recall its past. Adjacent is the sleepy village of Caledonia. The focal point is the Caledonia Congregational Church, which was built in 1894 (Harvey 1924, 92).

BRAIDWOOD

The town of Braidwood was named by John H. Daniels in honor of James Braidwood, a civil engineer and coal mine operator, who was born in Everton, Scotland, in 1831 and died in Braidwood in 1879 at the age of forty-seven (Donna 1957, 323). In 1865 Braidwood built the first miners' home on the north side of what is now Main Street near the intersection with School (97, 323). James Braidwood, Jr., was the first person to be buried in Braidwood's Protestant Cemetery (277).

Coal miners from Pennsylvania and such countries as Scotland, England, Wales, Canada, Belgium, France, Italy, Germany, Austria, Poland, and Bohemia settled in Braidwood (10). In 1898 Illinois could claim 889 mines in fifty-two counties that employed almost 40,000 workers. Increasingly the United Mine Workers union

Street signs, Argyle (above)

played an important role. Its original membership consisted largely of Scots, Welsh, Irish, and English immigrants and their descendants (Howard 1972, 411). At that time Braidwood, a one-industry town, had a population of 15,000. John H. Walker was a native Scot who organized a miners' local in Grundy County and emerged as one of the Illinois' mining community's most forceful leaders (412).

A report from 1881 in the *Chicago Tribune* described the "black and grimy" conditions that these immigrants worked under. It further stated that they spoke "with a peculiar accent of their own" and then went on to contain a poor rendition of a Scottish accent, "Na, na, mon—we ha no wish fur any ther work, and we could na live at a' wi out our black diamonds" (Keiser 1977, 62).

William H. Steen, a native of Renfrewshire, Scotland, was an alderman, city clerk, city attorney, and one-time mayor of Braidwood. In 1894 he was elected a member of the Illinois legislature, serving two terms. Four years later he was appointed postmaster of Braidwood by President William McKinley. Steen worked in the coal mines of his native Ayrshire as a young child. He then moved to Kilmarnock for several years until, at the age of sixteen, he emigrated to America. He settled in Pennsylvania and Ohio before moving to Braidwood in 1870. He was a miner there until 1883, when he entered the insurance and real estate business. In 1901 Steen was chosen as chieftain of the Royal Scottish Clans at their twenty-fifth biennial convention. He was also a founding member of the First Presbyterian Church. He died in 1930.

Many Scots played prominent roles in the city's history. James Crichton, who was mayor from 1918 to 1939, served the longest term as the city's chief executive (Donna 1957, 50). Even the names of the mines reeked of old Scotia, such as the Thistle Mine and Skinner's Slope Mine (69). Other prominent Braidwood families of Scots descent were the Barrs, the Skinners, the Pattersons, the Bains, the Bowies, the Braydens, the Barrowmans, and the Walkers. Robert Barrowman was the goalkeeper of the Braidwood World's Champion Soccer Football Team of 1893–94 at the World's Columbian Exposition (137, 244). Additional Scottish members of the team included John Stewart, Dick Walker, Chuck Walker, and Willie Kelso (243). Allan Cameron, of the Braidwood team, won first prize at the fair for the longest kick of a football, then a world record (244). The 1894 team consisted of ten Scots and one Belgian: Robert Barrowman, James Cameron, A. Walker, John Cunningham, Alex Cameron, George Littlejohn, A. Young, David Young, J. Walker, and George Cunningham (245).

The Braidwood Soccer Football Club was formed in 1890. It didn't take long before it joined the Chicago Area Football League

Entering Caledonia, Illinois (above)

and started winning several championships (244). Not surprisingly, the Braidwood players were mostly miners.

A major landmark of the area is the Diamond Monument, which was erected by the United Mine Workers' Union and dedicated on September 5, 1898, in memory of the victims of Braidwood's greatest mining disaster (79). It was not until Labor Day 1926, however, that a bronze plaque listing the victim's names was completed (80). Of the seventy-four known victims, fifteen were Scots. Most were young men in their twenties and thirties although two, Hugh Nesbit at sixteen and Robert Stewart at fourteen, were mere teenagers (81).

In 1910 a historic event took place in nearby Coal City. On October 1, 1910, hundreds of people watched William E. Somerville, the mayor of Coal City, attempt to fly a biplane. The craft was forty-eight feet in length and was "superb in workmanship," according to the *Kankakee Daily Republican*. The frame was made of ash and hemlock; each joint was set with an aluminum socket. The paper indicated that Somerville had spent two years studying airplanes and had "probably the most complete library of any who soar the air."

Despite Somerville's knowledge and apparent expertise, the first flight failed—an axel broke on one of the wheels—but Somerville vowed to try again as soon as repairs were made.

The following year he received patents for his designs and then resigned from his job with the Macomber Whyte Company wire rope factory. He leased a large tract of land and built a hangar and workshop. He then took in partners and formed the Illinois Aero Construction Company. Within a few months they had built a "load-carrying tractor biplane" that was operated by an eighty-horsepower engine and able to carry two passengers. According to the paper, Somerville was considered "the first and only mayor in the United States to build and fly a plane."

Somerville was born at Harthill in

Preparing for flight, August 4, 1912 in Coal City (above)

Lanarkshire, Scotland, on April 12, 1879. He was trained as an electrician and marine engineer. He came to the United States in 1892. Three years later he attended the funeral of his brother in Coal City. While there, he accepted an offer to become the electrical engineer of the town. In 1900 Somerville became superintendent of the Macomber Company and was also elected mayor.

In 1908 Somerville began experimenting with scale model airplanes. Within two years he made a biplane, which contained a new feature that used wing warping. The ends of the wings were upturned to offer greater stability in flight. Somerville would later design and fly four types of aircraft.

DUNDEE

Dundee was named in honor of the hometown of a young Scots millworker, Alexander Gardiner.

Most of the Scots who came to Dundee were Lowlanders. Some were employed as spinners and weavers in their native land but forced to emigrate when the new technology made them obsolete (Dupre 1985, 79). Quite a few came from fairly well-off families, and many accumulated lucrative land holdings within a few years of their arrival. Among the early Scots settlers were the McCullochs, Crichtons, Todds, Binnies, Duffs, McNeils, Archibalds, Howies, and Weirs (81–82) The Todd brothers—Hugh, Robert, and James—worked for several months on the Illinois and Michigan Canal in 1837 before moving west to Dundee. Other Scots families included the Forrests, Griffiths, Campbells, McKendricks, Allisons, Rankins, Thompsons, Hodgesses, and Hills (83).

But no one was as famous as the Pinkertons.

Allan Pinkerton was the town's first cooper—that is, barrelmaker—as well as credited as the person who established the U.S. Secret Service and founded the Pinkerton national detective agency.

Pinkerton came to Dundee in 1843, after living in Chicago for one year. On Third Street, just off Main Street, he opened his first cooper shop. He would later recall the humble times of his early years:

> *The town itself did not contain probably over three hundred inhabitants all told, the business portion only consisting of a few country stores, a post office, a blacksmith shop or two, a mill, and two small taverns able to accommodate a few travelers at a time. . . .*
>
> *There was then one rough bridge across the river, built of oaken beams and rude planks, in a cheap, common fashion; and at either end of this were clustered, each side of the street, all the stores and shops of the place, save one. That shop was my own; for there I both lived and labored, the "Only and Original Cooper of Dundee."*
>
> *The shop of mine was the farthest of any from the business center of the village, and stood just back of, and facing, the main highway, upon the crest of a fine hill, about three hundred yards distant from the bridge. After the manner of the Scottish custom it was both my home and my shop.* (Dupre 1985, 83–84)

The Scots of Dundee were abolitionists, and Pinkerton, as the community's leader, was perhaps the most avid. There are stories of a houseful of African Americans in Pinkerton's little shop who were learning the cooper trade (84).

In 1935 Dundee celebrated its centennial with a parade and day-long festivities. Part of the activities included a three-act play entitled *The Canny Cooper,* based on the life and times of Allan Pinkerton (333).

Early Scots churchgoers in Dundee wore the accustomed top hats and dressed in black. The women brought with them the dresses that they had made in Scotland. The first Scottish emigrant in the community to join the already settled colony of Hoosiers and New Englanders was Alexander Dempster (77). Born in Keith, near Aberdeen, in 1811, Dempster contributed a series of sketches to the *Dundee Record.* His livelihood in his adopted land was farming.

INVERNESS STREET NAMES

Abbotsford Drive
Aberdeen Lane
Ayrshire Lane
Balmoral Circle
Bannockburn
Barra Lane
Berwick
Blair Lane
Bonny Lane
Bonny Glen Gates
Braeburn Road
Brodick Lane
Cawdor Lane
Cheviot Drive
Common Ridings Way
Craigie Lane
Crichton Lane
Direlton Lane
Drummond Court
Dumfries Court
Dunbar Road
Dunbarton Drive
Dundee Road
Edinburgh Court
Fife Court
Firth Road
Gaelic Court
Galloway Circle Drive
Glamis Lane
Glen Eagles Court
Glenmore Court
Grayfriars Lane
Great Glen Court
Guthrie Court
Heather Lane
Highland Road
Inverray Road
Inverway Road
Kelso Glen
Kirkwall Court
Knox Court
Lamond Drive
Lanark
Lauder Lane
Loch Lomond Drive
Lochleven Lane
Macalpin Circle
Muirfield Court
Prestwick Drive
Rob Roy Court
Rosslyn Lane
Selkirk
Shetland Road
Skye Lane
St. Andrews Lane
Stonehaven
Summer Isle Lane
Tweed Road

He also apparently had quite a voice. His renditions of the songs and poetry of Robert Burns were much in demand (78).

Scottish connections are still evident in Dundee. In 1968 a marker was placed at the site of the Pinkerton cooper shop at Third Street and West Main Street in West Dundee. A dedication ceremony was held and the Dundee Scots Marching Band participated in the festivities. (The Dundee Scots had changed their name from the Dundee High School Marching Band.) Two years later they adopted kilts as their official uniform and began to receive recognition as a national championship band. They performed at presidential inaugurations and at sporting events, and, in 1976, they even marched in the Macy's parade in New York City (288–89).

In 1984, when Dundee High School closed, the Dundee Scots merged with the Crown Imperials from Crown High School to form the Imperial Scots. To symbolize the coming together of the two schools, a mock wedding was held. A truck from each band decorated as the "bride and groom" paraded down Main Street as part of the Dundee Days parade (289).

Even the local golf club has a Scottish name. The Bonnie Dundee Golf Course and Country Club in East Dundee was established in 1924. And on the main street of town, visitors and residents alike can quench their thirst at the Scots Inn.

ELGIN

James T. Gifford, an early pioneer of Scots descent from central New York and considered the city's founder, built his log cabin in 1835. Gifford reportedly chose Elgin not after the Scottish town of the same name but after a favorite Scottish hymn (Alft 1980, 10). As early as 1842 Gifford laid out the town's design. Gifford and his brother Hezekiah came to the settlement but for altogether different purposes: Hezekiah to establish a farm and James to build a town along the Fox River. Elgin was chosen

SELECT SCOTTISH SITES IN CHICAGO AREA

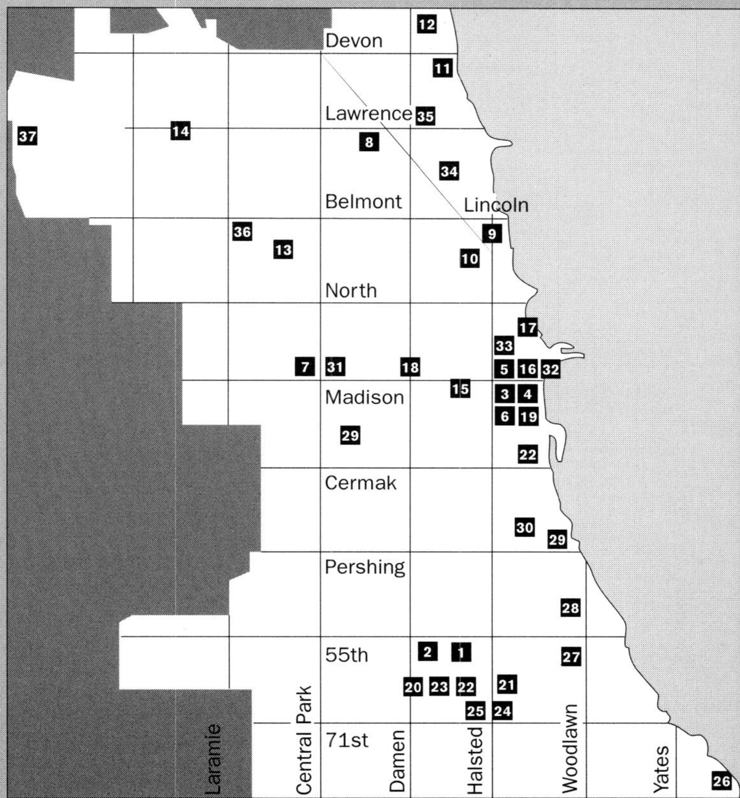

Businesses

1. O'Gara and Wilson Bookshop, 1131 E. 57th St.
2. John Crear Library, University of Chicago, 5730 S. Ellis
3. former site of British-American Co., Pontiac Building
4. Encyclopaedia Britannica, 310 S. Michigan
5. Carson, Pirie, Scott & Co., State and Madison
6. Ernst and Young, 233 S. Wacker
7. former site of Robert Burns Hospital, 3807 W. Washington
8. Kelmscott Gallery, Lincoln and Wilson
9. Duke of Perth, Clark near Diversey
10. Deacon Brodie's, Lincoln, Fullerton and Halsted
11. St. Andrew's Inn, 5938 N. Broadway'
12. Charles H. Kerr & Co., 1740 W. Greenleaf
13. Stewart Tea Co., 4110 W. Wrightwood
14. Gaelic Imports, Lawrence and Austin

Churches, Halls, Organizations and Societies

15. former site of Scotch Presbyterian Church, Adams and Sangamon
16. former site of Masonic Temple, 32 W. Randolph
17. Fourth Presbyterian Church, Michigan and Chestnut
18. former site of St. Andrew's Church, Washington and Robey (Damen), c. 1899
19. Second Presbyterian Church, 1936 S. Michigan
20. former site of Drexel Park Presbyterian Church, 64th and Marshfield
21. former site of Englewood Presbyterian Church, 64th and Yale
22. former site of South Side Masonic Temple, 64th and Green
23. former site of Prospect Hall, 64th and Ashland
24. Englewood Masonic Temple, 68th and Yale
25. Anderson Hall, 69th and Halsted

Historic Sites

26. Donald Culross Peattie house, 7660 South Shore
27. Oak Woods Cemetery, 1035 E. 67th
28. Dr. John McGill house, 4938 S. Drexel
29. Stephen A. Douglas Monument, E. 35th
30. former site of Camp Douglas
31. Burns Monument, Garfield Park
32. Kinzie plaque, near Michigan and Wacker
33. former site of Lake House, between Rush and Kinzie
34. Graceland Cemetery, Irving Park and Clark
35. Rosehill Cemetery, 5800 N. Ravenswood
36. Laughlin Falconer house, 4830 W. Wellington
37. Alexander Robinson family burial site, Lawrence and East River

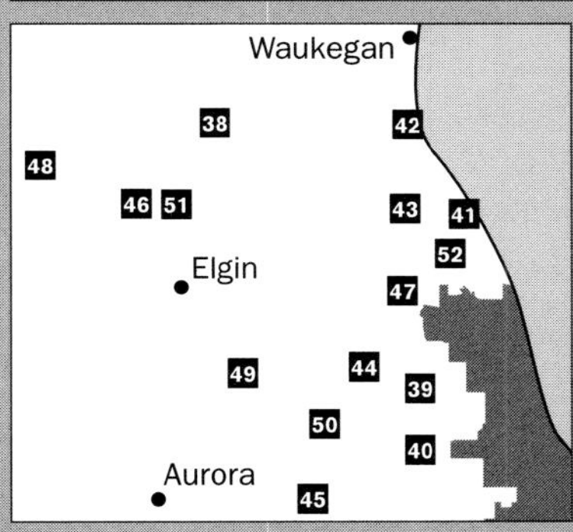

Businesses

38. *The Highlander,* Barrington
39. Scottish Home, North Riverside
40. Scottish Modern Enterprises, Summit

Historic Sites

41. former site of "Craigie Lea," Glencoe, Archibald MacLeish's childhood home
42. Sylvester Lind house, Lake Forest
43. Kennicott house, "The Grove," Glenview
44. Charles H. Kerr house, Glen Ellyn
45. Naper Settlement, Naperville
46. Allan Pinkerton house plaque, West Dundee

Golf and Country Clubs

47. Glen View Club, Golf
48. Rob Roy Golf Course, Prospect Heights
49. St. Andrew's Country Club, West Chicago
50. Chicago Golf Club, Wheaton
51. Bonnie Dundee Golf Course, East Dundee
52. Tam-O-Shanter Golf Course, Niles

because it was situated between the lead mines of Galena and the growing frontier town of Chicago (6). Gifford's cabin later served as the town's first school, first church, and first post office.

There are several sites associated with Gifford in modern-day Elgin. There's a Gifford Park, a plaque, a portrait of Gifford in the Elgin Area Historical Society Museum, and the Stone Cottage. The Stone Cottage at 363–65 Prairie was Gifford's third home in Elgin. Gifford died soon after the house was completed. His widow, daughter, and son-in-law lived on the premises for many years. In 1903 it was renovated, and years later, in 1980, the house was placed on the National Register of Historic Places (7).

Much of Elgin's earlier wealth was a result of the tremendous success of the Elgin National Watch Company. In 1891 the firm employed 3,000 people, turning out 60 percent of all the fine jewelry produced in the United States (1). In the 1880s the city's elite hired domestic servants, many of whom were German or Scandinavian immigrants (5).

Elgin's first foreign-born mayor, David F. Barclay, was also a Scot. The homes at 363 and 359 Park Street were built for his sons (34).

The Elgin Historical Society Museum has a woodcut of the James T. Gifford cabin by Dean Chipman, a watercolor of the cabin by C. A. Reber, as well as portraits of James T. and Laura Gifford by artist Sheldon Peck.

ELMIRA

The tiny community of Elmira in central Illinois was settled in 1838 by both Lowland and Highland Scots. Early Scottish settlers included the Turnbulls, Olivers, Armstrongs, McLennans, Buchanans, and others. The Gaelic-speaking Highlanders in particular soon needed the services of a preacher. Because it was so difficult to find a Gaelic-speaking minister, the families were compelled to apply to the Synod of the Presbyterian Church of Canada. Reverend Duncan McDermid served the congregation for a short time. During the next few years a succession of Canadian ministers came to the little community, including Reverends Adam McKay and Lochlin Cameron. In 1868 another Canadian, Reverend Alexander McKay, became the church's first permanent pastor.

The first services of the Gaelic church were held in the homes of the members or in the Methodist Episcopal Church until 1866. In July 1868 the Knox Gaelic Church was established. In the 1880s, the church was disbanded and eventually destroyed. Over the years, Elmira saw numerous Presbyterian churches come and go until 1929, when the two remaining churches, the United Presbyterian and the Presbyterian, joined together.

INVERNESS

Although the first settler was George Ela in 1836, Arthur T. McIntosh was the original developer of Inverness. McIntosh was a resident of Kenilworth, but he saw much potential in the Inverness area. In 1926 he bought a farmhouse and some 1,500 acres of farmland. He continued to purchase additional land and named the community Inverness after his ancestral home in Scotland. Some even felt that this area of Illinois bore a striking similarity to the Inverness area of Scotland.

McIntosh had a vision of creating a distinctive community that would be affordable for young married couples. House exteriors and the placement of homes had to be approved by the McIntosh Company.

In 1962 Inverness was incorporated as a village. New developments were created with such Scottish-sounding names as Muirfield I, Bonny Glen, Cheviot Hills, Shetland Hills, and Lauder Hills. Eventually homes became bigger and more expensive while still keeping the traditional flavor of the area intact.

ZION

Zion, Illinois, was the site of a failed religious utopian community founded by a fanatical Scot named John Alexander Dowie. At the age of thirteen, Dowie emigrated with his father from Scotland to Australia. Trained in Edinburgh in the Congregationalist ministry, he returned to Australia to establish a ministry in Adelaide. An epidemic outbreak that killed most of his congregation persuaded him to consider faith healing. He became determined to try to establish a ministry elsewhere, though, and so emigrated to the United States, settling in Chicago. Dowie gained public attention when he opened a ministry near the grounds of the World's Columbian Exposition in 1893. So successful was he that he rented large halls at such places as the mammoth Central Music Hall and the Auditorium for his mass meetings. His headquarters were located at Twelfth Street and Michigan Avenue (Duis and Holt 1979, 116).

The always cynical Chicago press was suspicious of Dowie and his motives, calling him a hoax. The public, too, was beginning to have doubts. More than a hundred lawsuits were filed against him in 1895 alone, say Duis and Holt, and he was subject to attacks by "howling mobs." Weary of the harassment, Dowie began to scout for land in order to establish and control his own city.

Shiloh House, Zion (above)

Dowie bought a 6,500-acre site just north of Waukegan and established a bank. Buyers purchased long-term leases rather than actually buying land. Dowie's dream was to establish the spiritual equivalent of the Pullman community on Chicago's South Side (118). Ultimately he was able to build a 6,000-seat wooden hall called Shiloh Temple, a 350-room hotel, a milling and baking plant, a lace factory, a school, and a mansion for himself. In the meantime, though, Dowie continued to preach in Chicago, thus maintaining close ties with the city.

Dowie proclaimed himself "Grand Overseer" of his thriving spiritual kingdom. He ruled absolutely. He would brook no dissent. Those who dared to differ were expelled from town and lost their investment (ibid). Eventually, though, Dowie began to slowly lose control. Restricted finances compelled him to allow private companies into town while in 1905 failing health forced him to turn the future of the town to one of his most trusted followers, Wilbur Glenn Voliva. Voliva soon betrayed Dowie, however, informing the townspeople not only about Dowie's financial difficulties but also about his profligate lifestyle—including the use of his expensive mansion. He even discussed Dowie's alleged marital infidelity (119). All this was too much for the residents to take. They rejected the once indestructible leader with a chorus of boos and hisses. Dowie, already weak from a stroke and now suffering a broken heart, died on March 9, 1907.

Before Dowie's death, the town had already fallen into bankruptcy. Within a few years, though, Voliva had managed to "buy back" almost everything that had been lost and returned to the autocratic rule of the Dowie years. Stringent "blue laws" were more strictly enforced. But by 1933 Zion had again ended up in bankruptcy court, and Voliva lost control of the local government. He died in 1942 (ibid).

Yet the presence of John Alexander Dowie continues to be felt in Zion. There's a street named after him, John Alexander Dowie Memorial Drive, that circles Shiloh Park, and the city's religious history is still very much alive. Since 1934 the community has sponsored the annual Zion Passion Play each spring.

Dowie was an avid book collector. In April 1910 the Chicago firm of A. C. McClurg and Company published a catalog of books from his personal library. Among the books of Scottish interest in his collection were Robert Burns's *The Land of Burns,* John Lorne Campbell's *Popular Tales of the West Highlands,* Robert Chambers's *A Biographical Dictionary of Eminent Scotsmen,* Andrew Lang's *The History of Scotland,* R. R. McIan's *The Clans of the Scottish Highlands,* a complete set of the *Edinburgh Review,* and Dowie's own *The Coming City,* a fortnightly newspaper that he published from June 27, 1900, to June 23, 1901.

OTHER COMMUNITIES WITH SCOTTISH CONNECTIONS

KENILWORTH

In 1889 businessman and philanthropist Joseph Sears purchased a tract of land near Lake Michigan with the purpose of building a model community that would combine the best of city and country living. When the population of the little community reached 300 in 1896, it was incorporated. The inspiration for the village came from Sir Walter Scott's romantic novel *Kenilworth.* The street names, too, were drawn from Scott's fictionalized world (Ebner 1988, 64–67).

LAKE FOREST

Lake Forest is an affluent community located along Chicago's North Shore. A number of the town's mansions have Scottish-sounding names, such as Cyrus McCormick III's "Argyllshire" or insurance brokerage president Donald R. McLennan's "Sturnoway." On a much humbler level is the Alex Robertson House, a Queen Anne–style dwelling on Oakwood Avenue. Robertson was a Scottish immigrant.

SLEEPY HOLLOW

Sleepy Hollow was named after Washington Irving's children's story *The Legend of Sleepy Hollow.* Floyd T. Falese, a member of Carpentersville's Italian American community, wanted a name that had strong romantic associations and was charming and historically significant at the same time. Hence, Sleepy Hollow seemed the perfect choice. Irving was the son of an Orcadian emigrant who settled in New York. The village of Sleepy Hollow was incorporated in 1958 (Dupre 1985, 171).

NAPERVILLE

Naperville was named after Joseph Naper, a pioneer in northern Illinois who was of Scots descent. In early histories his name often appears as "Napier," a more common Scottish spelling (MacMillan 1919, 52). Naper and his brothers arrived in Chicago in 1831 and claimed land along the banks of the DuPage River, establishing a settlement at what is now Naperville. He served as a captain during the Black Hawk War.

LANARK

Lanark is a pleasant community in western Illinois. It began life as a railroad town, and several of the investors who provided financial support for the Chicago-Milwaukee Railroad came from Lanark, Scotland, and named their new home after the land of their birth. Originally it was called Glasgow. Today Lanark is largely a farming community with a population of about 2,400.

A Scottish landmark of sorts in Lanark is the Standish Bed and Breakfast at 540 Carroll Street. The building was erected in 1882 by Joseph Laird, the son of one of the original Scottish investors. According to Norman Standish, a direct descendant of Captain Myles Standish, who came to

America on the *Mayflower,* Laird built it for a woman he had planned to marry in Scotland. However, she rejected his offer, and he lived out his life in the eleven-room house by himself.

Other Scottish place names in the Chicago area include the bedroom suburb of Bannockburn and south suburban Midlothian. Some say Glencoe, the affluent North Shore suburb, is named after Glencoe, Scotland. Scattered throughout the state are Glasgow, Edinburg, Gillespie, Dunfermline, Dundas, Berwick, and Cameron. There's even a little community in central Illinois bearing the name of Scotland.

EPILOGUE

Saint Andrew's Day Greeting

I have felt the tugging of those invisible fingers and heard the whispering of those voices. . . .

For I have seen the hills of Scotland moist with mist; I have seen the sheep on the hills and the heather in bloom; have heard the skirling of the pipes down the glen and the gurgling of the burn over the rocks . . . I have seen pictures that will never fade, and sounds that will never die away.

I have wanted to hear again the gentle low voices of the women and the music of the Gaelic tongue . . . "Guid save us a' . . ."; to smell the delicate fragrance of bluebells in the spring; to hear the mavis sing . . . and the lark.

I have wanted to see the long twilights, to look out over the waters of the Firth, and be grateful to God that there was still more of Scotland beyond.

Author Unknown

APPENDIX

THE ILLINOIS SAINT ANDREW SOCIETY PRESIDENTS

1845	George Steel
1846	Alexander Brand
1847	James Michie
1848	Alexander Brand
1849	George Steel
1850–51	Alexander Brand
1852	George Anderson
1853	John McGlashen
1854	John H. Kedzie
1855–56	John Alston
1857	Robert Hervey
1858	Andrew Harvie
1859	John R. Valentine
1860	Dugald Stewart
1861	Robert Hervey
1862	Daniel Cameron
1863	William James
1864	Robert Hervey
1865	William Stewart
1866	Hugh Macalister
1867	John Macalister
1868	Robert Hervey
1869–71	John McArthur
1872	Robert Clark
1873–74	Robert Hervey
1875–76	Godfrey Macdonald
1877–78	Daniel R. Cameron
1879–81	Alexander Kirkland
1882	R. Biddle Roberts
1883–84	Andrew Wallace
1885–86	Robert Clark
1887–88	Egbert Jamieson
1889–90	Andrew Carr Cameron
1891–92	John Alston
1893–95	John J. Badenoch
1896–97	William Gardner
1898–1900	Donald L. Morrill
1901–5	Walter Scott Bogle
1906–7	Thomas C. MacMillan
1908	John C. Hunter
1909–11	John Williamson
1912	John Crerar
1913–15	Dr. John A. McGill
1916	James B. Forgan, Sr.
1917–18	Joseph Cormack
1919–21	Dr. John A. McGill
1922–24	Dr. William Ferguson Dickson
1925	James R. Glass
1926–28	Robert Black
1929–30	William Lister
1931	John A. Williamson
1932–33	Gilbert Alexander
1934	William Cameron
1935	John T. Cunningham
1936–40	James Berwick Forgan, Jr.
1941–43	Alexander Shennan, O.B.E.
1944	William F. G. Ross
1945–47	Robert Black
1948–49	George C. Buik
1950	Don M. Compton
1951–53	John C. Clasper
1954	John Henry Hutchinson
1955–56	Samuel J. Smith
1957	Robert Crawford
1958–59	John Henry Hutchinson
1960–62	Edmund Leavenworth McGibbon
1963–65	Hughston McBain
1966–69	Angus John Ray
1970–72	Angus Macdonald
1973–74	Dr. James Currie McLeod
1975–76	Frank Clark Drysdale
1977–78	Robert Lewis William Graham
1979	Harvey Huston
1979–80	James C. Thomson
1981–82	David Lee Fargo
1983	Reverend James Wayland McGlathery
1984–85	Robert Bruce Graham
1986–87	Donald Alastair Gillies
1988–89	Robert James Black
1990–91	Nancy LeNoble Strolle
1992–94	Edward C. Rorison
1995–96	Alexander D. Kerr, Jr.

EYEWITNESS ACCOUNT OF THE GREAT FIRE OF 1871

The following eyewitness account of the Great Fire of 1871 by a Society member was contained in the Society's annual report of 1871:

The telegraph has already told to the world the story of the terrible fire in Chicago. "Send us food for the suffering, our city is in ashes" is the appeal of the Mayor and his brief description of the scene. To that cry for help, tremendous force is given by the statement of a few of the details of the great calamity. At present, we have no trustworthy estimate of the total value of the property destroyed or of the lives lost. One report states that the total loss can scarcely fall below one hundred fifty million dollars, and it is believed that over one hundred thousand persons have been rendered homeless and destitute by the calamity. Over an area four miles long and one mile wide, the fire swept, reducing all the finest public buildings in the city, the churches, hotels, theaters, banks, railroad depots, newspaper and telegraph offices, to ashes. For a long time it seems as if there was no chance of saving anything within the city limits, as the wind, after blowing the flames in one direction, turned and carried the destroying element in another. Fortunately, as we learned by the latest accounts on hand, on Monday evening, October 9, the wind lulled, and at three o'clock on Tuesday morning, the rain, so fervently prayed for, came. It did not rain long, but the roofs of houses and the ground have been wet, so that now it is possible to have fires and cook food for the multitudes.

From the numerous dispatches received, it appears that there were two fires. The first broke out in the western division of the city and consumed four blocks before it was extinguished. On Saturday night, October 8th, about ten o'clock, another fire commenced not far from the ruins left by the former, and the flames, urged by a strong south-west wind, and fed by blocks of wooden buildings and miles of wooden streets, rushed with irresistible fury over the river, through the very heart of the city, leaped the Chicago river a second time, and, with widening current, swept everything before them, until their course was stayed by the waters of Lake Michigan. Then the wind changed to the north, and the southern portion of the city was threatened with destruction. During the whole of Saturday night, all day Monday, and Monday night, the fire continued to burn, and it was only on Tuesday morning that its progress was stayed. Among the valuable buildings, reduced to ashes, we may mention the Court-House, Post-office, Exchange Hall, Tremont House, Sherman House, Bigelow Hotel, Palmer House, Pacific Hotel, all the wholesale stores in the city, and all the largest retail stores, every newspaper office, every theater, the six largest elevators, the immense depots of the Michigan Southern and of the Illinois Central Railroads (both the passenger and freight depots of the latter), more than a score of churches, and much of the shipping in the river was destroyed. Men who were millionaires are penniless today; but more terrible than all is the awful certainty that many human beings have perished in the flames—How many, no one can tell. Perhaps, no one will ever be able to tell? But it is known that some have perished, and there is only a heart sickening fear that the victims of the fiery monster may be counted by the scores. Hundreds of horses and cows have been burned in stables, and on the north side, numbers of animals, though released from confinement, were so bewildered and confused by the sea of fire which surrounded them, that they rushed wildly to and fro, uttering cries of fright and pain, until scorched and killed. Any attempt at a description of the scenes of this appalling calamity would be idle. The simple facts that the once great city of Chicago is destroyed, that hundreds of millions of active capital have vanished, and that nearly one-third of Chicago's inhabitants were houseless dependents, are enough.

Any attempt to embellish would be a mockery. Regarding the origin of the fire, on Sunday evening, there are various unreliable rumors. The flames spread very rapidly. The engines were waited for, and when they arrived, the firemen, stupefied by their exertion at the first fire, on Saturday night, worked slowly and clumsily. Their efforts were unavailing; the wind, from the southwest, blew a gale; rapidly the flames shot from house to house, and it was only after considerable delay that the firemen and city authorities perceived the magnitude of the calamity that threatened the city, and began to exert themselves. But the opportunity had been lost. The time when thorough organization could have blown up buildings, or prepared for the emergency, was neglected, and it was now a fight for life. A very few minutes sufficed to destroy the most elaborately built structure. The walls melted, and the very bricks were consumed. The wooden pavements took fire, making a continuous sheet of flame, two miles long by a mile wide. No human being could possibly survive many minutes. Block after block fell, and the red hot coals shot higher and higher, and spread further and further, until the north side of Lake street was a vast sheet of flame from the river to the lake, at one time, and so hemmed the people that it was expected that thousands must perish. Sherman,

Tremont, and other hotels, were emptied of their guests, and a remarkable sight presented itself in the hurrying of throngs with trucks, sacks or bags on their shoulders, fleeing amid flames for their lives.

This was the sight by night. One fireproof building, the Chicago Tribune building, seemed likely to escape, but by ten o'clock in the forenoon this remaining block was in ashes. Now was to be seen the most remarkable sight ever beheld in this or any country. There were from fifty to seventy-five thousand men, women, and children, fleeing by every available street and road to the southward and westward, attempting to save their clothing and their lives. Every available vehicle was brought into requisition for use, for which, enormous prices were paid, and the streets presented a sad sight—thousands of persons and horses inextricably commingled; poor people of all colors and shades, and of every nationality, from Europe, China, and Africa, mad with excitement, struggling with each other to get away. During Monday, a renewal of the fires, on the west side, was looked for, and a change of five degrees in the direction of the wind, at any time, would have led to that result. There would have been no refuge in the city for any. Everybody had their clothing packed, ready to start for the prairie at any moment, but God averted this last possible addition to the disaster.

Among the numerous remarkable incidents connected with the disaster, we may notice a protracted meeting on Monday night, held in the First Congregational Church, on West Washington Street, at which, measures were concerted to protect what property was left, and to provide for the homeless. On that night, fifteen hundred citizens were sworn in as an extra police force, and the Secretary of War, authorized General Sheridan to employ all the available troops for guard, and issued an order for one hundred thousand rations. Five hundred soldiers were placed on duty. This precaution was necessary, for, remarkable as it may seem, there were fiends who still sought to extend the disaster. Two men, caught in the act of firing houses on the west side, were arrested, and immediately hung to lamp-posts—one on Twelfth street, near the river, and the other, three miles away, on Clybourne avenue, north side. This summary action checked the thieves and murderers.

The condition of the population, at the date of our last reports, were deplorable. There were a thousand people camped about the artisan well, four miles out, and perhaps, as many more at the lake, and on Fullerton and Victor avenues, near the prairies. The people were being fed in the remaining churches, schoolhouses, in sheds, and by the roadside. It was cold and chilly, causing great suffering, but instead of this being welcome, the people were praying, earnestly for more rain, so fearful were they of a continuance of the flames. This was the situation at noon, on Tuesday.

Measures for the relief of the sufferers have been already taken in all the large cities. On Monday and Tuesday, aid in men to extinguish the flames, and in food and clothing to relieve the destitute, were hurried forward by all the railways and steamboats running to Chicago. On Monday, calls were issued in a number of the largest cities for relief meetings. In Cincinnati, an immense mass-meeting was held, and hundreds of thousands of dollars were subscribed. The Chamber of Commerce gave $5,000. Many leading firms gave $1,000 each. At night, a special train left Cincinnati with four carloads of provisions. Announcements were received in Chicago from all parts of the West and Southwest of liberal subscriptions of money and provisions. Trains, laden with fire engines and provisions, were sent from all points, with promises of more to follow. Wheeling, Columbus, Cleveland, Toledo, Detroit, Indianapolis, Terre Haute, Evansville, Memphis, and Nashville, as well as larger cities, contributed liberally. In St. Louis, $70,000 was raised in one hour. The Buffalo City Council authorized the issuance of $100,000 of city bonds for the immediate use of the Chicago sufferers. The officers and exhibitors at the International Industrial Exhibition raised ten thousand loaves of bread, to be forwarded at once for the relief of the sufferers. Owen's bakery, the largest in the city, was authorized by the city officials, to commence, without delay, and bake night and day, until further orders, for Chicago. The City Council of Elizabeth, N.J., voted an appropriation of $1,000. On Tuesday, the city of Brooklyn placed $100,000 at the disposal of the Mayor of Chicago. The New York Stock Exchange contributed $50,000, and the New York Underwriters' Agency made preparations to pay, immediately upon adjustment, all losses which they incurred by the fire. At noon, the New York Chamber of Commerce held a special meeting, and appointed a committee to collect funds for the relief of the sufferers, and to select the best method for distribution. Over $100,000 were subscribed at the meeting, and the officers of the Chamber were instructed to communicate by telegraph with the leading merchants of the principal cities in Great Britain, informing them of the extent of the calamity that had befallen Chicago, and asking for aid. The members of the New York Produce Exchange, of the Importers and Grocers Board of Trade, of the Cotton Exchange, and numerous public bodies, have been equally prompt and liberal. From the President of the United States, and the Governors of several of the States, throughout all classes and organizations of citizens, and from every city, town, and village in the country, offers of assistance and money are flowing towards Chicago, and it seems as if the most destructive fire recorded in history, will be followed by an outpouring of charitable contributions for the relief of the sufferers which will bear comparison with any previous display of charity in any age or country, will reflect honor on Christianity. In this work of charity, we believe that Scotsmen of America can do, is to take care that their countrymen, in Chicago, shall not suffer long from the late terrible disaster.

SCOTTISH STREET NAMES IN CHICAGO

ABERDEEN STREET. Named after Scotland's third largest city.

ARGYLE STREET. James A. Campbell, alderman and real estate speculator of Scottish descent named it in honor of Archibald Campbell, Marquis, First Duke of Argyll.

BALMORAL AVENUE. Balmoral Castle; named by John L. Cochran, a real estate developer of Scottish descent who came to Chicago from Philadelphia in 1881.

CAMPBELL PLACE. Named after Alderman James Campbell, who was born in Caledonia, New York, and moved to Chicago in 1862.

ELLEN STREET. Named after Ellen Marion Kinzie, the daughter of John Kinzie and Eleanor McKillip.

GLENROY AVENUE. Named for a valley in the northwest of Scotland.

IRVING PARK ROAD. Named after Washington Irving.

KEDZIE AVENUE. Named after John Hume Kedzie (1815–1903), an attorney who was born in Stamford, Connecticut, the son of Scottish immigrants who came to Chicago in 1847.

KENNETH AVENUE. Named after Kenneth MacAlpine, the first king of Scotland.

KENWOOD AVENUE. Dr. John A. Kennicott, the first settler of Kenwood, named his estate "Kenwood" in honor of his mother's birthplace in Scotland.

KINZIE STREET. Named after John Kinzie, of Scottish descent.

KIRKLAND AVENUE. Probably named after Scots-born Alexander Kirkland, commissioner of the Department of Public Buildings in 1879.

LIND AVENUE. Named after Sylvester Lind, a Scots carpenter who settled in Chicago in 1837 and later became mayor of Lake Forest in 1868–84.

MARION COURT. Named after Ellen Marion Kinzie.

MELROSE STREET. Named after Melrose Abbey, founded in 1136 in Melrose, Scotland, in the Border country.

MONTROSE AVENUE. Named after James Montrose (1612–50), famous Scots military leader.

NAPER AVENUE. Named after Captain Joseph Naper, the founder of Naperville.

ROBINSON STREET. Probably after Alexander Robinson, an early Chicago pioneer of Scots and Indian descent.

ST. CLAIR STREET. Named after General Arthur St. Clair, a Scottish-born soldier in the Revolutionary War and the first governor of the Northwest Territory.

(Source: Hayner and McNamee 1988)

REFERENCES

Invaluable information has been culled from the collection of the Illinois Saint Andrew Society. Of particular historical importance are the Margaret Baikie scrapbooks, which are also part of the Society's collection.

Album of Genealogy and Biography, Cook County, Ill. Chicago: La Salle Book Company, 1899.

Alft, E. C. *The Elgin Historic District.* Elgin, Ill.: Elgin Area Historical Society and Gifford Park Association, 1980.

Aman, Elizabeth. *The Scottish Americans.* The Peoples of North America series. New York: Chelsea House, 1991.

Anderson, Margaret. *My Thirty Years War: An Autobiography.* New York: Covici, Friede Publishers, 1930.

Angle, Paul M. "George Rogers Clark: Illinois and the American Revolution." *Chicago History* 4, no. 1 (Spring 1975): 4–13.

Bach, Ira J., and Mary Lackritz Gray. *A Guide to Chicago's Public Sculpture.* Chicago: University of Chicago Press, 1983.

Bailyn, Bernard. *Voyagers to the West: A Passage in the Peopling of America on the Eve of the Revolution.* New York: Vintage Books, 1986.

Berthoff, Rowland. *British Immigrants in Industrial America, 1790–1950.* Cambridge, Mass.: Harvard University Press, 1953.

Brander, Michael. *The Emigrant Scots: Why They Left and Where They Went.* London: Constable, 1982.

——. *The World Dictionary of Scottish Associations.* Glasgow: Neil Wilson Publishing, 1996.

British-American, February 20, 1932.

Chicago Landmark Commission. *Site of Camp Douglas.* Chicago: Chicago Landmark Commission, 1976.

Collier, James Lincoln. *Benny Goodman and the Swing Era.* New York: Oxford University Press, 1989.

Constitution and By-Laws of the Chicago Caledonian Club. Chicago: Fergus Printing Company, 1872.

Cromie, Robert. *The Great Chicago Fire.* New York: McGraw-Hill, 1958.

Currey, Josiah Seymour. *Chicago: Its History and Its Builders, A Century of Marvelous Growth.* Chicago: S. J. Clarke, 1912.

Currie, William. "Bagpipers hold last fling in Stock Yard Inn." *Chicago Tribune,* October 25, 1976.

Darling, Sharon. "Arts and Crafts Shops in the Fine Arts Building." *Chicago History* 6, no. 2 (Summer 1977): 79–85.

Dedmon, Emmett. *Fabulous Chicago: A Great City's History and People.* Rev. ed. New York: Atheneum, 1983.

Directory of the First Scotch Presbyterian Church of Chicago. Chicago: James Barnet, Printer and Publisher, March 1876.

Donaldson, Emily Ann. *The Scottish Highland Games in America.* Gretna, La.: Pelican Publishing, 1986.

Donaldson, Gordon. *The Scots Overseas.* London: Robert Hale, 1966.

Donaldson, Scott. *Archibald MacLeish: An American Life.* Boston: Houghton Mifflin, 1992.

Donna, Modesto Joseph. *The Braidwood Story.* Braidwood, Ill.: Braidwood History Bureau, 1957[?]

Drury, John. *Old Illinois Houses.* Springfield, Ill.: Illinois State Historical Society, 1948.

Duis, Perry, and Glen E. Holt. "God in Illinois: Zion's leader 'cured' his flocks wallets more often than their diseases." *Chicago Magazine,* March 1979, 116–19.

Dunbar, Olivia Howard. *A House in Chicago.* Chicago: University of Chicago Press, 1947.

Dupre, Irma, Beatrice Brittain Braden, and Carolyn J. Bullinger. *Dundee Township 1835–1985.* Dallas, Tex.: Taylor Publishing Company, 1985.

Ebner, Michael H. *Creating Chicago's North Shore.* Chicago: University of Chicago Press, 1988.

Edelstein, T. J., ed. *Imagining an Irish Past: The Celtic Revival 1840–1940.* Chicago: David and Alfred Smart Museum of Art, The University of Chicago, 1992.

Ferguson, Fergus. *From Glasgow to Missouri and Back.* Glasgow: T. D. Morison [etc.], 1878.

Forgan, James B. *Recollections of a Busy Life.* New York: The Bankers Publishing Company, 1924.

Freshman, Garry. "Chicago in the Civil War." *Chicago Reader,* August 27, 1982.

Frueh, Erne R., and Florence Frueh. *The Second Presbyterian Church of Chicago: Art and Architecture.* Chicago: Second Presbyterian Church, 1988.

Fyfe, Gordon. *A Short History of the Village of Golf.* Golf, Ill.: N.p., 1971.

Gilbert, Paul Thomas, and Charles Lee Bryson. *Chicago and Its Makers.* Chicago: Felix Mendelsohn, 1929.

Gottlieb, Amy Zahl. "The Influence of British Trade Unionists on the Regulation of the Mining Industry in Illinois, 1872." In *Labor History* 19, no. 3, New York Tamiment Institute (Summer 1978): 397–415.

Graham, Ian C. C. *Colonists from Scotland: Emigration to North America, 1707–1783.* Ithaca, N.Y.: Cornell University Press, 1956.

Hansen, Harry. *Midwest Portraits: A Book of Memories and Friendships.* New York: Harcourt, Brace, 1923.

Harmon, Ada Douglas, comp. *The Story of an Old Town—Glen Ellyn.* Glen Ellyn, Ill.: Anan Harmon Chapter D.A.R., 1928.

Harrison, Rev. Jack. *150 Years of Faith: History of Argyle and Willow Creek Presbyterian Church.* Argyle, Ill.: Willow Creek Presbyterian Church, 1995.

Harvey, Daniel G. *The Argyle Settlement in History and Story.* Beloit, Wisc.: Daily News Publishing, 1924.

Hasse, Roald. *The Story of Encyclopaedia Britannica.* Chicago: Encyclopaedia Britannica, n.d.

Hayner, Don, and Tom McNamee. *Streetwise Chicago: A History of Chicago Street Names.* Chicago: Loyola University Press, 1988.

Hewitson, Jim. *Tam Blake & Co.: The Story of the Scots in America.* Edinburgh: Canongate Press, 1993.

Hibbard, Angus. *Associations of Choice.* New York: Rand McNally & Company, n.d.

——. *Songs of the Glen View Club.* Chicago: N.p., July 1934.

Hirsch, Susan E., and Robert I. Goler. *A City Comes of Age: Chicago in the 1890s.* Chicago: Chicago Historical Society, 1990.

Holt, Glen E., and Dominic A. Pacyga. *Chicago: A Historical Guide to the Neighborhoods, the Loop and South Side.* Chicago: Chicago Historical Society, 1979.

Howard, Robert P. *Illinois: A History of the Prairie State.* Grand Rapids, Mich.: William B. Eerdmans Publishing, 1972.

Irvine, James W. *Up-Helly-Aa: A Century of Festival.* Lerwick, Shetland: Shetland Publishing, 1982.

James, Alton. "Robert Kennicott: Pioneer Illinois Natural Scientist and Arctic Explorer." In *Papers in Illinois History* (1940): 22–39.

Jensen, George Peter. *Historic Chicago Sites.* Chicago: Creative Enterprises, 1953.

John Crerar Foundation. *Great Is the Gift that Bringeth Knowledge: Highlights from the History of the John Crerar Library.* Chicago: University of Chicago Library, 1989.

Johnston, David. *Autobiographical Reminiscences of David Johnston, an Octagenarian Scotchman.* Chicago: N.p., 1885.

Karamanski, Theodore J. *Rally 'Round the Flag: Chicago and the Civil War.* Chicago: Nelson-Hall Publishers, 1993.

Keiser, John H. *Illinois Vignettes.* Springfield, Ill.: Sangamon State University, 1977.

Koenig, Rev. Msgr. Harry C., S.T.D. *A History of the Parishes of the Archidioceses of Chicago.* Vol. 1. Chicago: Archdiocese of Chicago, 1980.

Kokmen, Leyla. "Scottish Immigrants Find a Home Away from Home: Retirement Facility Keeps Culture Alive." *Chicago Tribune,* December 1, 1995.

Lanctot, Barbara. *A Walk through Graceland Cemetery.* Chicago: Chicago Architecture Foundation, 1988.

Logan, James. *Notes of a Journey through Canada, the United States of America, and the West Indies.* Edinburgh: Fraser and Company, 1838.

Maass, Alan. "The Little Red Book House." *Chicago Reader,* October 17, 1986.

MacArthur, John D.: *The Man and His Legacy.* Chicago: MacArthur Foundation, n.d.

MacDougall, D. *Scots and Scots' Descendants in America.* (Reprint 1917). Baltimore, Md.: Clearfield Company, 1992.

McFarland, Ron, and Hugh Nichols, eds. *Norman Maclean.* American Authors Series. Lewiston, Idaho: Confluence Press, 1988.

McGowen, Thomas. *Island within a City: A History of the Norridge-Harwood Heights Area.* Harwood Heights, Ill.: Eisenhower Public Library District, 1989.

Mackie, J. D. *A History of Scotland.* New York: Penguin Books, 1978.

MacMillan, Thomas C. *The Scots and Their Descendants in Illinois.* In Illinois State Historical Society Transactions no. 26. (1919): 31–85.

Macrae, David. *The Americans at Home: Pen-and-Ink Sketches of American Men, Manners and Institutions.* 2 vols. Edinburgh: Edmonston and Douglas, 1870.

Malone, Dumas, ed. *Dictionary of American Biography. Vol. 2.* New York: Charles Scribner's Sons, 1933, 551–52.

Maxwell, William. *Ancestors: A Family History.* New York: Vintage Books, 1971.

Mayer, Harold M., and Richard C. Wade. *Chicago: Growth of a Metropolis.* Chicago: University of Chicago Press, 1969.

Monroe, Harriet. *A Poet's Life: Seventy Years in a Changing World.* New York: Macmillan, 1938.

O'Neill, Francis. *Irish Minstrels and Musicians: The Story of Irish Music.* Cork: Mercier Press, 1987.

Patton, Patricia. Letter to Wayne Rethford, March 12, 1991.

Pick, Grant. "The MacArthur Manner: How the Foundation Picks Its Grants." *Chicago Tribune Magazine,* December 3, 1995.

Pierce, Bessie Louise. *A History of Chicago. Volume 1: The Beginning of a City 1673–1848.* New York: Alfred A. Knopf, in conjunction with the University of Chicago Press,1937.

——. *A History of Chicago. Volume 2: From Town to City 1848–1871.* New York: Alfred A. Knopf, in conjunction with the University of Chicago Press, 1940.

——. *A History of Chicago. Volume 3: The Rise of a Modern City 1871–1893.* New York: Alfred A. Knopf, in conjunction with the University of Chicago Press, 1957.

Redmond, Gerald. *The Caledonian Games of Nineteenth-Century America.* Rutherford, N.J.: Fairleigh Dickinson University Press, 1971.

Regan, John. *Western Wilds of America.* 2nd ed. Edinburgh: John Menzies and W. P. Nimmo, 1859.

Regnery, Henry. *Creative Chicago: From The Chap-Book to the University.* Evanston, Ill.: Chicago Historical Bookworks, 1993.

Rice, C. Duncan. *The Scots Abolitionists 1833–1861.* Baton Rouge, La.: Louisiana State University Press, 1981.

Riess, Steven A. *City Games: The Evolution of American Urban Society and the Rise of Sports.* Urbana, Ill.: University of Illinois Press, 1989.

Robertson, William, and W. F. Robertson. *Our American Tour, Being a Run of Ten Thousand Miles from the Atlantic to the Golden Gate in the Autumn of 1869.* Edinburgh: W. Burness, 1871.

Ruff, Allen M. "Socialist Publishing in Illinois: Charles H. Kerr & Company of Chicago, 1886–1928." *Illinois Historical Journal* 79 (Spring 1986): 19–32.

Runnion, Dale F. *The Saddle and Sirloin Portrait Collection: A Biographical Catalog.* Louisville, Ky.: Kentucky Fair and Exposition Center, 1992.

Sawyers, June Skinner. *Chicago Portraits: Biographies of 250 Famous Chicagoans.* Chicago: Loyola University Press, 1991.

Sclair, Helen. *Greater Chicagoland Cemeteries: A Self-Guided Tour.* The Association for Graveyard Studies Conference Guide Series. Guide #3. Worcester, Mass.: Association for Graveyard Studies, 1994.

Scottish-American (New York). May 21, 1890; July 2, 1890; October 21, 1891; August 23, 1893; February 7, 1894; April 8, December 9, 1896; November 22, 1905.

Shirreff, Patrick. *A Tour through North America; together with a Comprehensive View of the Canadas and United States as Adapted for Agricultural Emigration.* Edinburgh: Oliver and Boyd, 1835.

Spencer, LeAnn. "Grove gift adds to a suburban oasis." *Chicago Tribune,* December 13, 1995.

Stevenson, Robert Louis. *From the Clyde to California: Robert Louis Stevenson's Emigrant Journey.* Edited by Andrew Noble. Aberdeen: Aberdeen University Press, 1985.

Thernstrom, Stephan, ed. *Harvard Encyclopedia of American Ethnic Groups.* Cambridge, Mass.: Belknap Press of Harvard University Press, 1980.

Viallet, Jean B. "Highland Games: Blaring Pipes and Bonny Plaids." *Chicago Magazine,* July 1985.

Virden, Jenel. *Good-bye, Piccadilly: British War Brides in America.* Urbana, Ill.: University of Illinois Press, 1996.

Wade, Louise Carroll. *Chicago's Pride: The Stockyards, Packingtown, and Environs in the Nineteenth Century.* Urbana, Ill.: University of Illinois Press, 1987.

Ward, Martindale C. *A Trip to Chicago: What I Saw, What I Heard, What I Thought.* Glasgow: A. Malcolm and Company, 1895.

Weimann, Jeanne Madeline. *The Fair Women.* Chicago: Academy Press, 1981.

Wendt, Lloyd. *Chicago Tribune: The Rise of a Great American Newspaper.* Chicago: Rand McNally and Company, 1979.

Western British American, "Scottish Pioneers," February 7, 1914.

Wind, Herbert Warren. "Golfing in and around Chicago." *Chicago History* (Winter 1975–76): 244–51.

Zabel, Craig. "George Grant Elmslie and the Glory and Burden of the Sullivan Legacy." In *The Midwest in American Architecture.* Edited by John S. Garner. Urbana, Ill.: University of Illinois Press, 1991.

ADDITIONAL READINGS

Anderson, Carlyle E. *Glen View Club 1897–1987.* Golf, Ill.: Glen View Club, 1987. Booklet.

Andreas, A. T. *History of Chicago from the Earliest Period to the Present Time.* 3 vols. Chicago: A. T. Andreas, 1884–86.

Artner, Alan G. "British Art Is Looking Up: A New Generation of Painters Loudly Refuses to be Marooned on the British Isles." *Chicago Tribune,* January 29, 1989.

Aspinwall, Bernard. *Portable Utopia: Glasgow and the United States 1820–1920.* Aberdeen: Aberdeen University Press, 1984.

Bailyn, Bernard. *The Peopling of British North America: An Introduction.* New York: Vintage Books, 1986.

Bancroft, Hubert Howe. *The Book of the Fair: An Historical and Descriptive Presentation of . . . the Columbian Exposition at Chicago in 1893.* 10 vols. Chicago: The Bancroft Company, 1893–95.

Berthoff, Rowland. "Under the Kilt: Variations on the Scottish-American Ground." *Journal of American Ethnic History* 1, no. 2 (Spring 1982): 5–34.

Black, George Fraser. *Scotland's Mark on America.* New York: Published by the Scottish Section of "America's Making," 1921.

Blades, John. "Standard of Impurity: James Kelman has become both a literary giant and a dirty word in his native Scotland." *Chicago Tribune,* February 9, 1995.

Bonner, Thomas. *History of Medicine and Surgery and Physicians and Surgeons of Chicago 1803–1922.* Chicago: Biographical Publishing Corporation, 1922.

Bruce, Duncan A. *The Mark of the Scots: Their Astonishing Contributions to History, Science, Democracy, Literature, and the Arts.* Secaucus, N. J. : Birch Lane Press, 1996.

Burton, J. C., ed. *Arthur Young and the Business He Founded.* New York: Arthur Young & Company, 1948.

Carbutt, J., comp. *Biographical Sketches of the Leading Men of Chicago Written by the Best Talent of the Northwest.* Chicago: Wilson & St. Clair, 1868.

Carr, Clark E. *Stephen A. Douglas: His Life, Public Services, Speeches and Patriotism.* Chicago: A. C. McClurg, 1909.

Cook, Frederick Francis. *Bygone Days in Chicago: Recollections of the "Garden City" of the Sixties.* Chicago: A. C. McClurg, 1910.

Cumming, Elizabeth, and Wendy Kaplan. *The Arts and Crafts Movement.* New York: Thames and Hudson, 1991.

Currie, William. "The Passionate Piper." *Chicago Tribune Magazine,* October 21, 1973, 18–21.

Darling, Sharon. *Chicago Metalsmiths.* Chicago: Chicago Historical Society, 1977.

Darnell, Don. "Martie." *Chicago Tribune Sunday Magazine,* January 20, 1991.

Davis, Allen F. *Spearheads for Reform: The Social Settlements and the Progressive Movement, 1890–1914.* New York: Oxford University Press, 1967.

Drury, John. *Old Chicago Houses.* Chicago: University of Chicago Press, 1975.

Erickson, Charlotte. *Leaving England: Essays on British Emigration in the Nineteenth Century.* Ithaca, N.Y.: Cornell University Press, 1994.

Finlayson, Iain. *The Scots.* Oxford: Oxford University Press, 1988.

Finley, John H. *The Coming of the Scot.* New York: Charles Scribner's Sons, 1940.

Flinn, John J. *The Handbook of Chicago Biography.* Chicago: Standard Guide Company, 1893.

Gale, Edwin O. *Reminiscences of Early Chicago and Vicinity.* Chicago: F. H. Revell Company, 1902.

Garden, Mary, and Louis Biancolli. *Mary Garden's Story.* New York: Simon & Schuster, 1951.

Gottlieb, Amy Zahl. "British Coal Miners: A Demographic Study of Braidwood and Streator, Illinois." *Journal of the Illinois State Historical Society* 72 (August 1979).

Hallwas, John E. "John Regan's Emigrant Guide: A Neglected Literary Achievement." *Illinois Historical Journal* 77, no. 4 (Winter 1984): 269–94.

Hansen, Marcus L. *Atlantic Migration 1607–1860.* Cambridge, Mass.: Harvard University Press, 1940.

Hecht, Ben. *Charlie, The Improbable Life of Charles MacArthur.* New York: Harper & Bros., 1957.

Horan, James D. *The Pinkertons: The Detective Dynasty That Made History.* New York: Crown Publishers, 1967.

John, Mark. "Motorola Putting Another $387 Million into Scottish Plant," *Chicago Sun-Times,* September 7, 1994.

Johnson, Geoffrey. "Little Captain of the Ragged, the Mad Army of Poets." *Chicago Reader,* September 6, 1985.

Johnson, Rossiter, ed. *History of the World's Columbian Exposition Held in Chicago in 1893.* 4 vols. New York: Appleton, 1897.

Jouzaitis, Carol. "A Vision Runs Through It: Redford hopes filming fly fisherman's classic novel will help save rivers." *Chicago Tribune,* September 17, 1991.

Kelly, H. Michael. "Captain Colin P. Kelly, Jr.: The First Scottish American Hero of World War II." *The Highlander* 33, no. 2 (March/April 1995): 44–46.

"Kintyre Settlers in America: History of Argyle, Illinois, A Unique Scottish Community." *Campbeltown Courier,* n.d. From a newspaper clipping sent to the Chicago Historical Society, February 23, 1921.

Kinzie, Juliette A. *Wau Bun, the "Early Days" of the Northwest.* Chicago: Caxton Club, 1901.

Kirkland, Caroline. *Chicago Yesterdays.* Chicago: Daughaday & Co., 1919.

Kirkland, Joseph. *The Story of Chicago: Bringing the History Up to December, 1894.* 2 vols. Chicago: Dibble Publishing, 1895.

Kogan, Herman. *The Great EB: The Story of the Encyclopaedia Britannica.* Chicago: University of Chicago Press, 1958.

Lake Forest, Illinois: A Preservation Foundation Guide to National Register Properties. Lake Forest, Ill.: The Lake Forest Foundation for Historic Preservation, 1991.

Lewis, Lloyd, and Henry Justin Smith. *Chicago: A History of its Reputation.* New York: Harcourt, Brace, 1929.

Leyburn, James G. *The Scotch-Irish: A Social History.* Chapel Hill, N.C.: University of North Carolina Press, 1962.

Lyon, Christopher. "Scottish Expression." *Chicago Sun-Times,* July 13, 1984.

Macdonald, Charles Blair. *Scotland's Gift: Golf; Reminiscences by Charles Blair Macdonald, 1872–1927.* New York: Charles Scribner's Sons, 1928.

MacLeish, Andrew. *Life of Andrew MacLeish, 1838–1928.* Chicago: Privately printed, 1929.

Morn, Frank T. *The Eye That Never Sleeps: A History of the Pinkerton National Detective Agency.* Bloomington, Ind.: Indiana University Press, 1982.

Mullin, Earl. "Iowa and Scots to Present Fair Programs Today." *Chicago Daily Tribune,* September 30, 1933, 6.

Oliver, John H. *The Elmira Centennial and Scottish Pioneers 1838–1938.* Elmira, Ill.:, n.p., 1938.

Pierce, Bessie Louise, ed. *As Others See Us: Impressions of Visitors, 1673–1933.* Chicago: University of Chicago Press, 1933.

Poole, Ernest. *Giants Gone: Men Who Made Chicago.* New York: McGraw-Hill, 1943.

Quaife, Milo. *Checagou: From Indian Wigwam to Modern City, 1673–1835.* Chicago: University of Chicago Press, 1933.

Ross, Peter. *The Scot in America.* New York: Raeburn Book Company, 1896.

Sawyers, June. "Brush with the Art of the Highlands." *Chicago Tribune,* August 28, 1988.

Sawyers, June Skinner. "Scotia's Children: Scottish Societies in Chicago" in *Chicago Sketches: Urban Tales, Stories, and Legends from Chicago History.* Chicago: Loyola Press, 1995.

Scottish Musical Club. Program notes, May 4, 1905. In Chicago Historical Society.

Smith, Henry Justin. *Chicago's Great Century, 1833–1933.* Chicago: Consolidated, 1933.

Thomson, George. *Impressions of America.* Arbroath, Scotland: T. Bunele and Company, 1916.

Thomson, James Casement. *Great Scots! The Scottish American Hall of Fame.* North Riverside, Ill.: Illinois Saint Andrew Society, 1996.

Watson, John. *Souvenir of a Tour in the United States of America and Canada, in the Autumn of 1872.* Glasgow: Privately published, 1872.

Weber, Eleanor Cady. *Women's Club of Inverness.* Edited and updated by Angelo J. Polvere with the assistance of Sandy Johnson. Inverness, Ill.: Women's Club of Inverness, 1989.

Williams, Ellen. *Harriet Monroe and the Poetry Renaissance: The First Ten Years of Poetry, 1912–22.* Urbana, Ill.: University of Illinois Press, 1977.

Wood, David Ward. *Chicago and Its Distinguished Citizens or the Progress of Forty Years.* Chicago: M. George & Company, 1881.

INDEX

Boldface type denotes photographs.

CREDITS

PHOTOGRAPHY/ILLUSTRATION

Courtesy of Chicago Historical Society: pp. 17, 26, 28, 30, 35, 76, 86, 94

Courtesy of the Cliff Dwellers: p. 66 *(top left)*

Courtesy of Illinois Saint Andrew Society: pp. v, 9, 12, 24, 40, 42, 44, 53, 56, 58, 59, 60, 61 *(top and bottom),* 62, 63, 64 *(top and bottom),* 69, 70, 71, 72, 78 *(top and bottom),* 79 *(top and bottom),* 80, 81 *(top and bottom),* 82, 83, 85, 88, 89, 92, 104, 110, 114, 115, 116, 123, 128, 129, 130, 131, 132, 133, 134, 136, 137, 138, 152

Courtesy of Charles H. Kerr Publishing: p. 98

Courtesy of Loyola Press: pp. 27, 32, 70, 100, 124, 127

Courtesy of the MacArthur Foundation: p. 96

Photo by Donald H. Amidai,
courtesy of Timothy Cleavenger: p. 66 *(top right)*

Photos by Terry Lee: p. 118 *(top left, top right)*

Photos by June Skinner Sawyers: pp. iii, xii, 15, 18, 21, 31, 50, 99, 145, 146, 149 *(top left, top right),* 150, 151, 157

Maps by Tammi Longsjo: pp. 148, 155

Cover Photo: Margaret Baikie, 1933. Courtesy of Illinois Saint Andrew Society

AUTHOR BIOGRAPHIES

Wayne Rethford is executive director of the Scottish Home in North Riverside, Illinois.

June Skinner Sawyers is an editor and freelance writer.

BOOK AND COVER DESIGN

Michael L. Anderson